THE OFFICIAL P.F.A.
FOOTBALLERS
HEROES

THE OFFICIAL P.F.A.
FOOTBALLERS
HEROES

All the Award Winners and their Stories

Tony Lynch

Stanley Paul
LONDON

First Published 1995

1 3 5 7 9 10 8 6 4 2

© PFA Enterprises and Tony Lynch, 1995

Tony Lynch has asserted his right under the
Copyright, Designs and Patent Act, 1988 to be
identified as the author of this work.

First published in the United Kingdom in 1995
by Stanley Paul
Random House, 20 Vauxhall Bridge Road,
London SW1V 2SA

Random House Australia (Pty) Limited
20 Alfred Street, Milsons Point, Sydney,
New South Wales 2061, Australia

Random House New Zealand Limited
18 Poland Road, Glenfield, Auckland 10,
New Zealand

Random House South Africa (Pty) Limited
PO Box 337, Bergvlei, South Africa

Random House UK Limited Reg. No. 954009

A CIP catalogue record for this book is
available from the British Library

ISBN 0091791359

Designed by Stuart Perry Associates
Printed and bound in Portugal by Printer
Portuguesa

CONTENTS

Foreword by Gordon Taylor

FOOTBALLERS' HEROES tells the story of the PFA Awards which began in 1974. The book contains full details of the Awards nights and the Players' Player of the Year Award together with the Young Player of the Year Award and the PFA Merit Award, which is the footballers' hall of fame. There are some extremely good interviews with Players' Player of the Year Award winners – and Tony Lynch provides a wonderful insight into the background of their achievements.

There are also full details of the Divisional Awards for each of the four divisions of the full-time professional leagues, and the reader will no doubt enjoy tracking the paths of today's Premier League players who have come from those valuable breeding grounds at the lower end of the scale.

Tom Watson, the great American golfer, once said what he aimed for in life was the recognition and respect of his fellow professionals. Indeed, there can be no finer accolade than being chosen by your peers as the best.

The annual PFA Awards presentation has become the finest social occasion in the football calendar, and *Footballers' Heroes* reflects over two decades of excellence in the game. I hope you the reader has as much pleasure in reading it as the recipients had in receiving their Awards.

Gordon Taylor, PFA Chief Executive

THE PLAYERS' CHOICE

Every footballer wants one – the PFA Players' Player of the Year Award, the Young Player of the Year Award and the Merit Award. Since its inauguration in 1974, the PFA's annual event has grown to become an integral part of the football calendar, a celebration of the good things in the game. And, to a man, all PFA Award winners are immensely proud to be so honoured by their fellow professionals

At the midway stage of the English league season – when the title race and the promotion and relegation issues are starting to shape up and when the bigger clubs have joined the FA Cup competition – it would be a pretty safe bet to assume that debate in the dressing rooms of the 92 League clubs will soon turn to the outstanding players of the season so far.

For it is in late-January – early-February that each current member of the Professional Footballers' Association receives a ballot paper on which he is invited by the Chairman to cast his votes for the current season's PFA Players' Player of the Year, the Young Player of the Year – and for a team of Divisional Award winners comprised of the best players in each position in the member's own Division.

Clive Allen, the 1987 Player of the Year, is someone who has observed the voting process in more dressing rooms than most. 'It has become something of a ritual', he says. 'Suddenly you'll find it's that time of year again.

You'll see some players going off in groups of three or four to talk about it, others will go off on their own. The Divisional team is usually chosen first. They are looking at the individual contribution that such-and-such a player has made to his team – and at how successful that team has been. As for the Player of the Year, some years one individual obviously stands out, in other seasons the choice is a lot closer between a handful of outstanding players.'

Since the completed papers are not normally due to arrive at the independent scrutineers until the end of February, the players have several weeks in which to ponder their decisions (any papers received after the official closing date are deemed spoiled). A measure of the high regard in which the Awards are held by the membership is reflected in the participation of players from all 92 clubs.

The votes are counted in conditions of utmost secrecy at the offices of the independent scrutineers. The results, known only to a select few at PFA headquarters in Manchester, are not publicly revealed until the PFA Awards Annual Presentation (although it has occasionally been necessary to disclose to a player that he has won – to ensure his attendance at the Award ceremony).

The ceremony is usually held in early April at the Grosvenor House Hotel (the venue since 1986) on London's Park Lane and attended by more than 1000 dinner-jacketed players and guests of the Association.

In addition to the two current player- and Divisional honours, the PFA also makes a Merit Award each year, at the discretion of the Management Committee, to a notable figure who has made 'an outstanding contribution to the game' – recipients have included such luminaries as Bobby Charlton, Denis Law, Bill Shankly, Sir Matt Busby, Tom Finney, Sir Stanley Matthews and Brian Clough. In this way the ceremony manages to encompass the best of both past and present.

The original concept for the Awards came in 1972 when PFA Chairman Derek Dougan, while researching material for a book on the inner workings of football, called his good friend Eric Woodward who had recently been appointed commercial manager at Aston Villa. 'The Doog' first asked Woodward to enlighten him on the extra-curricular commercial potential of the game (that particular art was still in its infancy).

Their discussion later turned to the topic of the PFA itself, and resulted in Woodward promising to come up with some ideas to enhance the public profile of the Association. By far the most exciting of his subsequent suggestions was 'The PFA Awards', which arose from the question: why are the players themselves the only people who don't acknowledge their best?

The premise was simply to reflect the players' own perspective on the various merits of their fellow professionals, as expressed in the dressing rooms, on the training grounds and down on the pitch in the thick of the action. In no way was the intention to detract from the esteemed and

---

The rules of the PFA ballot are as follows:

● Players may not vote for any of his clubmates in any category.

● A player is only eligible to receive an Award providing that players from his club have participated in the Ballot.

● The age limit for Young Player Award contenders is twenty-three.

● No player can win the Player of the Year Award and the Young Player of the Year Award in the same season. In the event of one player topping both polls, he will be deemed the winner of the senior Award, and the person polling the second highest number of votes in the Young Player category will be named Young Player of the Year.

● In the Divisional Awards category, a member can only vote for players from his club's current Division.

● Only PFA members are eligible to vote, and to receive votes.

---

prestigious Football Writers' Association Footballer of the Year Award, which had been in existence since 1948 when it was first won by Stanley Matthews. Indeed, the PFA has always acknowledged and appreciated the tremendous input made to the game by the best of the professional pundits.

Yet it was felt by Dougan and Woodward that there *was* room in the game for another annual Awards ceremony. Together they took the idea to PFA secretary Cliff Lloyd, the Union's Solicitors and finally the Management Committee of the day. Everyone involved saw the obvious merits of the concept and the green light was given.

The ITV network, a body which obviously recognised the televisual potential of such an event, quickly came on board through executive producer Bill Ward and producers Gerry Loftus and John Bromley. Subsequently the first Awards ceremony was scheduled for the spring of 1974, and would be broadcast live.

Meanwhile there was much work to be done behind the scenes. The trophies for the Players' Player and Young Player Awards were commissioned from Richmond Trophies of Birmingham, whose managing director Harry Darlaston designed and made them from Eric Woodward's original rough sketches. The Divisional Award medals were minted by another Midlands-based company, HB Sale Ltd. Ballot papers were printed by the Peerless Press, a company specialising in matchday programmes, and distributed throughout the PFA membership. The Hilton Hotel in London was chosen as the venue for the first awards dinner and the date was set – 3 March 1974 . . .

The medals table at the 1992 PFA Awards. PFA Divisional Awards are presented to those players voted best in their position in each of the four divisions

THE PROFESSIONAL FOOTBALLERS' ASSOCIATION

The body which eventually became known as The Professional Footballers' Association was founded in December 1907, at a meeting in Manchester, chaired by the famous Welsh international winger Billy Meredith. Several attempts to form an effective players' union had been made since the legalisation of professionalism within the game by the Football Association twenty-two years earlier, but each had foundered against the resistance of the clubs, the various Leagues, and a certain amount of apathy among the players themselves.

But, nineteen years after the formation of the Football League and almost two years after the first £1,000 transfer deal had been completed, the players at last found an effective voice in the administration of the game.

Since those days the avowed aim of the organisation has been to 'systematically protect and improve the conditions and status of [our] members'. Landmarks in the PFA's history include the abolition of the maximum wage system in 1961; the 'Eastham Case' of 1963 which saw off the old 'retain and transfer' system; and, in 1978, the establishment of a player's right to transfer at the end of his contract.

These days, led by its redoubtable Chief Executive Gordon Taylor, the PFA involves itself in many aspects of the professional game ranging from advice and negotiating skills on contracts and commercial interests, through representing players at disciplinary hearings, to providing vocational training courses, insurance and pensions.

PFA Chairmen

1907–10	Harry Mainman
1910–11	Evelyn Linott
1911–18	Colin Veitch
1919–21	Charlie Roberts
1921–29	Jimmy Fay
1929–30	Howard Matthews
1930–31	Arthur Wood
1931–36	Dave Robbie
1936–	Albert 'Sid' Barrett
1937–46	Sammy Crooks
1946–57	Jimmy Guthrie
1957–61	Jimmy Hill
1961–63	Tommy Cummings
1963–66	Malcolm Musgrove
1966–67	Noel Cantwell
1967–70	Terry Neill
1970–78	Derek Dougan
1978–80	Gordon Taylor
1980–82	Alan Gowling
1982–84	Steve Coppell
1984–88	Brian Talbot
1988–90	Garth Crooks
1990–94	Brian Marwood
1994–	Pat Nevin

PFA Secretaries

1908–10	Herbert Broomfield
1910–13	Alfred Sydney Owens
1913–29	Harry Newbould
1929–53	Jimmy Fay
1953–81	Cliff Lloyd OBE
1981–	Gordon Taylor MA BSc (Econ) *(Chief Executive since 1989)*

NORMAN HUNTER
LEEDS UNITED

PLAYER OF THE YEAR

1974

In January 1974, as the PFA membership began voting for the Association's first-ever Awards, Bill Shankly's Liverpool were the reigning League Champions, Second Division Sunderland held the FA Cup, and the League Cup stood in the Tottenham Hotspur trophy cabinet. But the team of the moment was Leeds United.

Don Revie's disciplined and highly professional side had led the 1973–74 First Division table virtually from the start; by New Year's Day they remained undefeated and were looking uncatchable. Given those circumstances and the timing of the vote, it was a near certainty that a Leeds player would collect the first Players' Player of the Year Award: the erstwhile skipper Billy Bremner, perhaps? The ball-playing Irish midfielder Johnny Giles? "Play-anywhere" Paul Madeley or goal ace Allan Clarke?

When the votes were counted a Leeds man was indeed crowned Player of the Year but, to the surprise of many pundits, it was 'hard man' defender Norman Hunter who took the prize. How, they asked, could such a physical, aggressive and seemingly graceless player come top of the poll?

Hunter dodged the flak. 'Criticism was par for the course,' he recalls. 'I got a lot of stick from the press who were asking why the players had picked somebody with a "reputation"? But I was the players' own choice and couldn't have been happier. And I was delighted that people in the game recognised that Leeds, who were not exactly the most popular club in the world, had such a good team.'

Hunter had been part of the Elland Road revolution ever since Don Revie had succeeded Jack Taylor in the manager's chair in March 1961. 'I'd been on the groundstaff since leaving school. But when my seventeenth birthday came around Jack Taylor said I wasn't big enough or strong enough to be a professional and it looked as though I was on my way out. Luckily for me Jack only lasted a couple more weeks before Don took over. He saw things differently – I remember he signed Albert Johanneson one morning and me that afternoon.'

The young Hunter started out as a midfielder, but readily admits he wasn't quick enough in that position. 'Our coach Sid Owen recognised my strengths, he told me: "You can't run, you can't head the ball but you can get it and give it to somebody else". He moved me into defence, though I'll never forget my first game as a central defender – a 2–2 draw with Manchester United Reserves. I had to mark Albert Quixall and I scored an own-goal.'

From such an unpromising start he developed into a fine defender and made his first team début in the Second Division, a 2–0 win at Swansea in September 1962. 'Paul Reaney débuted in the same game, and a lad called Rodney Johnson who played up front and scored one of the goals. Gary Sprake was making his second appearance.

'People still can't believe that someone with my reputation won it,' says Hunter. 'I've become a regular quiz question: Who was the first PFA Player of the Year? Nobody ever gets it right.'

Billy Bremner and Jack Charlton were in the side – they were the only pre-Revie signings who would remain throughout Revie's reign. My next game was at Elland Road against Chelsea who were managed by Tommy Docherty and were the team to beat that season – we won 2–0.'

Largely inspired by the midfield trio of Billy Bremner, Bobby Collins and Johnny Giles, and bolstered by the arrival of centre forward Alan Peacock from Middlesbrough, Leeds won the 1963–64 Second Division Championship. 1964–65 saw them finish as First Division runners-up on goal difference to Manchester United, and as FA Cup runners-up to Liverpool who won 2–1 after extra time at Wembley. 'It went on from there,' says Hunter. 'We were always involved and we had many disappointments. Every time we'd come close to the title Don would pick us up and we'd go and do it all over again.'

Norman had nothing but the utmost respect for the manager who transformed Leeds United's fortunes. 'Don and I got on very well although there was this distance with him, which there always seems to be with great managers. It was always a teacher and pupil relationship as far as I was concerned. I thought the man was brilliant – his man-management and organisation were outstanding – and I would have done anything he told me to do. Looking back, and he admitted it himself, he was perhaps just a bit too cautious and superstitious at times.'

Norman made his England début as a substitute for Joe Baker in a magnificent 2–0 victory over Spain in Madrid in December 1965; it was the first time Alf Ramsey employed a 4–4–2 formation and the Spanish had no answer to it. 'Alf Ramsey was a totally different individual to Don Revie – although they both paid great attention to detail. The peripheral things – the Press and so on – didn't really matter to them; they were more interested in their players and winning games.'

In all, Hunter would collect 28 caps – a total that might easily have doubled but for the consistent presence in the side of Bobby Moore. 'People say Bobby kept me out of the team – but that doesn't bother me. I knew I wasn't going to play too often with him around. He was one of the best players I've ever seen and I didn't mind being his understudy one little bit.'

Norman played three times for England in 1966 and was included in Ramsey's World Cup Finals squad although he did not appear in the tournament. His first international goal was a vital one, the winner in Madrid against Spain in

the 1968 European Nations Cup qualifying tournament, which took England into the semi-finals against Yugoslavia in Italy.

That year also brought Leeds' first triumphs under Don Revie: the 1968 League Cup against Arsenal and the European Inter-Cities Fairs Cup against Ferencvaros. Next came the 1968–69 League Championship, won with a then-record 67 points. Hunter was right there at the heart of things. The enthusiastic ferocity of his tackling made him the talk of the League and no attacker, no matter how brave, could possibly have relished confronting the man they dubbed 'Bites Yer Legs'.

For the next three seasons Leeds finished as League runners-up. In 1970–71 they won the Inter-Cities Fairs Cup once more, beating Juventus on the away goals ruling over two legs. In 1972 Hunter won an FA Cup winners' medal, putting in a splendid defensive performance as Leeds beat Arsenal 1–0 in the FA Centenary Final.

Twelve months later United were back at Wembley, this time as outright favourites to beat Second Division Sunderland. But the Rokerites, managed by Bob Stokoe, pulled off the biggest FA Cup surprise of all time by winning 1–0. Eleven days later, in Salonika, United lost the European Cup Winners' Cup Final to a disputed AC Milan goal – and Hunter ended the most frustrating of seasons by being sent off.

In October 1973, as Leeds were flying high once more, he was selected by Alf Ramsey for the vital World Cup qualifier against Poland at Wembley. With almost an hour gone England, who had to win to go through to the 1974 Finals in West Germany, were dominating the game and it seemed just a matter of time before they broke the deadlock. Then, in an uncharacteristic lapse of concentration, Norman fluffed a clearance near the half-way line. The ball fell to Gadocha who raced down the left flank before feeding a pass to Domarski whose low shot skidded through Emlyn Hughes' legs and under Peter Shilton's diving body. England equalised six minutes later with an Allan Clarke penalty, but there were to be no more goals that night. England were out, and Hunter was virtually inconsolable.

Ever the consummate professional, he was back in the thick of the action for Leeds on the following Saturday afternoon as they beat Liverpool 1–0 at Elland Road to consolidate their place at the top of the table. It was this professionalism along with his first-rate defensive qualities: tremendous tackling, a fine sense of

timing, a never-say-die attitude and an undoubted and uncompromising commitment to his club which earned him the most votes from the PFA's membership.

Norman's 'hard man' qualities seemed to desert him on 3 March 1974, the evening of the Awards presentation at the Hilton Hotel in London. 'Don was certain a Leeds player would win and had booked a couple of tables for the whole team and some of the backroom people. I was very, very nervous – I prepared a speech in my mind, as I had a feeling I was in with a chance. When Dickie Davies announced my name, I went up to receive the trophy from Sir Matt Busby. As I got to the stage Dickie whispered "Cut it short, Norman, we're running late", which totally threw me. It was the first time I'd ever spoken in front of a large group and I remember thanking people and then getting back to my seat as fast as possible.'

The following weekend, Norman and Leeds were back in business, with a 1–0 home win against Manchester City. Two more points were in the bag and the Championship was well within sight.

Norman 'Bites Yer Legs' Hunter, the scourge of attackers in the '60s and '70s, an Elland Road folk hero – and the first recipient of the PFA Players' Player of the Year Award. 'People still can't believe that someone with my reputation won it,' he says . 'I've become a regular quiz question: Who was the first PFA Player of the Year? Nobody ever gets it right.'

In 1976 he moved on to Bristol City after Jimmy Armfield had succeeded Brian Clough at Elland Road. 'Jimmy thought some of us were too old and wanted to move us on. He got rid of Billy Bremner, Johnny Giles, Terry Cooper and myself. But, as time proved, Terry went on to play another three years at Middlesbrough; Johnny took West Brom up and was even then one of the best midfielders in the country; and I had another three years with Bristol City where I absolutely loved battling to stay in the First Division.'

Norman's playing career ended with Barnsley where he became manager. He later managed Rotherham United and coached at West Bromwich Albion, Leeds and Bradford City. These days he divides his time between summarising Leeds United's games on local radio and after-dinner speaking

KEVIN BEATTIE
IPSWICH TOWN

YOUNG PLAYER OF THE YEAR

1974

On the opening day of the 1972–73 season 19-year-old Kevin Beattie made his League début for Ipswich Town, in a 2–1 victory over Manchester United at Old Trafford. Two weeks later Ipswich travelled to Leeds where Beattie scored his first League goal in a gripping 3–3 draw. On the opposing side that day was Norman Hunter who recalls Don Revie's words after the match: 'That Beattie's a good player – he's got power and pace and he's good in the air,' observed the Leeds manager. 'He'll play for England one of these days.'

Born in Carlisle in December 1953, Kevin was a product of the Ipswich youth policy, masterminded by Bobby Robson, which would also produce the likes of Brian Talbot, George Burley, Terry Butcher. and future PFA Player of the Year John Wark.

The East-Anglian side finished the 1972–73 campaign in fourth place, their best showing since winning the Championship eleven years earlier. Young Beattie had played 38 League games in central defence, had scored five goals and was by now firmly established as a creative force, a tenacious battler and a great favourite with the Portman Road crowd.

In the first half of the 1973–74 campaign, Beattie stood out in an Ipswich side hovering at first in mid-table, then climbing to sixth place. So impressed were his fellow professionals that they elected him as the first-ever PFA Young Player of the Year, an award presented by his great admirer Don Revie.

At the season's end Ipswich again finished fourth and Beattie, along with skipper Mick Mills, was one of the two players who had started in all 42 league games for the club.

The following season saw Don Revie appointed manager of England in succession to Joe Mercer's seven match caretakership. For his fourth match in charge Revie backed his judgement of the young Ipswich star by selecting him in the heart of the defence. The game was England's celebrated European Championship qualifier against Cyprus at Wembley, in which Malcolm Macdonald created a post-war record by scoring all the goals in a 5–0 win. Beattie almost got his name on the scoresheet too, but in the process of putting the ball in the net he had fouled the goalkeeper.

He would go on to collect nine caps for England, all but one of them under Don Revie's management.

Between 1972 and 1978 Kevin Beattie, the PFA's first Young Player of the Year, went on to complete 228 League appearances and score 24 League goals for Ipswich Town. In 1978 he was a member of the team which achieved such a memorable FA Cup Final victory over Arsenal. He later played briefly for Colchester United and Middlesbrough before injury brought his playing career to a premature end in 1982

CLIFF LLOYD *OBE*

Cliff Lloyd was one of the many footballers whose playing career was effectively put on hold by the outbreak of World War II. Born in Ellesmere Port in November 1916, the fourth of six brothers, he was a promising left-back who signed for Liverpool in 1937. He then moved to Wrexham, making 13 League appearances and scoring two goals before war was declared.

Cliff joined the Army Physical Training Corps, and was stationed at Sidcup in Kent. Between 1939 and 1945 he 'guested' for Wrexham, Fulham and Brentford and played in several representative matches. When the football programme resumed in 1946 his career continued with Fulham, although the best of his playing days were gone. He also spent some time coaching in Norway before returning in May 1950 for one more season, with Bristol Rovers.

But it as one of the game's most able administrators that Cliff Lloyd will always be remembered. While with Fulham he had become the club's PFA delegate, the player who collects his team-mates' subs and keeps them informed on union matters, and in 1950 he was voted on to the Management Committee. Three years later, and much to his surprise, he was appointed Secretary to the PFA as successor to Jimmy Fay who had served in the post since 1929.

Lloyd was to help steer the PFA through some of its most turbulent and triumphant times – the abolition of the maximum wage in 1961, the 'Eastham Case' of 1963 (which spelled the end of the old 'retain and transfer' system) and the creation of the Players' Cash Benefit scheme. No one was more deserving of the PFA's inaugural Merit Award presented to him by Tom Finney.

Cliff retired from office in 1981 and was awarded the OBE in recognition of his services to football.

MERIT AWARD WINNER

1974

PFA leader Cliff Lloyd (left) with George Eastham

BOBBY CHARLTON *CBE*

**MERIT
AWARD
WINNER**

1974

On 28 April 1973 Chelsea beat Manchester United 1–0 at Stamford Bridge, a result somewhat overshadowed by the poignancy of the occasion. It was Bobby Charlton's last game for United and each of the 44,000 spectators, reds and blues alike, felt they had witnessed the end of an era.

Being a nephew of Newcastle United star 'Wor' Jackie Milburn meant that football was in Charlton's blood right from the start. And, as his elder brother Jack readily admits, the 'Bobby Dazzler' was always the most talented kid in their north-east neighbourhood. Bobby became a schoolboy international and, at fifteen, joined Manchester United as a junior. At the time several other top clubs expressed interest in the gifted youngster, but his mind was set – he was staying at Old Trafford.

He turned professional in 1954, becoming for a while the youngest of the celebrated 'Busby Babes'. On 6 October 1956 he made his first team début away to Charlton Athletic, and scored twice in a 4–2 win. In all, young Bobby scored ten times in 14 League appearances that season and collected the first of his many honours as United stormed to their second successive Championship. He also played in his first FA Cup Final as United lost 2–1 to Aston Villa.

The 'Double' was snatched from United's grasp when Peter McParland charged into goalkeeper Ray Wood rendering him unable to carry on.

In 1957–58 Charlton began to assert himself in the first team. On 18 January 1958, he struck a fine hat-trick in a 7–2 drubbing of Bolton Wanderers at Old Trafford. A week later he scored both goals in United's 2–0 FA Cup Fourth Round victory over Ipswich Town, and on 1 February he notched another in a famous 5–4 win against Arsenal at Highbury. The following Wednesday saw United renewing their quest for European glory with a 3–3 draw away to Red Star Belgrade, enough for a 5–4 aggregate win and a place in the European Cup semi-finals.

Next day, 6 February, the aircraft carrying the team back to Manchester landed for refuelling at snow-bound Munich. During a third attempt to take-off again the plane left the runway, crashed through a fence, crossed a road and struck a house. Eight United team members were killed, as were three club officials, eight journalists, an aircrew member and two other passengers.

Bobby Charlton, who had been sitting in the middle of the plane, was thrown clear and escaped with superficial cuts. Within weeks he was a vital factor in United's rebuilding plans, initially watched over by assistant manager Jimmy Murphy as Matt Busby recovered from his injuries in a Munich hospital.

United finished the 1957–58 League campaign in 9th position. They also reached the FA Cup Final for a second successive year. Bolton Wanderers were the opponents and once again United lost in a match tinged with controversy. This time keeper Harry Gregg was barged over the line, ball and all, by Nat Lofthouse for Bolton's second goal.

By then Charlton had made a memorable full England début in which he scored a spectacular volleyed goal in a 4–0 victory against Scotland at Hampden Park.

He became the cornerstone of United, and Matt Busby continued to shape the team around him throughout the '60s. The additional purchases of the likes of Denis Law and Pat Crerand, and the irresistible rise of George Best made United one of the most formidable clubs of the day. Bobby was at the heart of things as they won the FA Cup in 1963, the League Championship in 1965 and 1967, and was at his inspirational best in the 1968 European Cup

> *Bobby Charlton, arguably the world's most famous footballer, played 606 League games for Manchester United and 106 times for England*

campaign. In the final, against Benfica at Wembley, he scored twice in the 4–1 victory.

By then, of course, Charlton also had a footballer's greatest prize in his trophy cabinet – a World Cup winners' medal, won in England's 4–2 defeat of West Germany in 1966. He went on to amass 106 international caps, and score a record 49 goals for England.

Following that last game in United's colours he joined Preston North End as player-manager, playing a further 38 games and notching eight more goals before finally hanging up his boots.

Bobby then joined the board at Old Trafford and has continued to serve football in general and Manchester United in particular, ever since. In 1994 he became 'Sir Bobby' when knighted for his services to the game.

COLIN TODD
DERBY COUNTY

**PLAYER OF
THE YEAR**

1975

'You always know when you're playing well, and I was having a great season in 1974–75,' says Colin Todd, recalling the campaign in which Derby County secured their second League Championship in four years.

At centre back Colin was a vital member of Dave Mackay's team, which tended to play fairly square in defence and often relied on his phenomenal pace to clean things up in an emergency situation. But Todd had much more than speed to rely upon: he was a master of the art of interception; his tackling was precise, he was cool under pressure and he could read the game as well as anyone.

Born in Chester-le-Street in December 1948, Colin had grown up a Newcastle United supporter idolising the likes of Len White and Ivor Allchurch. Yet when the time came to seriously consider his footballing future, the youngster showed a maturity beyond his years. 'In those days clubs couldn't approach a lad until he

was fifteen, and that's when Newcastle and Sunderland both declared an interest in me. I looked at both clubs and there seemed to be more youngsters coming through at Sunderland, so I became a Roker Park apprentice straight from school.'

Alan Brown, a man with a reputation for discovering fine young players, was Sunderland's manager at the time. 'He was a disciplinarian. Very strict. Not much of a sense of humour,' Colin recalls.

But it was to be another prominent Rokerite, Brian Clough, who would have the most significant influence on young Todd's early development. After being sidelined by the serious knee injury which would ultimately bring his playing career to a premature end, Clough had been given the first opportunity to practise his mercurial management and motivational skills, as coach to the Sunderland Youth team which he led to the semi–finals of the FA Youth Cup.

By the time Colin became a professional player in December 1966, Clough had moved on to begin his managerial career with Hartlepool; but manager and player were destined to meet again in more elevated circumstances. Alan Brown had been succeeded as Sunderland's manager first by George Hardwick and then by the former Scottish international boss Ian McColl.

'Ian McColl gave me my first team début when I was seventeen,' says Colin. 'I played two games in midfield but didn't do particularly well and was left out again. Then the opportunity came to play at centre back alongside Charlie Hurley – and from that day on I never looked back.'

During the next four years, while developing into the most polished of defenders, Colin

'Look at the players who've won it over the years – they've all been internationals in their own right.'

played 173 League games for Sunderland who stubbornly remained in the lower half of the First Division, before succumbing to relegation in 1970. 'I was ambitious, and definitely unhappy at the prospect of playing in the Second Division, so I put in a transfer request to Alan Brown, who had returned to Roker Park as manager in 1968.'

But more than half of the 1970–71 season passed before Colin was summoned one afternoon to Brown's house where the young player made a reunion with none other than Brian Clough. 'Brian said he wanted me at Derby. This meant a very big wrench for a lad of twenty-two, and of course I didn't know how it was going to turn out. I hadn't been married long and when I talked it over with my wife she decided the matter by saying she was quite happy to go wherever the football took me. So, I joined Derby for £170,000, which was a massive fee in those days.'

The Brian Clough revolution at the Baseball Ground had begun in 1967. In partnership with his old friend Peter Taylor, he had lifted County back into the First Division in 1969 – a feat achieved via a number of shrewd dealings in the transfer market. John O'Hare and John McGovern came from Sunderland and Hartlepool respectively, and so Clough was well aware of their potential. Roy McFarland came from Tranmere, Alan Hinton from Nottingham Forest. But the major factor in Derby's resurgence was

the signing of Dave Mackay from Spurs; his stirring example as team captain inspired the club to the 1968–69 Second Division Championship.

By the 1970–71 campaign County were a formidable force in the First Division as Clough continued to strengthen his squad with Archie Gemmill from Preston, followed by Colin Todd from Sunderland.

'I have the biggest admiration for Brian for putting me on the road to a successful career after spotting my potential in the Sunderland Youth team,' says Colin. 'He was very deep and it was difficult to get close to him, but you only have to look at his record to see that he got players to play for him. His style of management and his style of football were tremendous.'

Young Todd quickly settled into an awesomely efficient defensive partnership with Roy McFarland. In 1971–72 they became the cornerstone of the side which lifted the First Division title, Derby's first-ever success in the competition.

At the end of that victorious campaign, Colin's abilities were recognised at senior international level when Sir Alf Ramsey selected him at right-back in the England line-up for the Home International against Northern Ireland at Wembley. 'I'd played a number of time at Youth International and Under–23 levels, but winning my first full cap is something I'll never forget.'

In the event England lost the match 1–0 and Colin was not selected again until April 1974 against Portugal. In all he would appear 27 times in England's colours, and under three different managers: Ramsey, Mercer and Revie. 'I played just twice for Sir Alf, the second time – a 0–0 draw with Portugal in Lisbon – was his last in charge of the side. I was in all seven of Joe Mercer's games as caretaker boss. He was a lovely person, not a serious guy at all, he would just let you get on with the game. Don Revie was different, far more uptight, but he knew his football inside-out.'

By 1974–75 Todd and his Derby County team-mates had a new manager in their lives. Brian Clough, along with Peter Taylor, had left the Baseball Ground in October 1973 in a cloud of controversy and had been replaced by former Derby favourite Dave Mackay.

'Under Brian and Peter we had been brought up to keep clean sheets without being negative,' says Colin. 'They always said "we start off with a point, let's make sure we keep it". Dave wasn't as strict. He had his own style of management which allowed players to express themselves. He made some excellent signings – Charlie George, Franny Lee, Bruce Rioch – and he changed the team quite a bit.'

As the PFA membership voted for their second Player of the Year, Derby were going well in the league and Colin Todd was proving their most outstanding player – an opinion endorsed by the count which placed him top of the poll.

Several Derby County players were due to attend the Awards presentation at the Hilton Hotel on 2 March, but Colin had not intended to be among them, preferring to return home after County's match with Tottenham on Saturday 1st. Meanwhile, PFA Secretary Cliff Lloyd had called Colin's wife to ensure that the Player of the Year *would* be there. Eventually Lloyd had to ring back and tell Todd that he had won. 'That came as a big surprise. Although I knew I'd been playing well, it had never entered my mind that I might be the Player of the Year.'

In the event Colin received the coveted trophy from the Prime Minister Harold Wilson. 'Being voted best player by the other professionals is something I'll always cherish and remember. Look at the players who've won it over the years – they've all been internationals in their own right. My two sons still look at the trophy and remind me what a tremendous achievement it was.'

Colin Todd left Derby for Everton in September 1978. A year later he went to Birmingham City and in 1982 had yet another reunion with his old mentor Brian Clough who signed him for Nottingham Forest. His playing career wound down in 1984 after brief spells with Oxford United, the Vancouver Whitecaps and Luton Town. 'I played until I was thirty-five – you know in yourself when to call it a day,' he says. 'I felt I'd had enough of football and went back to Chester-le-Street hoping to go into a newsagent's business. But once I'd been out of the game for a while I realised what a mistake I had made.'

Colin returned to the game as assistant manager to his old friend Bruce Rioch at Middlesbrough, in 1985. Then came a spell in charge at Ayresome Park, following Rioch's departure in 1990. The two later teamed up again and steered Bolton Wanderers into the First Division in 1993

MERVYN DAY
WEST HAM UNITED

Born in Chelmsford in June 1955, Mervyn Day joined the West Ham 'football academy' as an apprentice a few days after his 16th birthday and later graduated to the England Youth team. Standing well over six feet tall, he was an agile goalkeeper with a mature attitude to the game and a certain coolness under pressure. However, his first team début, as a stand-in for Bobby Ferguson against Ipswich Town on 27 August 1973, was not a particularly auspicious one. The match was played in a heavy downpour, Mervyn conceded three goals (in a 3–3 draw) and was not selected again until some six weeks later, after Ferguson had a much-publicised falling-out with the club.

This time the youngster grabbed his chance to impress, with a degree of consistency that had manager Ron Greenwood enthusiastically declaring that Mervyn Day would be West Ham's first choice goalkeeper for the next decade. He finished the 1973–74 campaign with the valuable experience of 33 first team appearances under his belt. Throughout 1974–75, Mervyn was undoubtedly one of the most exciting goalkeepers in the First Division, as the Hammers struggled at first to maintain a mid-table position and then rose for a few weeks into the upper reaches of the table.

In March 1975 the PFA membership endorsed his sterling qualities by voting him their Young Player of the Year, at a time when he was being hailed as a future England international.

West Ham's League fortunes continued to fluctuate for the remainder of the season and they eventually finished in 13th position. Day had been ever-present throughout the campaign. He also played in all seven of West Ham's FA Cup matches *en route* to Wembley where they met Alec Stock's Fulham in the Final.

Throughout the Final Mervyn was his usual confident self. He made a two fine saves from John Mitchell, the first shortly before half time, the second late in the game – by which time the Cup was destined for the Upton Park trophy room, thanks to two opportunist goals snatched by Alan Taylor.

Mervyn Day remained with West Ham until the summer of 1979 when a £100,000 transfer took him to Leyton Orient, following the arrival of Phil Parkes at Upton Park. He later played for Aston Villa and Leeds United, playing 44 games and keeping 17 clean sheet as Leeds won the Second Division title in 1989–90. He also had brief loan spells with Luton Town and Sheffield United. Mervyn did not become a full England international, although he did make five appearances in the Under–23 side. In 1994–95 he was involved, as coach, in Carlisle United's promotion drive to the Second Division

YOUNG PLAYER OF THE YEAR

1975

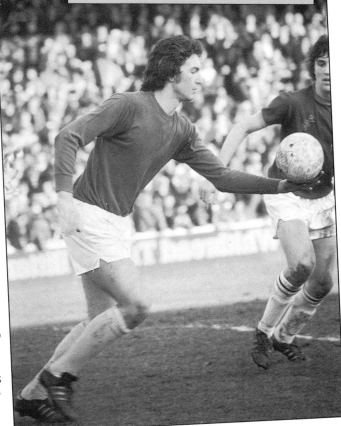

DENIS LAW

**MERIT
AWARD
WINNER**

1975

To see Denis Law going for goal, a look of intense concentration on his face and his shirt cuffs gripped firmly in his fists, was one of football's quintessential sights in the 1960s. Yet, as a boy, the young Law must have looked a most unlikely candidate for football stardom. Born in Aberdeen in February 1940, he was a skinny, slightly-built lad who had to wear glasses to correct a squint.

Like many youngsters in the '40s he honed his talents in street games. He was attack-minded right from the start – neither midfield or defence held much interest for him. He played for the Powis Street School team and was selected for the Aberdeen Schools XI and the Aberdeen Lads' Club.

In 1955 his talents were spotted by Archie Beattie, brother of Huddersfield Town manager Andy Beattie. After a trial period Denis was was offered a place on the Leeds Road ground staff.

When Huddersfield were relegated to Division Two in 1956, Andy Beattie was succeeded as manager by Bill Shankly who drafted the sixteen year-old Law into the first team. 'Shanks' described his protégé as 'a bloody terror – with ability'. That ability soon had a string of First Division clubs enquiring after the youngster and also brought him

international recognition in October 1958 when, at the age of 18 years, 236 days he became Scotland's youngest post-war cap, against Wales in Cardiff. Denis scored the first of his 30 international goals in the game. A few weeks later he had his first experience of the 'Hampden Roar' when he played against Northern Ireland.

Meanwhile, the ambitious Bill Shankly was becoming restless at Huddersfield and in December 1959 he moved to Liverpool. Law was also anxious to move on and might well have followed Shankly to Anfield if the Reds had been in the First Division. Instead, some three months after Shankly's departure, Denis was transferred to Manchester City for £47,500. He stayed at Maine Road for the 1959–60 season and was then on the move again – to Torino in Italy, for £110,000 and the prospect of a glittering future in the Italian sunshine.

But, despite scoring ten goals in 20 games for Torino, Law felt stifled by the overly-defensive style of Italian football and by the oppressive control wielded by the club over its players.

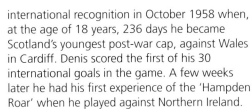

Things finally came to a head when Torino refused Law permission to play for Scotland. He walked out and flew back to Britain. In spite of Torino's strong protestations Law adamantly refused to return, thereby bringing about an inevitable transfer back to Britain, and in August 1962 he signed for Manchester United for £115,000. He blended perfectly into Matt Busby's squad of established and burgeoning stars.

His first success under Busby came in the 1963 FA Cup. A Third Round hat-trick in a 5–0 drubbing of his old club Huddersfield set United *en route* for Wembley where they eventually met Leicester City. Law was the man-of-the-match in the Final,

> *Like many youngsters in the '40s he honed his talents in street games. He was attack-minded right from the start – neither midfield or defence held much interest for him.*

scoring the first goal – a low drive on the turn from an inspired Paddy Crerand pass – and generally running the show as United cruised to a 3–1 victory. It was the beginning of good times again for Manchester United; Busby's post-Munich rebuilding plans were almost complete.

In 1963–64 Law was leading scorer with 46 goals in League, Cup and European Cup-Winners' Cup as United finished runners-up to Liverpool and reached the FA Cup semi-finals. Among that tally were no less than six hat-tricks and a four goal spree against Stoke City – all of which helped Denis being voted the 1964 European Footballer of the Year.

He was top scorer again in 1964–65 as United topped the League table to earn a place in the European Cup for the first time since 1958. They reached the semi-finals but were dismissed by Partizan Belgrade after two distinctly below-par performances.

Law again contributed more goals than anybody else (23) as Manchester United won the 1966–67 League title. In the following season's European Cup he scored twice in United's opening game of the competition, a 4–0 win against Hibernians of Malta. A knee injury kept him out of the next two ties, but he was back for the home leg of the semi-final encounter against Real Madrid, in which a George Best goal gave United a slender lead in the tie.

Law's knee problem worsened in the match and he found himself confined to hospital for the return leg, three weeks later, in which United battled through with a marvellous 3–3 draw – and was in hospital again when United defeated Benfica 4–1 in the Final at Wembley.

Denis Law continued to serve Manchester United until 1973 when he reluctantly accepted a free transfer to Manchester City. In an ironic twist of fate, it was Law's opportunist, back-heeled goal against United which won the game for City and helped condemn United to the Second Division at the end of the 1973–74 season. It was Denis Law's last League game.

That summer he also bowed out of the international scene. But he went out at the top, as a member of Scotland's World Cup squad in West Germany, making the last of his 53 appearances against Zaïre.

Manchester United's fans loved Denis Law's flamboyant goalscoring exploits, and dubbed him 'The King' of Old Trafford. Schoolboys all over the country imitated his sleeve grabbing style (Law claimed it simply made it easier to wipe his nose on his sleeve!). In 1975 he became the second ex-United hero in successive years to be honoured with a PFA Merit Award. These days Denis enjoys life as a football summariser on television

PAT JENNINGS
TOTTENHAM HOTSPUR

PLAYER OF THE YEAR

1976

On Sunday 29 February 1976 the Northern Ireland squad was due to fly to Tel Aviv for a friendly fixture with Israel three days later. Pat Jennings, the country's first-choice goalkeeper, fully expected to join his team-mates on the flight. But the timing of the fixture had left him in something of a dilemma. 'I knew I was one of the six contenders for the PFA's Player of the Year Award which was being presented on the Sunday evening,' he recalls. 'Kevin Keegan and Kevin Beattie were the hot tips that season and I honestly didn't expect to win. Then I got a call from Cliff Lloyd, who obviously knew the result of the poll and wanted to make sure I'd be at the "do".'

Pat explained to Cliff that he did not want to travel to Israel on his own simply for the sake of attending the dinner. 'But Cliff, who did everything except tell me I'd won

'Until the PFA introduced their Award, the big one had been the Footballer of the Year – but it was now equally as important to be chosen by your fellow professionals. I'm honoured to have won both Awards in my career.'

the Award, persuaded me to be there. He even rang back on the Saturday evening and on the Sunday morning to check that I was still in the country.'

On arriving at the Hilton Hotel Jennings was still convinced that he was an also-ran. 'A lot of people seemed to be congratulating Kevin Keegan in advance. I had no idea I'd won until my name was called out.'

The mild-mannered, softly spoken Ulsterman was a popular choice among his fellow professionals who were rewarding his consistent form which stood out in a Tottenham Hotspur side struggling in the lower half of the First Division. The PFA membership had, of course, long been aware of his goalkeeping qualities: supreme confidence, pinpoint timing, lightning reflexes, effective distribution, an enormous kick and the uncanny ability to make the most unortohodox of saves.

Pat's massive hands were the stuff of football legend too. Leeds United's Norman Hunter recalls a game played on a particularly windy day at Elland Road. 'The ball was pinged in and Pat came for it, intending to catch it in both hands. But the wind took it at the last moment so he was forced to use just one hand and it just stuck there in the middle of his palm. I couldn't believe it.'

Pat's career is peppered with many similar incidents relating near-impossible, one-handed saves. 'I was always confident that if I could get the tips of my fingers to the ball, rather than knocking it into more trouble, then I was capable of holding it,' he explains.

After the PFA ceremony, at which he was presented with the Player of the Year Award by the Duke of Kent, Pat flew out to Israel to make his 58th appearance for Northern Ireland.

Throughout the remainder of the 1975–76 season he continued to do his stuff as Spurs reached the League Cup semi-finals and climbed to ninth place in the table. 'That was quite an achievement, considering we had only just missed relegation the season before – we'd beaten Leeds 4–2 in the last match of the 1974–75 season to stay up. Now, more or less the same players had finished ninth.'

Pat Jennings has played on football grounds all over the world, but one venue holds pride of place in his memory. 'When I was eleven I played in an Under-19s street league in which all the teams were named after famous clubs – "Arsenal", "Celtic" and so on – my team was "Shamrock Rovers". We played in a meadow in Newry, my home town. It was a great little tournament which attracted big crowds, but it only lasted one season through lack of facilities. Some years later the local council renamed the field "Jennings Park".'

And with good reason, for the local hero had risen from that makeshift tournament to the dizzying heights of the World Cup Finals.

At 16 he had become an Irish Junior Cup winner with Newry United before progressing to Newry Town, then in the 'B' Division of the Northern Irish League. At that time he was working as a labourer in a timber gang and felt that a career in professional football was only a remote possibility. 'I didn't think it was something that would be available to me,' he says.

Then, in 1963, Pat was selected for the Northern Ireland Youth team in a Youth tournament in England. 'The preliminary games were played in Bognor Regis and we stayed at the Butlins Holiday Camp. We got through to the Final but lost 4–0 to England at Wembley.'

Nevertheless that Final proved a successful shop window for the young keeper. Among those to declare an interest was Coventry City manager Jimmy Hill, but by then a £6,000 deal had already been struck between Newry and Third Division Watford, managed by former Spurs favourite Ron Burgess, and so Jennings joined the squad at Vicarage Road. 'It had been the winter of the Big Freeze and the season had been delayed. There were still four games left to play when I signed and Watford were involved in the relegation battle. I played in the last two matches when they were safe. My first game was at the old White City, a 2–2 draw with Queens Park Rangers.'

Jennings was ever-present for the Hornets throughout 1963–64, the season in which he also made his senior Northern Ireland debut. Watford finished third in the Third Division, but the goalkeeper moved into the upper echelons when Tottenham's Bill Nicholson signed him for £27,500 in June '64.

Four seasons earlier Spurs had become the first club in the twentieth century to achieve the League and FA Cup 'double'. Now that great team was in the process of changing. Jennings was brought in to understudy Scottish international Bill Brown, a situation which prevailed until Brown moved on to Northampton Town in 1966 and Pat became Spurs' undisputed first-choice goalkeeper.

His first major honour came in 1967 when Spurs beat an unsettled Chelsea in the FA Cup Final. By then Nicholson's rebuilding job was complete; skipper Dave Mackay remained from the 'Double' winning side of 1960–61, and the impressive line-up now included such thoroughbreds as Cyril Knowles, Alan Mullery, Jimmy Greaves, Alan Gilzean and Terry Venables. That summer Pat wrote a unique chapter in the history of the Charity Shield competition as Spurs drew 3–3 with League Champions Manchester United at Old Trafford.

'We were awarded a free kick just outside our box. Dave Mackay slipped the ball to me and I tried to hit Alan Gilzean up front. United's keeper Alex Stepney obviously thought Gilly was going to control it and came out behind him. But the wind caught the ball, Alex was nowhere, and suddenly it was in the net. I couldn't believe it. I wasn't even sure it counted in the rules of the game.'

More honours followed for Jennings: a League Cup winners' medal in 1971, when Tottenham beat Aston Villa 2–0, and a UEFA Cup winners' medal won over two-legs against Wolves in 1972. In March 1973 Pat put on one of his finest-ever displays for Spurs, against League leaders Liverpool at Anfield. Twice he saved from the penalty spot and pulled off two other point-blank saves to help secure a draw. That performance added to his cause in a season of consistency in which he collected his second League Cup winners' medal following Spurs' 1–0 defeat of Norwich City at Wembley and was also voted 1973 Football Writers' Footballer of the Year.

Three years later he was the PFA's Players' Player of the Year. 'Until the PFA introduced their Award, the big one had been the Footballer of the Year – but it was now equally as important to be chosen by your fellow professionals. I'm honoured to have won both Awards in my career.'

In the summer of 1976 Pat Jennings was awarded the MBE for his services to football. In the '76–77 season he missed around twenty League games due to an ankle injury. This time Tottenham could not avoid the drop and at the end of the season he found himself transfer-listed by Keith Burkinshaw. 'It doesn't bear thinking about,' says Pat. 'One season you are the Players' Player of the Year, the next you're being sold for £45,000. I knew I could still play. I was thirty-two at the time, but I hadn't lost any pace or speed.'

Others felt the same. Bobby Robson's Ipswich Town were the first to declare an interest; Manchester United and Aston Villa were also keen to sign the man described as 'Britain's best goalkeeper since Gordon Banks'. But, to the disbelief of the White Hart Lane faithful, Jennings was eventually transferred to their arch-rivals Arsenal. 'On the day Jimmy Rimmer left Highbury to join Aston Villa, I joined the Gunners. Looking back it was obviously a fantastic move for me – three FA Cup Finals in my first three seasons, and the European Cup Winners' Cup Final against Valencia in 1980.'

Keith Burkinshaw later admitted his error in selling Jennings, who went on to become the first British player to make 1,000 first class appearances. He returned to White Hart Lane as a reserve keeper in 1984. In 1986 he played for Northern Ireland in the World Cup Finals in Mexico, making his 119th international appearance on his 41st birthday. That year also saw him awarded the OBE

PETER BARNES
MANCHESTER CITY

Peter Barnes had appeared in just three League games for Manchester City before the 1975–76 season. Then, in October 1975, following an injury to left winger Dennis Tueart, he was drafted into the first team by manager Tony Book for a League encounter with Burnley. Tueart was back for the next game, against Tottenham Hotspur, but young Barnes had impressed enough to be retained in the team and would remain in the line-up for most of the rest of the season.

Within weeks Peter's dazzling performances on the wing saw him earmarked by the Press as a prospective England international. He was fast, skilful, creative, a holy terror to opposing defences – and most definitely an exciting player to watch.

He was particularly effective in the League Cup, scoring City's opening goal in the 2–1 defeat of Newcastle United in the Final at Wembley on 28 February 1976.

The following day Peter was named PFA Young Player of the Year at the Hilton Hotel in London. The Award was presented to him by England's World Cup winning goalkeeper Gordon Banks.

In November 1977 Peter was selected for England for the first time, in a World Cup qualifier against Italy at Wembley. He had a fine game, attacking down the left flank (another débutant, Steve Coppell, had the same task on the right) as England won 2–0 in a performance described as their best in at least two years. It was the first of Peter's 22 international appearances.

Peter Barnes left Manchester City for West Bromwich Albion in July 1979. He would later play for several more clubs, including spells in Spain with Real Betis and Portugal with Farense and a return to Maine Road in 1987. He finally hung up his boots in 1989, having spent the 1988–89 season on the books at Bolton Wanderers and Sunderland

YOUNG PLAYER OF THE YEAR

1976

GEORGE EASTHAM OBE

MERIT AWARD WINNER

1976

All modern-day PFA members owe a great deal to the 1976 Merit Award winner, George Eastham, whose brave, pioneering efforts in the High Court in 1963 brought about the end of the old 'retain-and-transfer' system.

Eastham, the son of a former England international, was a slightly-built player who displayed a magnificent talent as an inside-right. His career began with the Northern Irish club, Ards, where his father was player-manager. A number of English clubs, among them Bolton Wanderers, Blackpool and Arsenal, were reportedly showing interest in the talented teenager and it was inevitable that he would soon return across the Irish Sea.

In April 1956 young George represented the Irish League against The Football League. The Irish side won 5–2, and Eastham was the star of the show. In the following month he signed for Newcastle United in a £9,000 transfer deal.

He rose quickly at St James' Park and within four seasons was numbered among the most talked-about players in English football. Here was a true artist with the ball, the most accurate of passers, who stood out in The Magpies' forward-line of the late '50s. His best season with the club was 1959–60 during which he was ever-present and had a tally of 18 League goals as Newcastle finished 8th in the First Division.

But this was not the Magpies of old, and the ambitious Eastham felt ready to move on to pastures new. Arsenal wanted him. Newcastle United refused to let him go. After all, argued the Tyneside club, they had

developed him into the player he was and under the prevailing system had every right to retain him on their books – even against his own wishes. No one knew it at the time, but this simple situation would lead to a fundamental change in the way in which professional footballers would be treated by their clubs.

In an unprecedented move Eastham steadfastly refused to play for Newcastle again and, despite efforts at reconciliation by the club, the £47,500 transfer finally took place in November 1960.

Encouraged by the PFA Eastham then decided to pursue the case in court, demanding that footballers be granted the same rights as workers in other walks of life – namely the freedom to change one's place of employment. The case was eventually heard in the High Court in June and July of 1963, under the jurisdiction of Judge Wilberforce who eventually decreed that clubs who denied a transfer request when a player had served out his contract were indeed in restraint of trade. Eastham had won the day and the path was cleared towards freedom of contract.

George continued with Arsenal until the end of the 1965–66 season. During his stay at Highbury he became an England international, under Alf Ramsey, winning 19 caps and scoring two goals. He played his last game for England in July 1966, just before the famous World Cup Finals campaign got under way.

For the last seven years of his playing career he enjoyed a degree of success with Stoke City, most notably scoring the winning goal in the 1972 League Cup Final against Chelsea.

George Eastham of Ards, Newcastle United, Arsenal and Stoke City – a great player who struck a blow for players' rights

ANDY GRAY
ASTON VILLA

Andy Gray described the 1976–77 season as his 'Golden Year'. It was also the season in which the Aston Villa striker changed the PFA rules.

Born in Drumchapel, Glasgow, in November 1955, Andy was the youngest of four football-mad brothers, all of them Rangers supporters. His enthusiasm for the game and his competitive spirit were apparent from very early on and it seemed he was an almost intuitive goalscorer. He played for Scotland Schoolboys and in local League soccer for the Clydebank Strollers. At 17 he was spotted by Maurice Friel, a Dundee United scout, who invited him to a trial at Tannadice – but he failed and returned dejected to Glasgow, convinced he would never make it as a professional footballer. However, Friel kept faith with Andy and persistently reported his progress back to United's manager Jim McLean who gave him a second chance less than twelve months later. This time he was offered terms.

Within weeks of turning professional in July 1973 Andy made his first team début as a substitute in a 4–0 Scottish League Cup defeat at Motherwell. His first goal came against East Fife, also in the League Cup. The goals continued to flow and within months Andy was attracting the attention of numerous clubs south of the border and being hailed as a future international star.

Then he picked up the first in a string of injuries that were to plague his career and was out of action for a few weeks, returning in time for the Scottish Cup quarter-final victory (after a replay) against Dunfermline. United went on to beat Hearts in the semi-finals and meet Celtic in the Final. 'We were beaten 3–0,' Andy recalls. 'It was the most disappointing moment of my career and the only time I've ever cried at a football match.'

Despite the disappointment he finished the season as the club's top scorer and was voted Player of the Year by the Tannadice faithful.

As Andy's career developed, it became almost inevitable that he would move on. In the summer of 1975 he almost became the first British footballer to play in the West German Bundesliga when Schalke 04 made a £150,000 bid for his services. But, after careful consideration, he turned the offer down and at the beginning of October moved instead to Aston Villa for £110,000.

Ron Saunders' side had just achieved promotion to the First Division, after finishing as Second Division runners-up behind Manchester United. Now in the process of strengthening the squad (a task that would ultimately bring European Cup success to Villa Park) Saunders had had Gray under surveillance for some time.

Andy fitted into the scheme of things straight away, making his club début in a 0–0 draw with Middlesbrough at Ayresome Park on 4 October. His home début and his first goal for Villa came four days later, in the League Cup third round tie against Manchester United, and although Villa lost 2–1 the Holte Enders took their new striker to heart. He also scored on his home League début in a 1–1 draw with Spurs.

Villa finished the 1975–76 season in a disappointing 16th place, but Andy was reasonably pleased with his own progress. 'I'd played three-quarters of the season, scored ten league goals and had begun to make one or two inroads towards making a reputation for myself,' he says.

PLAYER OF THE YEAR

YOUNG PLAYER OF THE YEAR

1977

The following season was to tell a different story for both club and player. 'A lot of the players were very keen to do well in 1976–77 – among them John Gidman, Brian Little, Gordon Cowans, Alex Cropley and myself. It was a really strong looking side and we all felt very confident. Villa were at last signalling to everyone that they were back in the big time.

'For me the season started full of promise. I got off to a flyer with two goals in the opening game against West Ham at Villa Park – and when a striker does that it lifts the pressure immediately and really gets him up and running.'

There were no Gray goals in the next two League games, against Manchester City and Everton, but in the fourth game of the season, at home against Ipswich, he hit a magnificent hat-trick in a 5–2 victory – and when the tables were computed Villa found themselves top of the League. Four days later Andy scored his first goals for Scotland, in his third international appearance. He struck twice in a 6–0 trouncing of Finland at Hampden Park.

'I had a magnificent September and from then till Christmas, I just couldn't stop scoring,' he recalls. 'Come the turn of the year I was way ahead of everyone else.'

When the votes were counted for the season's PFA Awards, the membership showed its appreciation of his goalscoring feats by voting him in ahead of everyone else in both the Players' Player and the Young Player categories. It was the first time such a situation had arisen. The history-making presentations were to take place at the Hilton Hotel on Sunday 13 March.

By then Aston Villa had battled through to the Final of the League Cup and were due to meet Everton at Wembley on the 12th. During the game, which ended in a 0–0 draw, Gray aggravated an ankle injury which would require treatment before the replay on the following Wednesday evening.

On Sunday morning Andy received a call at home in Sutton Coldfield, from Cliff Lloyd who was in London with Derek Dougan preparing for the evening's presentation ceremony. 'Cliff wanted to check that I'd be going to the dinner and then he dropped the bombshell that I'd won *both* Awards. You could have knocked me down with the proverbial feather – I'd known I was on the shortlist and thought I might be in with a chance of the Young Player title, but hadn't really given it much thought beyond that.'

That was the good news; next came the bad. Ron Saunders had refused Andy permission to travel to London that evening as the journey

might further aggravate his injury. 'It was quite a dilemma. But in the end I had to agree with my manager as it was important to win a major trophy and I desperately wanted to play in the replay later in the week. At the time the PFA Awards had only been in operation for four seasons and people were still getting to know the value of them. I was only twenty-one and couldn't really grasp what it meant to be voted best player by your peers.'

The PFA were in a dilemma too. Two awards, no recipient and the TV cameras standing by to broadcast the non-event. The telephones lines between London and Birmingham glowed as Derek Dougan first attempted to persuade the young footballer to put pressure on his manager. No chance, said Gray. They also contacted Saunders directly, but he steadfastly refused to change his mind. Villa Chairman Sir William Dugdale was also asked to intervene, but still Saunders refused. They even offered to fly the Award winner to London, but he would not go behind his boss's back.

At one stage Dougan desperately suggested that Gray relinquish his Young Player Award which would then be presented, on camera, to the second placed player in that category. 'For a brief, brief moment I nearly said yes,' recalls Andy. 'But something stopped me and I realised if I gave one up, then no-one would ever know it and I might have been passing up a piece of history. I said "Sorry, Derek. If I've won both, I want both".'

In the end a compromise was reached when Dougan arranged that a TV crew would come to Andy's home where he would receive the main Award, while the Young Player trophy would be accepted on his behalf at the Hilton ceremony. 'I lived in a small semi-detached house at the time and all the TV lights brought out the whole neighbourhood to see what was going on. My brother turned up with some of the Villa lads, and the skipper Chris Nicholl presented me with the trophy. It was great, but it was only when I went to the following year's PFA Awards, for the first time, that I realised what I'd missed and what an opportunity had been denied me by Ron Saunders. I was young and inexperienced at the time and now I know I'd take the situation in my own hands, turn up – and take the consequences later. It's the one big regret that I have.'

On the following Wednesday evening Andy was fit for the League Cup Final replay with Everton at Hillsborough. With seconds remaining Villa were ahead 1–0 thanks to an own-goal by Roger Kenyon, then Bob Latchford hit Everton's equaliser in a goalmouth scramble. After extra-time the scoreline remained at 1–1 and a second replay was scheduled for 13 April at Old Trafford.

By then Andy was out of action with his leg in plaster, following a ligament problem picked up in the previous League match against Derby at the Baseball Ground. Villa eventually won the League Cup, beating Everton 3–2 after yet another period of extra time.

Andy Gray returned to the fray two weeks later to help in Villa's push for a place in Europe. In the last game of the season, at home to West Brom, he blasted a hat-trick as Villa won 4–0 to finish fourth and book a UEFA Cup berth. Those three goals took his tally of League strikes to 25, making him the First Division's joint-top scorer with Malcolm Macdonald of Arsenal. It was the perfect end to Andy Gray's 'Golden Year'.

Meanwhile, back at PFA headquarters it was decided to adopt Derek Dougan's suggestion that no player would again win the Player of the Year Award and the Young Player of the Year Award in the same season. In the event of one player topping both polls in future, *he* would be presented with the Player of the Year Award, while the person receiving the second highest number of votes in the Young Player poll would be named *Young* Player of the Year.

Andy Gray, the man who made PFA history and the catalyst for a change in the rules, is listed among the most exciting goalscorers of modern times. He was also the most courageous of strikers, with a fiery, aggressive style which brought him several injuries throughout his career. His Villa days ended in September 1979 by which time he could no longer see eye-to-eye with manager Ron Saunders. He moved to Wolverhampton Wanderers for £1.5 million, a new British transfer record. In 1980 he scored the only goal in the League Cup Final as Wolves beat Nottingham Forest at Wembley. Unfortunately Wolves' financial troubles were just around the corner and with limited resources the club was unable to sustain its challenge for honours. In 1981–82 came relegation and the threat of receivership, but Wolves bounced straight back to the top flight only to struggle again with nine defeats and three draws in the first dozen games of the '83–84 season.

It was then that Everton stepped in and Andy moved to Goodison Park for the most glorious stage of his career which brought him an FA Cup winners' medal in 1984. In '84–85 he collected a League Championship medal and a European Cup-winners' Cup medal. Then came a return to Aston Villa for two seasons, a brief loan out to Notts County at the start of the 1987–88 campaign and a move to West Brom. But his playing career was destined to end on a high note, with his boyhood club Rangers. 'Spending my last year as a professional with Rangers and winning the Premier League Championship in 1988–89 was the icing on the cake, giving me Championship medals north and south of the border. It was great for me to take my family, all Rangers nuts, into the inner sanctum at Ibrox and for them to share it all with me.'

On hanging up his boots Andy transferred his vast experience of the game to television and, via Sky TV, has become the most enthusiastic of commentators

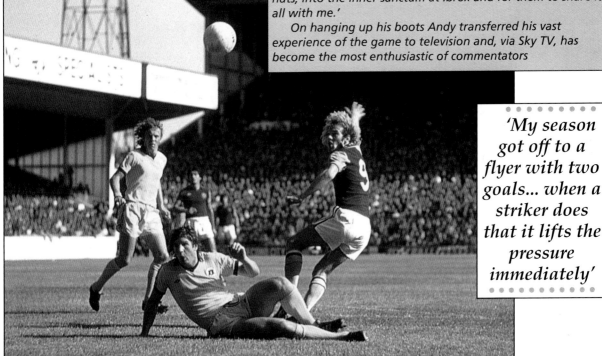

'My season got off to a flyer with two goals... when a striker does that it lifts the pressure immediately'

JACK TAYLOR *OBE*

**MERIT
AWARD
WINNER**

1977

Jack Taylor, a master butcher from Wolverhampton, is the only referee to be honoured with a PFA Merit Award. A man of unrivalled integrity he was a familiar figure at football grounds all over the country.

The big match highlights of Jack's career were the 1966 FA Cup Final in which Everton beat Sheffield Wednesday 3–2, the 1971 European Cup Final between Ajax and Panathinaikos at Wembley – and the World Cup Final between West Germany and Holland in 1974.

Jack made history that day – as the first referee to award a penalty in a World Cup final.

It happened in the first minute of the match when Holland's Johan Cruyff was brought down. Neeskens converted and the Dutch were ahead, without a single West German player so much as having touched the ball.

Jack belonged to that rare breed – a referee who was respected wherever he blew the whistle.

Jack Taylor (with ball) looks on as Johan Cruyff and Franz Beckenbauer exchange pennants before the 1974 World Cup Final

PETER SHILTON
NOTTINGHAM FOREST

There can hardly have been a more fortuitous place for an aspiring goalkeeper to learn his craft in the early–60s than Filbert Street, Leicester. It was there that the young Peter Leslie Shilton was invited, while still at primary school, to train with Leicester City whose resident keeper was, of course, the great Gordon Banks – the perfect role model and an absolute idol to the young Shilton.

Peter was born in Leicester in September 1949. By the age of ten, he had already decided to become a professional goalkeeper. He represented England for the first time as a schoolboy international, winning three caps before becoming an apprentice on the Leicester groundstaff in June 1965 and a protégé of Banks himself.

The England keeper quickly recognised Shilton's outstanding potential and offered his advice and encouragement. The impressive youngster was keen and willing to learn at the feet of the master and never shirked extra training; in fact he thoroughly enjoyed it. He also became dedicated to the cause of total fitness – an attitude that would ultimately bring him a playing career of great longevity – and he developed into a strong and strapping six-footer, weighing in at almost 13 stones and earning the nickname 'Tarzan' around Filbert Street.

On 4 May 1966, with Gordon Banks on England duty against Yugoslavia, manager Matt Gillies drafted Peter into Leicester's first-team for a home match against Everton. The 16-year-old

put in a particularly impressive and confident display as City recorded a 3–0 victory. Towards the end of the 1966–67 season Gillies had enough confidence in Shilton to allow the transfer of Banks – by then a World Cup winner – to Stoke City.

But Peter's run as Leicester's first-choice keeper almost came to an abrupt halt in only his third game of the 1967–68 season. He was stretchered-off following a collision with Manchester United's George Best in the dying minutes of a game at Old Trafford. The dive at Best's flying feet demonstrated Peter's courage; it also kept the scoreline at 1–1 and earned him a well-deserved standing ovation. Thankfully he recovered and returned to complete 35 League games as City held a mid-table position.

**PLAYER OF
THE YEAR**

1978

By 1978, when he was voted in as the PFA's Player of the Year, Peter Shilton was already a veteran of nearly thirteen seasons as a professional footballer ... but his incredible playing career was only just nearing its halfway point.

In 1968–69 as Leicester's form faltered, the ambitious Shilton, unhappy at the prospect of Second Division football, put in a transfer request, which he later withdrew on the advice of new manager Frank O'Farrell.

Leicester couldn't avoid the drop, but they did appear in the 1969 FA Cup Final against Manchester City. *En route* to the Final the nineteen-year-old Shilton had saved a Tommy Smith penalty at Anfield to help put Liverpool out in the Fifth Round. The only goal of the Final came from an unstoppable shot by City's Neil Young. In his disappointment Shilton again requested a transfer which was denied – thereby starting a long and drawn-out dispute with the club.

It was in his second season as a Second Division player that Peter made his full England début – on 25 November 1970 against East Germany at Wembley (it was England's first match after the World Cup Finals in Mexico in

which they had been eliminated at the quarter-finals stage by West Germany). He played exceptionally well in the 3–1 victory but, with Gordon Banks still prominent, Sir Alf Ramsey did not select him again until the Home International against Wales six months later, by which time Leicester had returned to the top flight.

In November 1974 Shilton again found himself in confrontation with the Leicester hierarchy and this time he was transferred – to Stoke City for £325,000, then a world record fee for a goalkeeper. The Potters had been a First Division club since 1963, when they had achieved promotion with the help of Sir Stanley Matthews, and in 1972 had won the League Cup with the help of George Eastham. But beyond that they were, like Leicester, rather a middle order club. In his three seasons at the Victoria Ground, Peter played in just three internationals (largely due to disagreements with Don Revie) while his great rival Ray Clemence became England's first-choice keeper. And in 1976–77 Shilton's club fortunes dipped dramatically with Stoke's relegation to the Second Division.

But rescue was close at hand in the shape of Brian Clough and Peter Taylor, the dynamic management team at Nottingham Forest – a club which had been promoted as Stoke went down. They paid a then-club record £250,000 to bring Shilton to the City Ground in September 1977. Forest had already won four of their five fixtures at the start of the 1977–78 League campaign when Peter took over from John Middleton who was simultaneously transferred to Derby County, in part-exchange for Archie Gemmill.

Under Clough's guidance Peter Shilton at last had the stage on which to display his prodigious talents week in, week out. Time and again he proved he was worth every penny of the huge fee paid by Forest. He played in all 37 of the club's remaining League matches, keeping no less than 23 clean sheets and conceding just eighteen goals. (Being 'cup-tied' because of a Second Round appearance for Stoke in August, meant that Peter played no part in Forest's other great campaign of the season – the goalkeeping duties in the victorious League Cup run went to young Chris Woods.)

Forest romped to the League title unbeaten at home and losing only three away games. They clinched the Championship with four matches of their programme left to play, leaving Liverpool and Everton floundering.

Midway through Forest's magnificent campaign the PFA membership acknowledged

Peter's dazzling consistency by voting him their Player of the Year for 1978, an Award presented to him by Lord Ted Willis, the creator of the long-running TV series *Dixon of Dock Green*.

Throughout 1977–78 Peter was surprisingly selected only twice for international duty, in victories against Wales and Hungary, as Revie's successor Ron Greenwood continued to keep faith with Liverpool's Ray Clemence. This friendly rivalry between England's two top keepers would continue until the 1982 World Cup Finals in Spain, when Shilton made the job virtually his own.

By 1978, when he was voted the PFA's Player of the Year, Peter Shilton was already a veteran of nearly thirteen seasons as a professional footballer. He was the second goalkeeper to win the top honour (no other keeper has since been named Player of the Year).

In 1978–79 Peter was ever-present throughout the League campaign in which Forest finished runners-up to Liverpool. He also played in the League Cup Final in which Forest beat Southampton 3–2, to take the trophy for a second successive year. On 30 May in Munich, he played in his first European Cup Final in which Forest beat Malmo 1–0. But his most outstanding contribution in the competition had come in the first leg of the quarter finals tie against Grasshoppers of Zurich. In the 75th minute, with Forest 2–1 ahead, he pulled off the save of the season with a superb dive to prevent the equaliser. Brian Clough later said 'It was an absolutely fantastic save considering Peter was stone cold, having been a spectator for most of the match. It even surpassed his normal brilliance ... and it underlined that he is the best goalkeeper in the world. We'll look back on it and say it was the moment we won the European Cup.'

Peter Shilton's incredible playing career was only just nearing its halfway point. He had many more seasons ahead of him – and he was to receive a PFA Merit Award in 1990

TONY WOODCOCK
NOTTINGHAM FOREST

**YOUNG
PLAYER OF
THE YEAR**

1978

On Saturday 18 March 1978 Nottingham Forest met Liverpool in the League Cup Final at Wembley. Prominent in Forest's line-up was 22-year-old striker Tony Woodcock who had so far contributed four goals in the campaign. He was an exciting player with incredible pace, lightning fast reflexes and a high degree of skill.

A local lad, born in Eastwood in December 1955, Tony had begun his career as a Forest apprentice. His League début came in the 1973–74 season and his experience had since been bolstered by brief loan spells at Lincoln City and Doncaster Rovers.

In October 1977 he made his England Under–21 début, scoring a hat-trick in an 8–1 defeat of Finland at Hull. By then he was well-established as a first team regular with Forest and a firm favourite of the City Ground faithful.

In the event the 1978 League Cup Final ended in a scoreless draw after extra-time – thanks largely to the heroic efforts of Forest's young keeper Chris Woods – and the teams

were due to meet again at Old Trafford four days later.

On Sunday 19th the PFA held its fifth annual Awards presentation at which Tony Woodcock stepped onto the stage at the London Hilton Hotel, to acknowledge the appreciation of the membership who had voted him the Young Player of the Year. The Award was presented to him by the England team manager Ron Greenwood.

On Wednesday the 22nd Tony was back in action in the League Cup Final replay against Liverpool. In the second half he provided a through ball to John O'Hare, who was subsequently brought down on the edge of the area by Phil Thompson. The referee awarded a penalty which was hotly disputed by the Liverpool players who were convinced that the incident had occurred outside the box. John Robertson converted the spot-kick for the only goal of the game – and Tony Woodcock collected his second major honour of the week.

In April he also picked up a League Championship medal as Forest romped home ahead of Liverpool and Everton – he had played 36 games in the campaign and finished with 11 League goals to his credit. In May he made his full England début in a 1–0 victory over Northern Ireland at Wembley.

Tony Woodcock and Nottingham Forest parted company in 1980 when he was transferred to FC Cologne of the West German Bundesliga. After two seasons he returned to England with Arsenal, but rejoined Cologne in 1986. His playing career ended with German club Fortuna Dusseldorf. Tony played 42 games and scored 16 goals for England

BILL SHANKLY *OBE*

**MERIT
AWARD
WINNER**

1978

Bill Shankly, the architect of the most successful English club side of all time, was one of the game's great motivators – a fact underlined by the long list of glowing tributes from players who served under him, and by the results they achieved.

'Shanks', the second-youngest in a family of ten children (five of them became professional footballers), was born on 2 September 1913 in the coal mining village of Glenbuck, Ayrshire. A tenacious half back of the 'hard man' school, and blessed with almost legendary stamina, his playing career began with Carlisle United who he joined in July 1932 after impressing with local clubs Cronberry and the Glenbuck Cherrypickers. A year later he moved on to Second Division Preston North End in a £500 transfer deal.

At the end of his first season at Deepdale the club was promoted to the top flight – as runners-up to Grimsby Town – and they were to remain there until 1948–49, the season he left. During his time with Preston he won five caps for Scotland.

Shankly's finest season as a player was 1937–38 when Preston finished third in the First Division and won the FA Cup by defeating Huddersfield Town 1–0, with a penalty in the last minute of extra-time (making up for the disappointment of losing to Sunderland in the previous year's final).

On hanging up his boots in March 1949, Shanks went straight into management with Carlisle United. He took them to third spot in the Third Division (North) in 1951. That summer he moved on to Grimsby Town, also of the Third Division (North), almost taking them to promotion in his first season. Workington was the next stop, in January 1954. Then, in December 1955, the Shankly learning curve took him into the First Division as assistant to Andy Beattie at Huddersfield Town, a club with an impeccable pedigree.

In 1953–54 Huddersfield were riding high, finishing in third place behind Wolves and West Bromwich Albion. 1954–55 saw them in mid-table, but '55–56 brought relegation and signalled the start of a decline from which they have yet to recover. Andy Beattie moved on in November 1956 and Bill Shankly took over, knowing that in order to restore the status quo the club needed to invest heavily in the transfer market. Unfortunately, funds were not forthcoming and in December 1959 the ambitious manager made the move that would eventually turn him into a football legend. He went to Second Division Liverpool as successor to Phil Taylor.

Since their relegation in 1954, the Anfield club has been close to a return to top flight football on three occasions. At the end of Shankly's first season in charge they were lying in fourth place. Next season saw them in third spot.

In 1961 Shankly discarded no less than twenty-four members of the Anfield playing staff and began to delve into the transfer market, buying Gordon Milne from Preston, Ian St John from Motherwell and Ron Yeats from Dundee United. This formidable trio added steel to the side, and in 1961–62 Liverpool stormed to the Second Division title, eight points ahead of nearest rivals Leyton Orient.

Two seasons later Shankly had further strengthened his squad with Peter Thompson from Preston and Willie Stevenson from Rangers. Goalkeeper Tommy Lawrence had been drafted in from the reserves as a replacement for Jim Furnell.

With four games of the 1963–64 season left to play, Liverpool needed just two points to ensure the League Championship title. The last three of these fixtures were away, and so Shankly urged his Reds to settle the matter in front of the Anfield crowd. Arsenal were the victims, in a 5–0 thrashing, and Liverpool's glory days had begun.

The following season saw Shankly's team lift the FA Cup against Leeds United in extra-time at Wembley – Liverpool's first success in the competition – and they were European Cup semi-finalists. In 1965–66 he called on just fourteen players (a then-record) as Liverpool again won the League Championship,

conceding a mere 34 goals and notching 61 points. The Reds also reached their first European final, in the Cup -Winners' Cup, losing 2–1 to Borussia Dortmund at Hampden Park.

A third League title followed for Shankly in 1972–73, along with the UEFA Cup, the club's first European trophy won with a 3–2 aggregate over two legs against Borussia Moenchengladbach. By then the Anfield squad boasted the likes of Kevin Keegan, Ray Clemence, Tommy Smith, Emlyn Hughes, Steve Heighway and John Toshack – all of whom would benefit from Shankly's influence for the remainder of their careers.

In 1973–74 Liverpool finished second in the League and won the FA Cup with a devastating 3–0 destroyal of Newcastle United at Wembley. After the match, and much to the astonishment of the Anfield faithful, the great manager announced his retirement and handed the reins to Bob Paisley. Shanks was awarded the OBE for his services to football.

Sadly he died in September 1981 after a heart attack. The 'Shankly Gates', adorned with the legend 'You'll Never Walk Alone', were erected at Anfield in his memory.

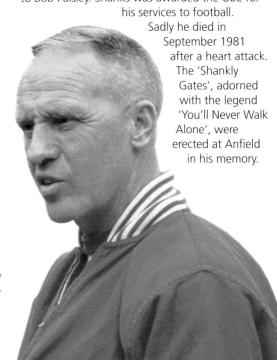

Bill Shankly – master motivator and expert team builder who combined shrewd acquisitions in the transfer market with a wealth of homegrown talent

LIAM BRADY
ARSENAL

Liam Brady was an exceptionally talented Dublin-born schoolboy, spotted by an Arsenal scout at the start of the 1970s. He was then invited to Highbury for a trial and subsequently became a Gunners apprentice in 1971.

'Highbury was a great place to learn my trade,' says Liam, 'Arsenal had just done the League and Cup "Double" and were the team of the moment.'

Liam made his first team début as a substitute for Jeff Blockley in a 2–0 defeat at Tottenham in October 1973 and went on to complete 13 league appearances that season as Arsenal finished in tenth position. He scored his first goal for the club in the last game of that campaign, a 1–1 draw at home to QPR. 'Alan Ball had joined the club by then and several of the double-winning team were still there – Charlie George, Ray Kennedy, Bob Wilson, John Radford, George Armstrong – they were all smashing players.'

When Bertie Mee stepped down from the Arsenal managership in 1976 after the club had narrowly escaped relegation, he was replaced by Terry Neill. 'A season later, Terry re-appointed Don Howe as coach and the club's fortunes really began to look up again,' recalls Liam.

Throughout 1977–78 Arsenal remained in contention for the title, which was eventually won by Nottingham Forest. They also reached the League Cup semi-final, and the FA Cup Final against Ipswich Town. 'Three or four of our players weren't quite right in the Final, including myself – I had an ankle injury and was substituted by Graham Rix with twenty-five minutes to go – Ipswich were the better team on the day and deserved their 1–0 victory.'

Despite the disappointments and frustrations of the season, 'Chippy' Brady was by now well-established as the Gunners' midfield general, the man with the 'educated left foot' who had proved the natural successor to Alan Ball. His ease on the ball was a joy to watch, and his unpredictability kept the Highbury fans on their toes: would he deliver the perfect pass, or would he use his dazzling array of skills to take on an opponent?

PLAYER OF THE YEAR

1979

'I think most of the players who have won the Award thank their team-mates and that's only right and proper'

By then he was also an international star – having made his debut for the Republic of Ireland against the USSR in May 1975 – and was already being hailed as one of Ireland's best-ever players.

His exceptional season in 1977–78 was recognised by the PFA membership and he found himself nominated for the Young Player of the Year Award which eventually went to Nottingham Forest's Tony Woodcock.

Liam began the 1978–79 season in great style, scoring both of Arsenal's goals in a 2–2 home draw with Leeds United. By the turn of the year he was leading the Gunners' scoring chart with eleven league goals and the club were once more enjoying life in the top four.

From the outset he was a contender for the Player of the Year title. 'I'd had a great run in 1977–78 and that continued into the following season. Those goals helped too. You get profiled a lot more if you are scoring regularly, you're remembered more easily. And it obviously helps if your team is doing well. I think most of the players who have won the award thank their team-mates and that's only right and proper, it wouldn't be possible without them.'

The 1979 PFA Awards dinner was scheduled for Sunday 18 March. The Arsenal party had booked a table well in advance of the ceremony, but then their FA Cup sixth round tie away to Southampton was scheduled for the 19th and they decided not to attend. Knowing he was one of the six nominees for the Players' Player Award, Liam asked Terry Neill to find out if he had won. 'If I hadn't, I would have gone down to Southampton with the team. But Terry came back with the news that I *had* won. So, I turned up at the Hilton with my best friend, expecting to be seated at our original table. But because of the cancellation and rearrangements there was just one seat available for me at the table. So my friend and I sat at the back of the room which meant it took a while for me to get up to the stage when the announcement was made.'

When he arrived on stage to accept the trophy from The Rt Hon George Thomas MP, Liam's legendary deft footwork momentarily deserted him and he managed to nudge the table on which stood the Divisional Award medals waiting to be handed out after the ceremony. 'The whole thing was televised and you could plainly see the medals moving behind Dickie Davies as he spoke,' recalls Liam. 'That little incident raised a good laugh among my Arsenal team-mates when I got down to Southampton.'

Arsenal drew 1–1 with the Saints, and then beat them 2–0 in the replay at Highbury two days later. They went on to reach the FA Cup Final against Manchester United, a game which turned into one of most dramatic Wembley Finals of all time, dubbed 'The Five Minute Final'.

'We were a good team on the counterattack and that's the way we played in the Final,' says Liam. 'United pushed forward and we hit them twice with counterattacks in the first half.'

Brady was at his mercurial best that afternoon, and later took the man-of-the-match accolades. He had a say in both those early goals, the first a 'joint' effort by Brian Talbot and Alan Sunderland (later credited to Talbot), the second an unstoppable header from Frank Stapleton after an inch-perfect cross from Brady.

'With five minutes to go we looked to be holding

Liam Brady was among the first British-based footballers to benefit from freedom of contract. 'In 1980 I played in my third FA Cup Fnal on the bounce and the European Cup Winners' Cup Final. But by then Kevin Keegan had made a great success of his move to the continent and I wanted the same thing for myself.'

The 16-year ban imposed by the Italian League on the import of foreign players was lifted in 1980 and, despite Arsenal's offer to make him the best-paid player in Britain, Brady moved to Juventus for £600,000, the maximum fee then allowed under EEC regulations. 'I joined a side full of world class players – Bettega, Tardelli, Cabrini, Scirea, Gentile – the basis of the Italian squad that went on to win the World Cup in 1982.'

Liam won Championship medals in his first two seasons with Juventus (his last-minute penalty ensured the 1981–82 title). He also played for Sampdoria and Inter Milan before making '... the only mistake of my career – joining Ascoli where the President was a law unto himself. I stayed just seven months before joining John Lyall at West Ham and getting to know why the Hammers have such a fine reputation in the game. Upton Park was a great place to end my playing career.'

them quite comfortably through good defence and with Pat Jennings looking unbeatable in goal. Then Gordon McQueen pulled one back after a free kick in our area and a bit of panic set in. We were so close – and then Sammy McIlroy equalised. Luckily enough they lost concentration for a split second and I took the ball into their territory in the last minute. Graham Rix was clear on the left and I let the ball run to him. He crossed and Alan Sunderland volleyed home the winner. 'Being voted best player by my fellow professionals in March and then collecting an FA Cup winners' medal in May capped a great season for me.'

CYRILLE REGIS
WEST BROMWICH ALBION

**YOUNG
PLAYER OF
THE YEAR**

1979

In mid-January 1979 West Bromwich Albion topped the First Division ahead of Liverpool and Everton, and many were predicting that the club's second League Championship was within sight – ending a long wait since 1920.

Things had begun to look up for Ron Atkinson's side in the previous season, when they finished sixth to earn a place in the 1978–79 UEFA Cup tournament. Prominent in Atkinson's impressive line-up were the likes of Bryan Robson, Brendon Batson, Laurie Cunningham and the striking partnership of Ally Brown and Cyrille Regis.

Twenty-one year-old Regis, in his second season at The Hawthorns, had arrived in a £5,000 transfer deal from Isthmian League side Hayes in May 1977. Weighing in at 13 stones and standing at six feet, he was a forceful, aggressive centre forward specialising in spectacular goals and looking every inch an international prospect. Indeed, he had already appeared for England in an Under–21 game against Denmark.

West Brom reached the quarter-finals of the UEFA Cup, but lost 1–0 to Red Star Belgrade in the away leg. A superb volleyed goal by Regis early in the return at The Hawthorns gave Albion renewed hope – but unfortunately the visitors scored with a late break to go through.

His dozen goals so far in the 1978–79 League campaign – including two in a 3–1 win against Leeds United at Elland Road in October, followed by another brace the next weekend in a 7–1 drubbing of Coventry City – caught the eye of his fellow professionals who voted him PFA Young Player of the Year for 1979. The Award was presented by England captain Kevin Keegan.

West Brom went on to finish third in the table with 59 points, behind Liverpool – who won the title with a record 68 points – and Nottingham Forest. Cyrille finished the campaign with 15 goals in 39 league appearances.

Cyrille Regis made the breakthrough at full international level in February 1982 as a substitute for Trevor Francis in a 4–0 win against Northern Ireland and went on to collect five England caps. He left WBA in October 1984 to join Coventry City for £300,000. In 1987 he played a part in the Sky Blues' greatest triumph when they beat Spurs 3–2 in the FA Cup Final. He later played for Aston Villa, Wolves and Wycombe Wanderers

TOM FINNEY *OBE*

Tom Finney was born in Preston in April 1922. A slight lad, he was football-daft from the off. He played in regular Sunday side competitions and represented his schools at all levels. His great idol was Alex James, the famous Scottish international inside-left who played for Preston between 1925 and 1929. Years later Tom would acknowledge the influence the little Scot had on his own style of play.

The youngster's relatively small stature was to keep him on the sidelines at important matches during his schooldays – at fourteen he was a reserve for the Preston Town team which shared the 1936 All-England Schools Shield with West Ham.

A sportsmaster at Deepdale Modern School was the first to recognise young Tom's potential. Finney applied to Preston North End for a trial, but again his slight physique was to bar his way. A year later his father persuaded Preston's coach Will Scott to give the boy a chance. Tom's skills impressed enough for him to be offered a job on the Deepdale groundstaff, although on his father's advice he declined in order to continue his apprenticeship as a plumber while playing as an amateur in Preston's 'B' team.

MERIT AWARD WINNER

1979

'Tom would have been great in any team, in any match and in any age – even if he'd been wearing an overcoat.'

He progressed to North End's Under–18s side, usually as a reserve inside-left. One Saturday he was drafted into the team at short notice, on the right wing. In this unfamiliar role the predominantly left-footed Finney made two of the goals in Preston's 3–0 defeat of Manchester United's Youth team, and from then on his destiny was set.

He turned professional in January 1940, but the duration of the War delayed his League début until 31 August 1946, when he scored in Preston's 3–2 home victory over Leeds United. The following month saw his international début in England's first match since the war, against Northern Ireland in Belfast. He was selected because Stanley Matthews was unfit. It was the start of one of the enduring debates of post-war soccer: who was best, Matthews or Finney? Tom celebrated with a memorable performance and scored England's fifth goal in a 7–2 victory. He also scored the only goal of the game on his next international appearance against the Republic of Ireland in Dublin.

In his first two seasons with Preston, Finney established himself as the undoubted star of the side. His team-mate Bill Shankly who played behind him for two seasons, said: 'Tom would have been great in any team, in any match and in any age – even if he'd been wearing an overcoat … he was the greatest player I ever saw.'

In 1948–49 North End were relegated and rumour had it that Tom was about to move to Manchester United or Blackpool. But his heart lay with Preston and after consultation with the club chairman, who promised to strengthen the squad, he agreed to stay. In 1952 a lucrative offer from Sicilian club Palermo was rejected by Preston – Finney later said that even if freedom of contract had been in place at the time, he would probably have decided against the move anyway.

By then Preston were back in the top flight, having returned in 1950–51 after a remarkable Second Division campaign which included a sequence of fourteen consecutive victories beginning on Christmas Day 1950 with a 4–1 away defeat of QPR and ending on 31 March in a 3–3 draw at Southampton.

That Second Division Championship medal marked Finney's only major honour in North End's colours. He almost added a First Division medal in 1952–53, but Preston were pipped at the post by Arsenal who had a marginally superior goal average.

1953–54 also proved a frustrating season for Finney. On 1 May 1954, having just been named Footballer of the Year by the Football Writers' Association, he captained Preston in the FA Cup Final against West Bromwich Albion. The press build-up to the game compared it to the previous year's Final in which Stanley Matthews had at long last won a Cup winners' medal. Could Finney now do the same? On the day, however, he was well below par and found himself effectively marked out of the game by West Brom skipper Len Millard and left-half Ray Barlow. Albion won 3–2; Finney blamed himself for the defeat and had to be content with a runners-up medal.

By then Finney had made 49 international appearances and had scored 23 goals for England. There had been many highlights, including the 10–0 drubbing of Portugal in 1947, the masterly 4–0 defeat of World Champions Italy in 1948, a 9–2 thrashing of Northern Ireland in 1949 and Finney's four goals in a 5–3 defeat of Portugal the same year.

He had also played through England's most painful ninety minutes, the 1–0 defeat by the USA in the 1950 World Cup Finals in Brazil, to which the England squad had gone woefully unprepared. Finney had come close to scoring in the game but his shot rebounded off the post. Of the forwards only he and Stan Mortensen retained their place for the next game against Spain (who won 1–0 and sent England home again).

There were another 27 international appearances to come for Tom Finney, including three in the 1954 World Cup Finals in Switzerland and one in Sweden in the final stages of the 1958 World Cup. His 76th and last cap came in a 5–0 defeat of the USSR in October 1958. In all he scored 30 international goals and now stands joint-fourth, with Nat Lofthouse, in the list of England scorers.

Tom Finney was one of England's all-time greats. Often described as 'the complete footballer', he was a gifted winger, equally capable of playing on either flank, or indeed in any attacking role. Nicknamed 'The Preston Plumber' he was often compared to Stanley Matthews, England's other great winger of the '40s and '50s and a perennial debate raged as to which of the two was the finer player. In truth England was lucky to have two world class players often vying for the same spot in the team

TERRY McDERMOTT
LIVERPOOL

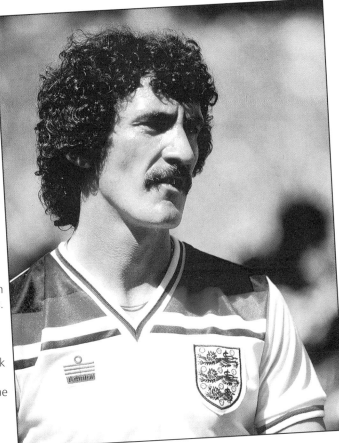

Early in March 1980 PFA Secretary Cliff Lloyd contacted three of the leading contenders for the Player of the Year title – Kenny Dalglish, David Johnson and Terry McDermott – to ask if they would attend the PFA Awards ceremony on Sunday 16th. 'I told him I didn't want to go,' recalls Terry, 'I'm not one for ceremonies or speeches – I'd sooner have a pint and a pie in a pub than go to a big function. I said the only reason I'd go was if I'd *won* it and he said "I think you better come then."'

The Liverpool trio were flown south late on the afternoon of the 16th and then driven to the Hilton Hotel where Terry was presented with the trophy by Norman St John-Stevas. 'I'd never got up to speak in front of people before,' he says. 'But it was a great occasion and I thoroughly enjoyed myself. We flew straight back to Liverpool afterwards and all my family were waiting to greet me at the local club – we celebrated till about four in the morning.'

Born in Kirkby, on Merseyside, in December 1951, Terry grew up as an avid Liverpool supporter and was a member of the Kirkby Boys' team in the late–60s. 'We had a very good side – John McLaughlin went to Liverpool, Jimmy Redfearn and Chris Duffey went to Bolton – they all got fixed up by big clubs. Me and Dennis Mortimer were probably the last out of the team to be picked up by anyone. We'd obviously been watched but it seemed that no-one fancied us. Then one evening when I got home from watching Liverpool play Burnley, I learned that the Bury scout Colin McDonald had come to our house to chat about the possibility of my going to Gigg Lane. He had left the apprentice forms for me to sign, which was quite an unusual thing to do considering he hadn't even spoken to me. He then went to Dennis Mortimer's home and did exactly the same (Dennis had also been at the

'I couldn't understand why a ragbag like me should be the first one to do it. And that's still my opinion.'

match) but he didn't sign – I thank my lucky stars that I did.'

Terry turned professional in October 1969 and quickly established himself as one of the most energetic, hard-working and skilful midfielders in the Fourth Division. In the winter of 1973 he caught the eye of Newcastle United scout Len Richley who persuaded his manager Joe Harvey to come and take a look for himself.

'Joe came to watch me in a game against Reading at Gigg Lane,' says Terry. 'But it was called off because of fog and he never actually saw me play. He signed me anyway, on the strength of Len's recommendation and when he did see me play in a reserve game shortly afterwards, he apparently exclaimed "What the Hell have I bought here!", or words to that effect.'

A few weeks later, however, an injury situation forced Harvey to select his new signing for first team duty, and from then on Terry did not look back. He quickly blossomed into one of the most impressive midfielders ever seen at St James' Park, and in retrospect the transfer fee of £22,000 that Newcastle had paid to Bury was considered one of football's best-ever bargains.

'I loved every minute of my time with Newcastle. In the twenty months I was at St James' Park we won the 1973 Anglo–Italian Cup which was a good competition in those days – we beat teams like Roma, Torino and Crystal Palace on the way to the Final which we won 2–1 in front of 45,000 in Fiorentina. And in '74 we won the Texaco Cup Final against Burnley, having won through against Morton, Birmingham City and Dundee United.'

In 1974 Newcastle also reached the FA Cup Final against Liverpool. Although they were somewhat overwhelmed by the dominant Merseysiders, who won 3–0, McDermott acquitted himself particularly well and six months later new Liverpool manager Bob Paisley paid Newcastle £170,000 to take him to Anfield. 'I would not have left Newcastle for anywhere other than Liverpool, and I had no second thoughts about going back to my home town and playing for the club I'd always supported as a lad,' says Terry.

But the transition was not a smooth one. He took a while to settle in at Anfield and was in and out of the side throughout the remainder of the 1974–75 campaign. 'Normally I'm quite a confident lad, but all of a sudden there I was, sharing a dressing room with Kevin Keegan, Emlyn Hughes, Tommy Smith, Chris Lawler, Alec Lindsay, Ian Callaghan … players I'd respected and idolised and had paid money to go and watch. I didn't think about it at the time, but maybe I was a bit overawed by it all.

'I know I didn't play to my capabilities in the first two years and consequently never played much in the first team, although sometimes I felt I was left out unfairly. I'd play well in a game and then Bob would leave me out for the next one – so I asked to leave. Luckily for me, as it turned out, he kept saying "No, I want you here". He just persevered with me.'

Terry played nine times in Liverpool's 1975–76 Championship success, not enough to qualify for a medal. In 1976–77 he became more established in the side, playing 26 times as Liverpool again took the title, a single point ahead of Manchester City. He also appeared in the 1977 FA Cup Final in which Liverpool's much-touted 'Treble' hopes were shattered by Tommy Docherty's Manchester United who won 2–1 at Wembley on 21 May. Four days later McDermott scored a brilliant opening goal in the 3–1 victory against Borussia Moenchengladbach in Rome, which marked Liverpool's first-ever European Cup Final triumph. Two-out-of-three trophies was not at all bad.

In 1977–78 Terry made 37 League appearances as Liverpool finished runners-up to Nottingham Forest, and he won the first of his 25 caps for England, in a 0–0 draw with Switzerland at Wembley. He was also a vital member of the Reds' second successive European Cup-winning team which beat Bruges 1–0 at Wembley.

By then Graeme Souness had joined the Liverpool line-up, and was firmly established as the central midfield general. The situation brought about a restructuring of the line-up and consequently allowed Terry to adopt a wider ranging role with more freedom of expression. In September 1978 his effectiveness was amply demonstrated in a 7–0 thrashing of Spurs at Anfield. Not only did he supply a perfect cross from which Ray Kennedy headed the third goal, he also initiated and finished the marvellous seventh goal. 'It started with a Tottenham corner,' he recalls. 'I was on the near post and got the ball away. Then I made my way to the Spurs' penalty area and was lucky enough to be on the end of an incredible move which involved Ray Kennedy, Dave Johnson, Kenny Dalglish and Steve Heighway. Spurs never had so much as a touch of the ball.' The goal was described by Bob Paisley as the best he had ever seen at Anfield.

Liverpool finished the 1978–79 season as Champions for the eleventh time, conceding just sixteen goals – a First Division record. 'We had one hell of team,' says Terry. 'We had strength everywhere, we had strength in depth, and practically everyone was an international. I don't think anyone in English football will ever dominate in the way Liverpool did throughout those years.'

That devastating success continued into

1979–80 – Liverpool again won the Championship and were also semi-finalists in the FA Cup and the League Cup. Throughout the season Terry revelled in his roving role. His passing was perfect, his renowned forward runs created panic in many a defence, he scored several vital goals – and of course, his outstanding contribution was recognised by the PFA membership.

Six weeks after his PFA success, Terry was at another swish function in London, this time to collect the Footballer of the Year trophy awarded by the Football Writers' Association. He was the first player to win both top player awards in the same season.

'Just before the Football Writers' votes went in we played Spurs in an FA Cup Sixth Round tie. The papers were billing it as "McDermott v Hoddle" – they said whichever of us had the outstanding game would probably be named Footballer of the Year. I was lucky enough to score the winning goal and that probably clinched it for me.' And what a goal it was. In the 38th minute, Terry collected a loose ball, flicked it up and then volleyed home from a near impossible angle.

Although he was obviously well aware that he had enjoyed a fine season, Terry was surprised by his historic personal 'Double'. 'I remember saying at the time that I couldn't understand why a ragbag like me should be the first one to do it. And that's still my opinion …'

It's an opinion he shares only with himself.

In 1980–81 Terry McDermott collected his third European Cup winners' medal when Liverpool beat Real Madrid 1–0 in the Final in Paris. He was also in the team which defeated West Ham 2–1 in the replayed League Cup Final at Villa Park. Another League Cup success followed in 1981–82 with a 3–1 victory against Spurs.

In September 1982, he made a surprise return to Newcastle United who were then in the Second Division. 'I went because Kevin Keegan had gone there. I remember watching him on TV in his first game for Newcastle against QPR. The ovation he got when he scored was incredible – I felt a tingle down my back and I thought if anyone can wake the sleeping Magpies, then he's the man to do it. Luckily enough, Arthur Cox came in for me and I stayed for two years and helped in the return to Division One.'

Terry's playing career wound down with Cork City and Cypriot club Apoel. In February 1992 when Kevin Keegan was surprisingly lured out of retirement to take on the management of Newcastle, he immediately appointed Terry as his assistant. Together they have made the Magpies into one of the top sides in the country

GLENN HODDLE
TOTTENHAM HOTSPUR

**YOUNG
PLAYER OF
THE YEAR**

1980

In Tottenham's 1979–80 season 22-year-old Glenn Hoddle stood out in a team which also included the likes of Steve Perryman and the two 'exiled' Argentinian World Cup stars Ossie Ardiles and Ricky Villa.

By 16 March 1980, when England manager Ron Greenwood presented him with the PFA Young Player of the Year Award at the Hilton Hotel, Hoddle had played in all 32 of Spurs' First Division games of the season so far and had scored 18 League goals, including a hat-trick against Coventry City and two each against Norwich City and Bristol City. Several had come from spectacular long-range shots, something of a Hoddle trademark, and six had been scored from the penalty-spot. (He would end the season as Spurs' top scorer, with 19 goals.)

By then, however, it was increasingly obvious that there was much, much more to young Glenn's game than straightforward goalscoring. He was generally regarded as the most skilful and talented of England's burgeoning stars and, as such, was something of a great white hope for the future. He had 'vision'. He was a thinking player, a playmaker,

who could change the course of a game with a perfectly weighted long pass. On the negative side, he was already being criticised for lack of commitment and defensive deficiencies, by those who ought to have known better. Fuelled by certain sections of the Press, this duality of opinion would continue to dog Hoddle throughout his playing career.

Born in Hayes, Middlesex, in October 1957, Glenn served a White Hart Lane apprenticeship before turning professional at the age of 17 in April 1975. Terry Neill gave him his league début, as a substitute for Cyril Knowles, in a 2–2 draw at home to Norwich City that August. Six months later he made his second appearance, away to Stoke City, scoring once in a 2–1 victory. By that time he was already a member of the England Youth team and had yet to be on the losing side in the national colours. Promotion to the Under–21 ranks followed in December 1976.

But disaster was to strike in 1976–77, his first season as a first-team regular, when Tottenham were relegated. It was Keith Burkinshaw's first campaign as manager and Spurs went down largely because of a leaky defence and an appalling away record from which they had collected just eight points.

Young Hoddle put the disappointment behind him and knuckled down to life in the Second Division. The Tottenham board kept faith with Burkinshaw and the club was rewarded with a third place finish behind Bolton Wanderers and Southampton, and an immediate return to the top flight.

Glenn Hoddle's Tottenham team-mate Ossie Ardiles rated him second only to Diego Maradona in the world's best-player stakes. On leaving Spurs in 1987, Glenn moved to the South of France where he enjoyed great success with AS Monaco. He returned to England in 1991 as player-manager of Swindon Town, steering them into the Premier League, before accepting the managership at Chelsea and taking them to the 1994 FA Cup Final against Manchester United

Hoddle continued to impress throughout the 1978–79 season and it seemed only a matter of time before he graduated to the full England side. But Ron Greenwood kept him waiting until England's second European Championship qualifying match against Bulgaria in November 1979.

The match was originally scheduled for Wednesday 21st, but was postponed until the following day due to dense fog. When the mist lifted, Hoddle underlined the wisdom of his selection by scoring England's second goal in a 2–0 victory. It came in the 70th minute when Glenn side-footed a Trevor Francis pass into the net from twenty yards. It was a glorious goal which no doubt lingered in the minds of the PFA membership when it came to voting for their Young Player of the Year a few weeks later.

Hoddle had to wait a further four games before Greenwood selected him again. It was the start of a frustrating international career in which he would win 53 caps. Many felt he deserved twice that number.

SIR MATT BUSBY CBE

MERIT AWARD WINNER

1980

The one-minute silent tribute to the late Sir Matt Busby before Manchester United's Premiership match against Everton at Old Trafford on 22 January 1994, marked a moving and emotional farewell to a football legend. The great manager had been involved with United for forty-nine years and had steered the club to its finest hour; he had also lived through the saddest period in Manchester United's history.

Born in Orbiston, Lanarkshire, in May 1909, Matt intended to emigrate to the USA as a teenager. Fortunately, his talents were spotted by Manchester City who persuaded him to join them in February 1928.

Initially he played as an inside-forward, but his conversion to wing-half in 1931 brought out the best in him. In 1933 he made his first FA Cup Final appearance when City lost 1–0 to Everton. Later that year he won his only cap for Scotland, in a 3–2 defeat by Wales. 1934 saw him back at Wembley, this time collecting an FA Cup winners' medal as City came from behind to defeat Portsmouth 2–1.

In 1936 after more than 200 games for City, Busby moved on to Liverpool in an £8,000 transfer deal. During World War II he served with the King's Liverpool Regiment and later with the Army Physical Training Corps. He 'guested' for several clubs and captained Scotland in unofficial wartime internationals.

Busby was well into his thirties when the war ended in 1945, but he was ambitious for managerial success and had formulated many ideas during his playing days; he saw football as a game of

expression and freedom allied to watertight strategy. Liverpool wanted him back as a player-coach, but Manchester United's chairman James Gibson offered him a three-year contract as club manager. Although it was an offer Busby couldn't refuse, he nevertheless stamped his authority right from the outset, arguing that he needed more time to produce a winning team and demanding a two-year extension to the contract. To assist him in the task ahead, he appointed his good friend Jimmy Murphy as his assistant.

Busby was the first of the 'tracksuit managers' and his squad responded with enthusiasm. In the first post-war season United finished just a point behind Champions Liverpool. They were second again in 1947–48, this time to Arsenal, but capped the season by winning the FA Cup, beating Blackpool – Matthews, Mortensen and all – 4–2 at Wembley in a game still remembered as one of the greatest finals of all time.

United finished as League runners-up twice more, in 1948–49 and 1950–51. Then Busby's plans finally came to fruition with the Championship of 1951–52 – the club's first title success in 41 years.

Aware that all the best teams inevitably dissipate, Matt determined that continuity and consistency would be the order of the day at Old Trafford. And while his first great team had been gathering glory, the foundations of another wave of fine players were being laid via United's youth policy. Under the watchful eye of Jimmy Murphy, a whole network of scouts were scouring the country for potential players who would be groomed and cultivated by United's coaching staff.

The 1952–53 season proved a tough one for Manchester United and Matt began to draft the first of his 'Busby Babes' into the team, among them Roger Byrne, Jackie Blanchflower, David Pegg, Dennis Viollet, Bill Foulkes, Jeff Whitefoot and a colossal, attack-minded wing-half called Duncan Edwards. Busby supplemented these emerging talents with the addition of centre-forward Tommy Taylor, signed from Barnsley.

After finishing 4th in 1953–54 and 5th in the next season everything went right for Busby in 1955–56. His brilliant young team won the Championship by an eleven point margin, ahead of Blackpool and Wolves. They repeated the feat in the following season, this time beating Spurs and Preston to the title, and also came within sight of the 'Double', only to lose the FA Cup Final 2–1 to Aston Villa in a match dominated by controversy. In the sixth minute United's 'keeper Ray Wood was recklessly charged by Villa winger Peter McParland. Wood suffered a broken cheekbone and was unable to play on.

Matt Busby had also realised another important part of his plans when in 1956–57, despite the disapproval of the Football League, United became the first English side to compete in the European Cup competition. They gave a good account of themselves, reaching the semi-finals only to be beaten on aggregate by Real Madrid.

As the 1957–58 season unfolded, Manchester United were undoubtedly the most exciting team in British football, attracting enormous crowds at home and away.

By 1 February 1958, they were flying high in the League, were through to the Fifth Round of the FA Cup and mid-way through a two-legged European Cup quarter-final tie with Red Star Belgrade. On that day they took on Arsenal in a League fixture at Highbury, a match which first demonstrated the sheer power of United's game and then brought out their fighting qualities, tenacity and team spirit. They were 3–0 ahead by half-time, with goals from Edwards, Charlton and Taylor, and looked to be cruising to victory. But in the second half Arsenal levelled the score at 3–3. With thirty minutes left United dug in again and scored twice more, through Viollet and Taylor. The Gunners scored again, but United took the points. The game was written up as a classic by the newspapers. It was also to prove a poignant epitaph for a great team.

The following week United flew to Belgrade for the second-leg of the European Cup tie against Red Star on 5 February. The game finished 3–3 and saw United through to the semi–finals with a 5–4 aggregate.

Next day the team was *en route* to Manchester, when their BEA Elizabethan airliner touched down for refuelling in ice-bound Munich. Two attempts to take-off again were aborted. A third attempt was made at 3.04pm but this time the aircraft careered through the airport perimeter fence, crashed into a house and then broke in two.

Twenty-three people died as a result of the crash. Eight were Manchester United players: Geoff Bent, Roger Byrne, Eddie Colman, Duncan Edwards, Mark Jones, David Pegg, Tommy Taylor and Liam Whelan. For several weeks Matt Busby lay in a critical condition in a Munich hospital, and twice the last rites were read to him.

Jimmy Murphy took over the managerial duties at Old Trafford. The next scheduled League fixture, against Wolves, was postponed as he attempted a rapid rebuilding programme. He signed Ernie Taylor from Blackpool and brought forward a number of inexperienced youngsters from the ranks including Ian Greaves, Freddie Goodwin, Ronnie Cope, Colin Webster, Alex Dawson, Mark Pearson and Shay Brennan.

These players, along with Munich survivors Harry Gregg and Bill Foulkes, were in the team for United's first post-Munich match, an FA Cup Fifth Round tie against Sheffield Wednesday, on 19 February, at Old Trafford. The eleventh place in the line-up was filled just an hour before kick-off when Murphy signed Stan Crowther from Aston Villa (the FA had relaxed its normal rule on 'cup-tied' players). Old Trafford became a virtual cauldron of emotion that evening, as 59,848 fans watched the new United win 3–0.

Inevitably United were to suffer in the wake of Munich – and they finished the League campaign in 9th position. However, they did reach the FA Cup Final against Bolton Wanderers. By then Bobby Charlton and Dennis Viollet had also returned to the side. And sitting beside Jimmy Murphy on the bench at Wembley was Matt Busby – aided by walking sticks, his recovery was almost complete.

For the second year in succession, the Cup Final was marred by controversy involving a Manchester United goalkeeper. United were already a goal down when, in the 55th minute, Bolton's bustling centre-forward Nat Lofthouse charged in and barged Harry Gregg as he attempted to parry a shot, sending him and the ball over the line. To everyone's amazement the referee awarded the goal. Bolton won 2–0.

Five days later United resumed their European Cup challenge, beating AC Milan 2–1 at Old Trafford. Six days after that, in their first trip abroad since Munich, they lost the second-leg 4–0.

Matt Busby returned to the manager's desk in time for the 1958–59 season. Although rebuilding was obviously his top priority, he did not delve into the transfer market until the end of September when he paid a then-record fee of £45,000 for inside-forward Albert Quixall from Sheffield Wednesday. United finished the campaign as runners-up to Wolves.

Three seasons later United had slumped to 15th place in the League, and again Busby wielded the cheque book, to make arguably his finest signing – paying a record £115,000 to rescue Denis Law from his troubled Italian sojourn with Torino. Another important Busby acquisition was that of half-back Pat Crerand for £43,000 from Celtic.

Despite these glamorous signings United's League form did not improve and they finished in 19th place in 1962–63. They did reach the 1963 FA Cup Final, but were considered underdogs to opponents Leicester City who had finished fourth in the League. Inspired by Denis Law scoring the first goal and playing at the top of his game, United upset the odds by winning 3–1 and bringing Matt Busby his first trophy since the Munich disaster.

Early in the 1963–64 season Busby drafted a new youngster into the team – a slightly-built Belfast lad named George Best, who would develop into one of the world's finest players and become a major factor in United's future success.

1964–65 brought United's sixth League Championship, won on goal average from Leeds United, and giving Busby another crack at the European Cup, for the first time since Munich. In the event United reached the 1965–66 semi-finals, disposing of Benfica *en route* with a 3–2 home win and a magnificent 5–1 away victory inspired by two-goal George Best. But the euphoria was to end against Partizan Belgrade who won with a 2–1 aggregate. Busby still had to wait for his European glory.

It came two years later, on 29 May 1968, when United when United battled through to the final at Wembley where they beat Benfica 4–1 after extra-time (*see 1993 Merit Award*). The following month the Queen honoured Matt Busby with a knighthood.

Almost a year later, after twenty-four years in the job, he announced his retirement – only to return again for a brief spell in 1970. Sir Matt became a member of the Manchester United board and later the Club President.

> *Matt Busby created three great teams at Old Trafford and brought the European Cup to England for the first time. No one was more pleased than he to see the re-emergence of United as a footballing power in the early '90s*

JOHN WARK
IPSWICH TOWN

I scored thirty-seven goals in all competitions in 1980–81,' says John Wark. 'It was my best ever season in football, the best for myself and one of the best ever for Ipswich Town. We won the UEFA Cup, we should have won the League as well and we *almost* reached the FA Cup Final.'

On the opening day of the season Bobby Robson's side beat Leicester City 1–0 at Filbert Street with John scoring the solitary goal. He also scored in Ipswich's second and fourth games, victories over Brighton and Everton respectively. And as the season progressed he continued scoring consistently as Ipswich challenged Aston Villa for the League Championship. In the end the East Anglians' effort petered out in a 2–1 defeat at Middlesbrough in the penultimate game of their campaign – and the title went to Villa, with Ipswich as runners-up.

John was Town's top League scorer with 18 goals, five of them struck from the penalty spot. He had also scored twice in the FA Cup, in which Ipswich reached the semi-finals before their elimination by Manchester City, and twice in the League Cup competition. He also scored Scotland's only goal in a 1–1 draw with Northern Ireland in March.

But it was in the UEFA Cup that he really hit the headlines, scoring a record-equalling 14 goals as Ipswich swept to success. Included in this tally were four goals struck against Aris Salonika in the First Round, a hat-trick against Widzew Lodz in the Third Round, a goal in each quarter-final leg against St Etienne, a semi-final goal against Cologne – and a goal in each leg of the final against AZ 67 Alkmaar of Holland. 'It was quite incredible,' says John. 'I equalled Altafini's European competition scoring record which he set with AC Milan in the 1962–63 European Cup. It's not been matched since I did it and I doubt if it ever will be, as it's so difficult to score in Europe nowadays.'

Midway through the season, the PFA membership showed their appreciation of John's magnificent form by voting him the Player of the Year. The Award was presented to him by Sir Stanley Rous CBE, on 15 March at the London Hilton Hotel.

'I knew I was among the top contenders,' recalls John, 'as were my Ipswich team-mates Paul Mariner and Frans Thijssen (who later won the 1981 Footballer of the Year Award from the Football Writers). So it seemed pretty likely that the winner would be an Ipswich player, that was also the feeling among the other players at the dinner beforehand. I knew I was perhaps the favourite because I'd scored so many goals from midfield. But I'd have been happy if either of the other two had won it, because Ipswich was such a great club. We all got along well together, there was a really good spirit about the place.

PLAYER OF THE YEAR

1981

'It was my best ever season in football, the best for myself and one of the best-ever for Ipswich Town.'

'We had a table at the dinner for the three of us who were in contention, most of the other players and the boss, Bobby Robson. We had a few drinks, as you do, and when my name was announced as the winner all the lads stood up and cheered. My best mate Mariner stood on a chair and really applauded. It was a great feeling to have the team behind me like that. We stayed at the Hilton that night and afterwards a lot of other players from other teams came up to my room and had a few drinks. It was a really good night.'

Born in Glasgow in August 1957, John had been a more than promising player at his school, Victoria Drive Secondary, and with the Drumchapel Amateurs Youth Club team (the club that also set Archie Gemmill, John Robertson and Asa Hartford on the road to success).

'I had trials with a few Scottish clubs and with Ipswich and Manchester City when Malcolm Allison was in charge. But I was most impressed with Ipswich – they seemed a friendly club, and they had a reputation for giving youngsters a chance in the game. I got on well with Bobby Robson, he was a marvellous manager and something of a father-figure to me in those early days.'

Consequently John became an Ipswich Town apprentice in September 1973 and was offered professional terms eleven months later. He made his League début in a 2–1 victory over Leicester City in March 1975, although he would make only five more League appearances in the course of the following year.

It wasn't until the 1976–77 season that he became a regular in the first team line-up, notching 10 goals from midfield in 33 League games as Ipswich finished third in the First Division, behind Liverpool and Manchester City.

Ipswich's form throughout the 1977–78 season was dictated by a string of injuries and consequently their First Division survival seemed in some doubt. John was among the victims and was not fit for action until the turn of the year. When he did return he was prominent in the FA Cup as Ipswich battled their way to the Final, beating Cardiff City, Hartlepool United, Bristol Rovers, Millwall and West Bromwich Albion *en route* to Wembley where they would meet Arsenal.

By the time of the Final on 6 May Ipswich had secured their First Division survival with three matches to spare, eventually finishing in 18th position. Consequently, they were considered the

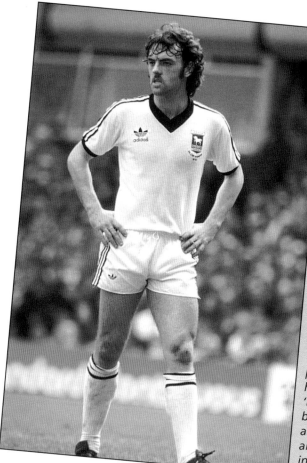

In the 1982 World Cup Finals in Spain John Wark was a member of Jock Stein's Scottish squad. 'That was quite an experience,' he says, 'although I never really played in my natural position – Graeme Souness played in the middle and I was on the right-hand side, which is not really me. Mind you, I would have played absolutely anywhere for my country.'

In the opening Group Six match he scored twice in Scotland's 5–2 victory over New Zealand – but despite that fine start, Scotland were destined for First Round elimination following a 4–1 defeat by Brazil and a 2–2 draw with the USSR. In all, John won 29 caps and scored 7 goals for Scotland. His last appearance in the famous dark blue shirt came against Yugoslavia in September 1984.

By then he was a Liverpool player having been signed for £450,000 by Joe Fagan – as a replacement for the soon-to-depart Graeme Souness. 'I was really sorry to leave Ipswich,' says John. 'They'd done well and built a new stand – but then they couldn't pay for it, so they had to sell players. I don't think I'd ever have left if they could have kept the same team.

'Liverpool was a big, big club and you had to do the business every week. At Ipswich we had a squad of around 14 or 15 players, but at Liverpool there were always half-a-dozen internationals waiting to step into your boots – so you were always playing under pressure.'

definite underdogs in the Final, with the Press rather overdoing the 'City Slickers v Country Bumpkins' angle.

In the event Ipswich ruled the game and were by far the better team on the day. John twice went close to scoring in the first half, but each time the ball rebounded off the woodwork. The deadlock was eventually broken in the 77th minute, when Roger Osborne latched onto a loose ball, fired home from ten yards and promptly passed out during the ensuing celebrations. The 1–0 victory earned John Wark his first major honour.

Ipswich were among the front runners again in 1978–79 and John was ever-present in a League campaign for the first time. In May 1979 his consistency was rewarded with his first full cap for Scotland (he had previously played at Youth and Under–21 levels) when he played in a 3–0 defeat by Wales in Cardiff.

John enjoyed another good season in 1979–80, scoring 18 goals as Ipswich challenged Liverpool and Manchester United for top place, eventually finishing third. Then came his 'best-ever season in football' and the 1981 PFA Player of the Year Award...

In 1984–85 John scored five goals on Liverpool's journey to the European Cup Final, including a hat-trick against Lech Poznan in the First Round, Second Leg. And he was in the team for the ill-fated Final against Juventus in the Heysel Stadium in Brussels on 29 May 1985. 'That was a terrible experience,' he recalls. 'Our dressing room was actually close to where the wall had collapsed, so we could hear a lot of screaming. We had to play the game, knowing what had happened. We had to go out, because if we didn't, there might have been even more trouble. It was a European Cup Final but it was played like a kickabout by both sides.'

In 1985–86 injury worries kept John on the fringes of Liverpool's famous 'Double' success. He made nine appearances in the League, not enough to earn a Championship medal, and he played in just three of the FA Cup ties – but not the Final. In January 1988, after 102 games and 42 goals for Liverpool, John returned to Ipswich in a £100,000 transfer deal. In August 1990 he moved again, to Middlesbrough for £50,000, staying a year at Ayresome Park before rejoining Ipswich yet again. 'I must like the place,' he says. 'I've come back again twice.' His new role at Portman Road was to have been on the coaching staff, yet in September 1991 he returned to first team action and played out the rest of the season in central defence as Ipswich won the Second Division Championship

GARY SHAW
ASTON VILLA

YOUNG PLAYER OF THE YEAR

1981

When the much-travelled, 29-year-old Peter Withe arrived at Aston Villa from Newcastle United in May 1980, he fully expected to form an attacking partnership with Brian Little. That, at least, had been manager Ron Saunders' plan before Little collected the serious injury which ended his playing career after 247 league appearances for his one and only club.

Gary Shaw, the 1981 PFA Young Player of the Year, was the only local-born player in Aston Villa's 1982 European Cup winning team. Villa beat Bayern Munich 1–0 in Rotterdam and young Shaw was named the best player in the tournament. Unfortunately, after such a magnificent start to his career, a serious knee injury was to hamper his progress. After 165 league games and 59 League goals for Villa, he moved on to Blackpool in February 1988 and later played for Klagenfurt in Austria, Walsall, Kilmarnock and Shrewsbury, finally hanging up his boots in 1991

Into his place stepped Gary Shaw, a 19-year-old, blond-haired striker with nine goals to his credit in 31 League games. Born in Birmingham in January 1961, Gary had been a Villa apprentice and an England Youth international.

Things began to look good for Withe and Shaw when they struck up a productive understanding in Villa's pre-season warm-up games. Withe, who had previously formed effective striking partnerships with Trevor Francis at Birmingham, Tony Woodcock at Forest and Alan Shoulder at Newcastle, took the youngster under his wing. They lined-up together in the opening game of the 1980–81 season against Leeds at Elland Road and Gary scored the second goal in Villa's 2–1 victory. From then on the two would lead the scoring chart for Villa as they battled for the Championship.

The supply line behind them included the magnificent midfield trio of Gordon Cowans, Dennis Mortimer and Des Bremner, each of whom would be ever-present throughout the League campaign – as were 'keeper Jimmy Rimmer, defenders Kenny Swain, Ken McNaught and winger Tony Morley. In fact, Saunders used just 14 players throughout the season, which eventually saw Villa lift the title with 60 points, ahead of Ipswich and Arsenal. It was the club's first League Championship for 71 years. Shaw ended the campaign with 18 goals. Eight weeks earlier, the PFA membership had voted him their Young Player of the Year, an Award presented by England's 1966 World Cup hero Geoff Hurst.

JOHN TROLLOPE *MBE*

In a playing career spanning twenty seasons and in an age when transfers became commonplace, left-back John Trollope remained a loyal one-club man with Swindon Town.

Born in Wroughton in June 1943, he turned professional with his local club, 'The Robins' in July 1960 and went on to make 770 League appearances, the record for one club, (including a consecutive run of 368 League and Cup matches between 1961 and 1968) before finally hanging up his boots in November 1980 at the age of 37. He was awarded an MBE for his services to football.

John spent most of his playing career in the Third Division, enjoying just a couple of forays into the Second. His proudest moment came at Wembley on 15 March 1969, when Swindon beat mighty Arsenal in the League Cup Final. The match was played in heavy, cloying mud, conditions which perhaps suited the lower division side more than the Gunners. But that aside, the Wiltshire club performed heroically to emerge after extra-time as 3–1 winners.

The presentation of John's PFA Merit award was made by ex-Portsmouth star Jimmy Dickinson, the previous holder of the one-club appearance record (764 League games).

MERIT AWARD WINNER

1981

> *John Trollope (left) celebrates Swindon's historic League Cup victory in 1969. Willie Penman also toasts the success*

KEVIN KEEGAN OBE
SOUTHAMPTON

**PLAYER OF
THE YEAR**

1982

In June 1977, after an illustrious career with Liverpool (three League Championships, an FA Cup winners' medal, two UEFA Cup wins, a European Cup success and the Football Writers' Footballer of the Year accolade in 1976), Kevin Keegan had joined SV Hamburg of the West German Bundesliga on a three year contract and for the then-British record transfer fee of £500,000.

He scored on his Hamburg début, in a 6–0 friendly victory over Barcelona in the Volkspark Stadium. But there was to be a difficult start for the England captain in the Budesliga itself, with an unsettled role in the team and a run of poor results. Eventually, however, Keegan became the key figure in Hamburg's midfield, dictating things from just behind the forwards. He went on to collect a West German Championship medal in 1979 and became the first player to be twice voted European Footballer of the Year in successive years (1978 and 1979).

Midway through the 1979–80 season the 28-year-old world famous soccer superstar announced that he was ready to move on to the next stage in his career. Rumours were rife of an imminent transfer to the New York Cosmos or the Washington Diplomats in the ultimately ill-fated North American League. But Kevin's sights were set on Juventus. The Italian giants were equally keen to sign the Englishman who had adapted so well to the man-to-man marking of continental football – they felt certain that he would perform equally as well in Serie A. However, Kevin's wife was opposed to the move, feeling that their two-year-old daughter would benefit more from a return home.

And so the focus of Press attention turned to England where the first club to declare an interest was Chelsea, managed by the 1966 World Cup hero Geoff Hurst, but nothing came of the approach. Arsenal were also keen; and a return to Anfield seemed to be on the cards for a while. It was an intriguing situation, but no one came close to guessing Keegan's ultimate destination.

The prime-mover in the drama was Lawrie McMenemy, the dynamic manager of Southampton FC. McMenemy was a man with a definite flair for publicity and a need to raise the profile of his club – a star of Keegan's stature would do just that, and keep the fans flocking to The Dell. Lawrie contacted Kevin and, using a softly-softly approach, gradually broached the subject of the player perhaps joining the Saints. Keegan was intrigued by the notion and eventually agreed to the move.

His decision was kept secret until 11 February 1980 when McMenemy invited the media corps to an hotel in Hampshire "to meet someone who will play a big part in Southampton's future". The news of the £400,000 transfer coup was sensational and everyone was looking forward to Keegan's contribution to the Saints' 1980–81 campaign.

But first there was unfinished business at SV Hamburg. The club was involved in a title chase with Bayern Munich and were heading for the European Cup Final in Madrid. In both instances they finished as runners-up, losing the European Cup Final 1–0 to Brian Clough's Nottingham Forest, who secured an early goal then shut up shop and efficiently kept out all of Hamburg's attempts to get back into the game.

Kevin then joined the England squad preparing for the 1980 European Championship in Italy. He had been a vital factor in England's qualification, playing seven times, scoring seven goals *en route* and striking up an uncanny understanding with West Ham's Trevor Brooking.

Despite worries about a niggling knee ligament problem, Kevin was available to play in the Finals, though it was felt he was generally below par. In the event, England were frustratingly eliminated in the First Round following a 1–1 draw with Belgium and a 1–0 defeat by Italy. A consolation 2–1 victory over Spain came too late to save the situation.

Kevin returned to England to face the new challenge of First Division football with Southampton whose 1980–81 squad also boasted such players as Steve Nicholl, Phil Boyer, Charlie George, Dave Watson, the precociously talented Steve Williams, the up and coming Steve Moran and Keegan's close friend Mick Channon.

23,320 fans squeezed into the Dell to witness Kevin's debut for the Saints, in a 2–0 victory over Manchester City. His first goal for the club came in the fourth League game of the season, a 3–1 home win against Birmingham City. The Saints finished the campaign in sixth place, earning themselves a UEFA Cup berth in the following season. Unfortunately Kevin's own season had been hampered by a string of niggling injuries which restricted him to 27 League appearances and kept him out of England's early World Cup qualifying games for the 1982 Finals to be held in Spain.

He played in a friendly against Spain at Wembley in March 1981, but was effectively marked out of the game which England lost 2–1. Two months later he was recalled by Ron Greenwood for World Cup duty against Switzerland in Basle. In a match marred by crowd trouble, England surprisingly lost 2–1 – a result which put a serious dent in their World Cup hopes. The next qualifier, against Hungary in Budapest, was therefore a vital one. But it was

against the odds that England would win; they had last recorded a victory in the Nep Stadium in 1909. However, the match turned into a glorious triumph for Ron Greenwood and his team. They won 3–1 with two goals from Trevor Brooking and a penalty from Keegan – and the World Cup Finals were in sight once again.

Kevin kicked-off the 1981–82 season with a goal for Southampton in a 2–1 defeat at Nottingham Forest. Despite the result it was the prelude to a brilliant run of form for him, and the beginning of a productive and exciting striking partnership with young Steve Moran. By the turn of the year Kevin had missed just one game and had netted 14 goals. And, to Lawrie McMenemy's delight, Southampton were serious title contenders.

By then Keegan he had also captained England in two more World Cup qualifiers – a shock 2–1 defeat by Norway in Oslo and a 1–0 home victory over Hungary at Wembley. That result, after a campaign of uncertainty, had finally booked England's passage to Spain in the summer of 1982.

The PFA membership were most definitely impressed with Kevin Keegan's form for club and country throughout the first half of 1981–82. They voted him the Players' Player of the Year, an Award presented at the Hilton Hotel on 14 March, by Neil Macfarlane MP. The presentation marked a memorable 'Double' for the Saints, with Keegan's team-mate Steve Moran named the Young Player of the Year.

Ironically, Moran had been out of action through injury since mid-January, and his absence from the team had coincided with a loss of form which saw the Saints' Championship challenge evaporate. They would eventually finish in seventh place, while Keegan finished as the First Division's top scorer with 26 goals.

In June 1982, just before he was due to depart with the England squad for the World Cup Finals Kevin was awarded the OBE for his services to football.

If not for the back injury which kept him out of England's 1982 World Cup Finals challenge, until the Second Phase match against Spain, Keegan's international career might have ended in a blaze of glory. But by the time he was fit enough for a recall to the ranks, England had to beat Spain by two clear goals in order to progress to the semi–finals ahead of West Germany. It didn't happen; England's World Cup challenge collapsed with a 0–0 draw. Kevin was a substitute in the game which marked his 63rd and final appearance for his country.

Back in England, he began the 1982–83 season with a new club, Newcastle United, in the Second Division. Within two seasons he would help the slumbering north-east giants back into the top flight before retiring to enjoy a few years in the Spanish sunshine while adamantly denying that he would ever turn to football management...

Joseph Kevin Keegan was born on St Valentine's Day 1951, in the mining village of Armthorpe, near Doncaster. A small boy, he was nevertheless an enthusiastic young footballer who started out with the aim of emulating England's Gordon Banks between the posts. But the realisation that a lack of height can be a serious barrier to the art of goalkeeping, turned his attention to making and scoring goals rather than stopping them.

He had trials with Coventry City and Doncaster Rovers, who both rejected him as "too small", before he struck lucky at Scunthorpe United where he became an apprentice, eventually turning professional in December 1968.

In three seasons at The Old Show Ground, Kevin toughened up with weight-training, cross-country running and the experience of 124 Fourth Division games for the Irons. In May 1971, after speculation that several top clubs were seeking his signature, Keegan's dedication to his craft paid off with a £35,000 dream move to Liverpool.

At Anfield he was to prove one of Bill Shankly's best-ever acquisitions and would develop into one of the world's finest players

STEVE MORAN
SOUTHAMPTON

Down at The Dell, in the first half of the 1981–82 League campaign 21-year-old Steve Moran was often seen upstaging the likes of Alan Ball, Kevin Keegan and Mick Channon as the Saints rode high in the First Division.

By the half way stage of the season the youngster had notched nine goals in 18 League games. Two of them, both scored at home, were exceptional. In a 4–0 win against Leeds in November Steve had beaten three defenders and gone around the goalkeeper before slotting the ball into the net. In a 3–2 victory over Manchester United two weeks later he controlled a headed pass from Kevin Keegan and beat two defenders in a single movement, then flicked the ball over the advancing keeper to score.

Moran's fine run of form was enough to earn him an appearance in the England Under–21 team against Norway; it also brought him the PFA Young Player of the Year Award for 1982, presented by the first-ever PFA Young Player Award winner Kevin Beattie. Unfortunately a serious back injury picked up in mid-January would keep Steve out for the rest of the season.

Born in Croydon in 1961, Steve had arrived at Southampton after being spotted as an 11-year-old by Lawrie McMenemy.

Legend has it that McMenemy promised to buy the boy a new pair of boots if he scored a second half hat-trick in a youth match. Moran duly obliged, became the proud owner of some spanking new footwear and was subsequently snapped up by the Saints at the earliest opportunity.

Steve made his first team début as a substitute in 4–1 home win against Manchester City in January 1980 and crowned the day by scoring with virtually his first kick of the game. A few months later, when he had proven himself a natural goalscorer with 17 goals in his first 19 appearances for Southampton, Lawrie McMenemy was full of praise for his young protégé. 'He has everything needed to take him right to the very top – pace, sharpness and, above all, he delights in scoring.'

YOUNG PLAYER OF THE YEAR

1982

Steve Moran left Southampton in September 1986 – after 78 League goals in 180 games – a £300,000 transfer took him to Leicester City. He later played for Reading, Exeter City and Hull City. Although widely tipped as a future England striker, he did not achieve full international status. In fact, his international career was limited to just one more appearance in the Under–21 side against France in 1984

JOE MERCER OBE

**MERIT
AWARD
WINNER**

1982

Everyone loved smiling Joe Mercer. One of football's comedians, he brought humour to a game often lacking in that particular quality. He was renowned too for the odd configuration of his legs, once described as being 'shaped like a pair of brackets ... made of thick wire'. And he was considered by many to be the finest left-half of his day.

Joe was born in Ellesmere Port, Cheshire in 1914. By the time he was eighteen he had graduated from the Cheshire Schoolboy ranks, through non-league football and onto the books of Everton, the club he would serve until he was 32. In 1938–39 he was the key figure in the Toffees' League Championship success. He had also gained international recognition, making his England début on 16 November 1938 in a 7–0 drubbing of Ireland. In the months befo start of the Second World War, he had accumulated five caps.

Then, like all professional footballer of the time, Joe's career was interrupted by the hostilities, although throughout the war he appeared in twenty-two unofficial internationals. In one of the last of these games, a Victory International against Scotland, he suffered a cartilage injury which later required surgery. In the aftermath of the operation he suffered both a crisis of confidence, and the loss of his place in the Ever line-up.

Joe was now in his early-thirties and it seemed likely that he would soon be employed full-time in his family's grocery business in Wallasey. But then, Arsenal's manager George Allison put in a bid of £7,000 for his services and Mercer signed for the Gunners in November 1946, although he continued to live in Cheshire.

Arsenal were perilously close to the foot of the table. Under the guidance of assistant manager Tom Whittaker, Mercer adopted a more defensive role than the one he had been accustomed to at Goodison Park, and with all his experience and his never-say-die attitude he was able to inspire a revival in the team's spirit and they finished the season in mid-table safety.

Twelve months later, with Whittaker

As a player Joe Mercer caused Everton to regret selling him to Arsenal at the age of 32, in 1946. At £7,000 he became one of the bargains of the century, captaining the Gunners to three major trophies over the next seven seasons; Everton won nothing in that period. As a manager smiling Joe took Manchester City to the top, and there were many who wanted to see him stay on in the England hot-seat. Sadly he died in August 1990

now in command and Joe Mercer as an inspirational captain, Arsenal won the 1947–48 Championship

In 1950 Joe, at 36, found himself leading Arsenal out at Wembley for the FA Cup Final against Liverpool (ironically, the northern-based Gunner had used the Anfield training facilities ever since signing for Arsenal). He was the Footballer of the Year and his man-of-the-match performance in the Final demonstrated just why he had been honoured by the Football Writers' Association. Arsenal won 2–0 with both goals scored by Reg Lewis. Joe led his team up to the Royal Box, collected the Cup from King George VI and his medal from Queen Elizabeth. He smiled as Her Majesty handed him a *losers'* medal – a mistake that was quickly rectified.

Two years later Joe was still going strong, and once again led Arsenal to the FA Cup Final. This time the opponents were Newcastle United, chasing their second Cup Final victory in successive seasons. A first-half injury to right-back Wally Barnes meant the Gunners played most of the match with ten men and, despite the exhortations and example of Mercer, were unable to keep out the Magpies who eventually broke them down with a George Robledo header six minutes from time. Newcastle had won the Cup – but Arsenal, Mercer in particular, stole the headlines.

1952–53 saw one of the closest League campaigns in history with Arsenal and Preston North End sharing identical results and finishing on 54 points apiece. But the Gunners had a goal average of 1.51, Preston 1.41, and Joe Mercer collected his third League Championship medal. He announced his retirement, but then changed his mind for one more battle.

Throughout the 1953–54 League campaign Joe was in and out of the Arsenal side. On 10 April 1954 he was making his 20th first team appearance of the season, against Liverpool at Highbury. In a freak collision with his own left-back, Joe Wade, Mercer's left leg was broken. As he was stretchered off in front of the 33,000 crowd he raised an arm to wave goodbye. He was 39 years old, and a remarkable playing career had come to an end.

Instead of going full-time into the grocery business as expected, he decided on the more precarious path of football management, joining Sheffield United in 1955. The club was relegated, swapping places with Sheffield Wednesday, and despite Mercer's efforts did not return to the top flight during his tenure. In 1958 he moved on to another troubled club, Aston Villa, who were

also relegated at the end of the 1958–59 season. But Joe's first managerial success was just around the corner. In 1959–60 he took Villa back to the top flight as Second Division Champions. A year later they became the first-ever winners of the Football League Cup, beating Rotherham United over two legs.

In 1964, it looked as though Joe's managerial career was at a premature end when he left Villa Park through illness. But with his usual tenacity he was back within a year – this time as manager of Manchester City, in partnership with the flamboyant coach Malcolm Allison. Together they steered City out of the Second Division and into the upper reaches of the First, thanks to such astute signings as Francis Lee, Mike Summerbee, Colin Bell and the remarkable Tony Book.

In the 1967–68 campaign City won an exciting race for the title ahead of Manchester United, Leeds United and Liverpool, and so booked the club's first excursion into Europe which ended with a First Round defeat by Turkish Champions Fenerbahce. In 1969 Joe was back on his old stomping ground, Wembley, as City beat Leicester 1–0 in the FA Cup Final with a Neil Young goal.

And there was more to come in the following season, as City lifted the League Cup, beating West Bromwich Albion 2–1 at Wembley. A month later they travelled to Vienna for the final of the European Cup-Winners' Cup against Polish side Gornik Zabrze. Goals from Neil Young and Francis Lee (a penalty) put City ahead by half-time and they eventually won the match 2–1, bringing to an end a remarkable run of success – four major trophies in three seasons – for Joe and his sidekick Allison.

In 1972 Malcolm succeeded Joe in the Maine Road hot-seat, as the elder statesman moved into the administrative side of the game as general manager of Coventry City. And there a fine career might have wound down, except that fate was about to deal another twist in the Joe Mercer story.

After England's failure to reach the 1974 World Cup Finals, Sir Alf Ramsey found himself out of a job. While the FA cogitated over his replacement, they decided to appoint a caretaker-manager and Joe proved the ideal choice. He was in charge for just seven games and by the time he handed over the reins to Don Revie, he had restored a great deal of spirit to the squad.

Joe had made it clear that, at 60, he did not want the job on a permanent basis.

KENNY DALGLISH MBE
LIVERPOOL

PLAYER OF THE YEAR

1983

Liverpool swept the board with a memorable hat-trick at the 1983 PFA Awards. Leading the charge was Kenny Dalglish, generally regarded as Anfield's finest-ever player and ranked among the best forwards ever produced in Britain.

'It was a great weekend for us,' Kenny recalls. 'We won the League Cup on the Saturday, for the third year running, then the three of us – Bob, Rushie and me – picked up PFA Awards at the Hilton Hotel next day. And in midweek I played for Scotland against Switzerland at Hampden Park.'

Kenny attributes his Player of the Year Award largely to the fact that he had been scoring regularly, even though his first goal of 1982–83 had not come until Liverpool's twelfth game of the season.

By 27 March, the day of the Awards ceremony, he had notched 19 goals in all competitions, including a hat-trick against Manchester City and two apiece against Brighton, Spurs, Notts County and Stoke City. 'A look at the list of PFA winners shows that a number of goalscorers have won the players' Award,' he asserts. 'Goals are what everybody wants to see, but you only get the good bit of putting it in the back of the net as a result of the efforts of everyone else in the team.'

Many PFA members voted for Dalglish not only for his goals, but for the determined and persistent way he had regained his form for Liverpool, and his international place, after a relatively poor showing for Scotland in the 1982 World Cup Finals.

Alvin Martin was among those who voted for Kenny in 1983: 'He battled his way back this term after being written off last season and I think he's as good as ever,' said the West Ham defender in an Awards night preview. 'I cannot remember seeing him play better than he's doing at this time.'

Kenneth Mathieson Dalglish was born in Dalmarnock, Glasgow, in March 1951. As a football crazy youngster he supported Rangers and in the '60s idolised the flamboyant Jim

Baxter and the fearless Ian McMillan among other Ibrox stars.

For a while the Dalglishes even lived in a flat overlooking the Rangers training pitch, and his family and friends felt it was only a matter of time before the talented youngster, who played twice for Scotland Schoolboys, would be snapped up by the 'Gers. But it was Celtic, the other half of the traditional 'Old Firm' rivalry, who first recognised the lad's potential when he proved a star turn for Glasgow United's Under–16s team, in a match against prospective Celtic signees, and was subsequently invited to train at Parkhead.

At Celtic's insistence he gained invaluable experience for a season with Cumbernauld United before signing professional forms in 1967. Managed by the formidable Jock Stein, Celtic was then the leading club in Scotland and had recently become the first British side to win the European Cup. Fate could not have placed the keen young Dalglish in a better place of learning.

Along with Lou Macari, David Hay and Danny McGrain, Kenny rose through the ranks at Parkhead as a member of Celtic's outstanding reserve side, dubbed 'The Quality Street Gang'. Within three years he had made his League début; within four he had won his first full cap

for Scotland, as a substitute for Alex Cropley in a 1–0 win over Belgium in Aberdeen.

Dalglish's Celtic career was studded with achievements: four championship medals, four Scottish Cup winners' medals and a Scottish League Cup winners' medal. By August 1977 he had scored more than a century of League goals and was the proud possessor of 49 Scottish caps. It was then that he was transferred, for a then-British record fee of £440,000, to Liverpool, as a replacement for Kevin Keegan who had departed to West Germany.

Those Anfield doubters who felt that Keegan was irreplaceable were soon delighting in the fact that Dalglish was a natural talent, equally as adept, and equally as capable of galvanising and inspiring the team as his predecessor had been. Manager Bob Paisley was delighted with his acquisition: 'From the off he read my team better than they understood him. That's the hallmark of a great player.'

Kenny scored on his Football League début against Middlesbrough and went on to hit 30 goals as the Reds became the first British club to retain the European Cup – beating FC Bruges 1–0 at Wembley, with a Dalglish goal. They also finished second in the 1977–78 League campaign and were runners-up to Nottingham Forest in the League Cup.

A year later Kenny was voted the Football Writers' Footballer of the Year for his part in Liverpool's eleventh League Championship success. Another championship medal followed in 1979–80 and a third in 1981–82. These achievements were supplemented by that trio of League Cup victories between 1981 and 1983.

'Obviously the most important awards for everyone, are the team awards,' says Kenny. 'But it's always nice to get a little bit of individual recognition as well, so long as you can keep your feet firmly on the ground afterwards. In my opinion, the PFA members could have picked anybody from that Liverpool side in 1983 – there were four of us nominated in the top six. It was a tremendous reflection on the club at the time.'

Liverpool, who had led the table since the end of October were destined to settle the matter eleven points ahead of closest rivals Watford. Kenny, who had been ever-present throughout the campaign, was voted Footballer of the Year by the Football Writers' Association for the second time. 'It was a tremendous season,' he says. 'A Championship medal, a Milk Cup winners' medal, Footballer of the Year and the players' own choice … I'll settle for that.'

'It was a tremendous season. A Championship medal, a Milk Cup winners' medal, Footballer of the Year and the players' own choice … I'll settle for that.'

Somehow the engravers managed to mis-spell Kenny Dalglish's name on the 1983 PFA Player of the Year trophy, omitting the second 'L'. 'That's fame for you,' he joked, when reminded of the error. 'I never really noticed. I wouldn't have given it back anyway, in case they changed their minds.' In fact the engravers fitted a correctly spelt nameplate shortly after the Awards ceremony.

Two years after becoming the PFA Players' Player of the Year Dalglish was appointed player-manager of Liverpool, winning the FA Cup and League Championship 'Double' in his first season in charge. His international playing career ended in 1987, by which time he had accumulated a record 102 Scottish caps and had scored 30 goals for his country (a record jointly-shared with Denis Law). When his playing career ended in 1990 he had played 353 League games for Liverpool. He scored 118 Football League goals, becoming only the second player to accumulate a century of goals on both sides of the border. In February 1991, after leading Liverpool to five major trophies in six years, he astonished the football world by resigning from his job at Anfield. Eight months later he became manager of Second Division Blackburn Rovers, a club he would quickly steer into the upper reaches of the Premiership, and to the title itself in 1994-95.

IAN RUSH
LIVERPOOL

Kenny Dalglish reckons that the most agonising part of winning an Award is having to make an acceptance speech at the presentation. However, on the occasion of the 1983 PFA Awards his nervous anticipation was somewhat lessened by the presence of the young player seated to his left.

'Rushie, who was nominated for the Player title and the Young Player Award, was an absolute bundle of nerves,' recalls Kenny. 'It was a confidence boost to me to have him sitting next to me.'

In the event the nervous Rush stepped up to receive the Young Player Award from his Welsh team boss Mike England.

In only his second full season for Liverpool, Ian was being hailed as the scoring sensation of the '80s. So far in 1982–83, he had scored 26 goals for the Reds who were sitting on top of the table and had just won the League Cup. This total included two hat-tricks, against Coventry City and Notts County, and four in Liverpool's 5–0 demolition of neighbours Everton in November 1982.

Born in St Asaph, North Wales, in October 1961, Ian was the second youngest in a family of ten children. Having overcome meningitis as a five-year-old, it was against the odds that he became a professional footballer. He arrived at Anfield in April 1980 for £300,000 from Chester City where he had caught the eye of Bob Paisley after scoring 14 goals in 34 League games. He had also impressed Wales boss Mike England

who selected him as a substitute for the match against Scotland in May '80 – *before* he had appeared in Liverpool's first team.

Ian did not score on his Liverpool début, against Ipswich at Portman Road in December 1980, nor in his next eight appearances – prompting many among the Anfield faithful to wonder what all the fuss had been about. The answer came in the 1981–82 campaign when Rush finished as Liverpool's top scorer with 17 goals in 33 League appearances, three in the FA Cup, eight in the League Cup and two in Europe. In the process he collected a Milk Cup winners' medal and a Championship medal.

Ian finished the 1982–83 season with another 30 goals to his credit, and it was increasingly apparent that winning prizes and making acceptances speeches was something the young striker would simply have to become accustomed to.

YOUNG PLAYER OF THE YEAR

1983

Liverpool striker Ian Rush. The 1983 PFA Young Player of the Year was destined to become one of the greatest goalscorers of all time

BOB PAISLEY OBE

MERIT AWARD WINNER
1983

On the afternoon before the 1983 PFA Award ceremony, Bob Paisley had been invited by Liverpool's skipper Graeme Souness, to collect the Milk Cup on behalf of the team at Wembley. It was Bob's twelfth major title since succeeding Bill Shankly in the Anfield hot-seat nine years earlier. It was the first time in Wembley's history that a manager had been accorded such an honour by his team.

Paisley had been a faithful Liverpool servant since his playing days in the late-40s and early-50s. He had joined the club in 1939, directly from amateur stardom with Bishop Auckland. The duration of the war delayed his official first team début until the 1946 FA Cup competition which saw Liverpool eliminated by Bolton Wanderers in the Fourth Round.

Shorter than the average player, Bob was nevertheless known as a tenacious tackler with a seemingly endless supply of energy, and was also something of a long throw-in expert.

In the 1946–47 season, when Liverpool won the first post-war League Championship in a neck-and-neck race with Manchester United, Wolves and Stoke City, Paisley made 33 appearances in the No. 6 shirt.

Three seasons later he scored the winner in Liverpool's 2–0 FA Cup semi-final victory over Everton at Maine Road, a cheeky lob which completely fooled George Burnett in the Everton goal. For the Final itself Paisley was replaced in a reshuffled line-up by Billy Jones – a selection which in hindsight was questioned as Liverpool lost 2–0. It was felt that Paisley's tougher

tackling ability might have coped better with the Gunners' Jimmy Logie.

Bob played on until the 1953–54 season when he hung up his boots after 278 games and 13 goals in all competitions for Liverpool. He then joined the Anfield coaching staff, under team boss Don Welsh. When Bill Shankly arrived as manager in 1959, he appointed Paisley as his assistant.

Throughout Shanks' revolutionary rebuilding of the Reds' squad, Paisley was there, offering advice and experience at every step of the way. And when Shankly announced his retirement in 1974, Paisley's appointment as his successor signalled a tradition of promotion from within which has continued at Anfield (with one notable exception) ever since. But simply stepping into the great man's shoes was no part of Paisley's philosophy. He was his own man, with his own ideas – a point underlined by his early conversion of Ray Kennedy from a striker to an effective midfielder, and later by the brilliant players he either nurtured from within the club or bought on the transfer market. They included Terry McDermott, Phil Neal, Joey Jones, Kenny Dalglish, Graeme Souness, Alan Hansen, Phil Thompson, Jimmy Case and David Fairclough.

Although no trophies came Anfield's way in Bob's first managerial season, Liverpool did finish as League runners-up to Derby County. Then, 1975–76 brought the club's ninth Championship, a success repeated in 1976–77 together with a magnificent 3–1 European Cup Final

victory over Borussia Moenchengladbach in Rome and an FA Cup Final berth against Manchester United. That summer Bob was awarded the OBE for his services to football.

In 1978 the Reds won the European Cup again, beating FC Bruges 1–0 with a Kenny Dalglish goal at Wembley. This was Liverpool's second visit of the season to the famous old stadium. In March they had played out a hard fought, extra-time draw with Nottingham Forest in the League Cup Final (they lost the replay 1–0 at Old Trafford).

Next came the most glorious spell of Paisley's reign, beginning in 1978–79 Liverpool won four of the next five League Championships, another European Cup and three consecutive League Cups. By 1983 when Bob handed the job to his long-time assistant, Joe Fagan, he had become the most successful manager in the English game with 13 major trophies. In cold black-and-white terms his achievements had eclipsed those of his mentor Bill Shankly.

Bob Paisley's quiet style – he preferred to let his team do the talking – may have been far removed from the charismatic brashness of his predecessor Bill Shankly, but the results were the same and the Liverpool success story continued to unfold throughout the 1970s and early '80s. The shy, retiring Paisley surprised guests at the 1983 PFA Awards dinner with a number of amusing anecdotes, including this gem which recalls his amateur days when his local team at Hetton-le-Hole won a trophy. It was, he said, the custom in those days to send results to the local newspaper via carrier pigeon. In honour of the occasion the team asked their President to do the honours. Overcome with emotion, the poor man released the pigeon without ringing the result slip to its leg. Realising his error, he yelled at the bird: 'Gan on, hinny, tell 'em we won 2–1'

IAN RUSH
LIVERPOOL

PLAYER OF THE YEAR

1984

Twelve months after lifting the PFA Young Player of the Year title, Ian Rush was back again – to collect the 1984 Players' Player of the Year Award. He was the first player to win the two trophies in successive seasons.

Rush and Liverpool were enjoying another brilliant season in 1983–84, this time under the management of Joe Fagan, a former 'boot roomer' who had succeeded Bob Paisley in June 1983. At the time of the PFA Awards ceremony on Sunday 25 March the club was lying second in the First Division, but only because of the welcome distraction of a League Cup Final appearance against Everton earlier that day at Wembley. The match had ended in a 0–0 stalemate after extra time, and the replay was set for the following Wednesday at Maine Road.

The situation meant that Ian was the only Liverpool player present at the ceremony. 'Because of the forthcoming replay Joe Fagan wanted the team back in Liverpool,' he recalls. 'But he gave me permission to stay in London to attend the dinner as I was one of the six contenders for the top Award – I sat with a friend and some of the Oxford United players.

'I was the first Welshman to get the Award, and it was a great honour to receive it

from another Welshman – Neil Kinnock.'

When the leader of the Labour Party had made the presentation, Ian nervously gave his second brief acceptance speech to an assembly of his peers from the PFA. 'It's funny,' he recalls, 'you don't mind playing in front of 100,000 people but to speak in front of a few hundred is terrifying. These days it's not so bad, but back then it was the most nerve-wracking thing. I

'If we scored three we wanted to score four. If we got four we wanted five. The whole team was hungry for success.'

thanked everybody who'd voted for me, and of course everyone at Liverpool. When I said how proud I was to be the first Welsh-born player to win the Award, Neil Kinnock seemed particularly pleased. Afterwards we had a long chat in the bar.'

No doubt the conversation touched upon the fine art of goalscoring, at which young Mr Rush was an undoubted master. He had already reached the 30 goals mark in all competitions for the third successive season.

Yet in the 1983–84 pre-season it had been touch and go whether Ian would actually play a part in Liverpool's defence of the League title and the League Cup. He was suffering from a groin injury picked up at the end of the previous campaign and the problem had remained throughout the summer. 'I went jogging to keep myself in some sort of shape, but I knew I had a problem when I reported for training,' he says.

His fears were confirmed during practise. 'It was the twisting and turning in match-play which gave me trouble and it seemed to get worse during a friendly in Dublin against Manchester United.'

The pre-season preparations continued in Holland, but Ian was unable to participate and on the team's return to Anfield he was put on a special exercise programme. Eventually Joe Fagan persuaded him to play in the Charity Shield game against Manchester United at Wembley. If the problem still persisted then the manager promised to rest him until Christmas.

Thankfully, Ian survived the game without further trouble and felt confident about playing in Liverpool's opening match of League campaign a week later, against newly-promoted Wolves at Molineux.

The new season was less than a minute old when Geoff Palmer blasted Wolves into the lead from the penalty spot. But the Reds fought their way back and on the hour Ian struck his first goal of the campaign to secure a draw. He also scored in three of the next five matches as Liverpool achieved a top four placing in the table.

But the groin problem was still troubling him and he failed to find the net in the next four games. On the eve of the home fixture against Luton Town on 29 October he almost pulled out of the team, for fear of letting his team-mates down. But assistant manager Roy Evans persuaded him to soldier on. 'I'm glad he did,' says Ian. 'Everything went right. I scored in the second and fifth minutes – and had a hat-trick by half time.'

He ended the afternoon with a personal best of five goals, as the Reds slaughtered the Hatters 6–0. The result lifted Liverpool to the top of the table.

In the League Cup, Ian scored eight times on the way to Wembley as Liverpool knocked-out Brentford, Fulham, Birmingham City, Sheffield Wednesday and Walsall, who had provided a real scare with a 2–2 draw in the first leg of the semi-final.

On the day after the PFA Awards, Ian travelled home by train and in the company of former Liverpool hero, Billy Liddell – no doubt they swapped some fascinating Anfield anecdotes.

Two days later the newly crowned Players' Player lined-up at Maine Road for the League Cup Final replay against Everton. Ian went close on a couple of occasions, but the match was won for Liverpool by a single goal from Graeme Souness. It was the Reds fourth successive League Cup win.

On the following Saturday Ian resumed the scoring habit with a goal in a 2–0 victory over Watford. The two points took Liverpool back to top spot where they would remain to become only the third club – after Huddersfield Town in the 1920s and Arsenal in the '30s – to win three Championships in successive seasons.

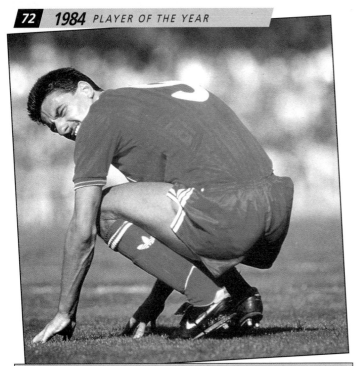

It's hard to believe, but when Liverpool first approached the young Ian Rush at Chester City, he actually turned them down. 'They came in for me in March 1980, just before the transfer deadline, but I honestly didn't think I was good enough to play alongside all those legendary players. So I said no. But they persisted and showed me around Anfield so I could see what a great place it was, and I eventually signed in April.'

It turned out, of course, to be wise move for Rush and one of the best signings Liverpool have ever made. In his fifteen seasons at Anfield Ian has contributed to five Championships, three FA Cup wins, five League Cup wins (he holds the record for League Cup-winners' medals) and a European Cup success. On the goalscoring front he is now Liverpool's all-time leading scorer. He has equalled Denis Law's record of FA Cup goals (41) and has scored the most FA Cup Final goals (5).

In 1987, Ian's Liverpool career was interrupted by a big money move to Juventus. But his Italian sojourn proved a personal disappointment, both on and off the pitch, and after a year he was recaptured by Kenny Dalglish for Liverpool for £2.8 million. 'Luckily Liverpool gave me another chance, and I'm still here. It was the best move I could have made,' says Ian.

Ian has played 69 times for Wales, a country which despite the wealth of talent available in recent seasons, has failed to find success. 'I've really enjoyed my international career, but it's been a big disappointment that we haven't qualified for a major tournament. That would be the icing on the cake for me. But for one reason or another we just don't follow through. We'll play really well in one game and then badly against a team we ought to beat.' Ian is now Wales' leading international scorer

Ian played in all but one game of the campaign and ended as the League's top scorer with 32 goals, included in that tally (in addition to that five goal haul in October) were four against Coventry City and a hat-trick against Villa. He was also top scorer in Europe and was later presented with the Golden Boot Award.

Ian had hit five goals on the Reds' journey to the European Cup Final. They had eliminated BK Odense, Atletico Bilbao, Benfica and Dinamo Bucharest and were to meet AS Roma in the Final to be played, of all places, in Rome. Despite the non-neutral venue Liverpool took early control of the game and scored first through Phil Neal on 14 minutes. Roma equalised with seven minutes to go and the game went through extra time still deadlocked, thereby bringing about the first-ever penalty shoot-out in a European Cup Final.

Steve Nicol insisted on taking the first kick – and promptly missed. Roma scored their first. Phil Neal scored. Then Bruno Conti missed for the home side to level the scores. Graeme Souness and Righetti scored. 'Then it was my turn to take the long walk from the centre circle,' says Ian. 'It was a great relief when my side-footed shot went in with the keeper diving the wrong way.'

Liverpool were now ahead and Graziani's miss for Roma meant that Alan Kennedy could settle the matter. With supreme confidence he did just that. Liverpool had won the shoot-out 4–2 and took the European Cup back to Anfield for the fourth time.

'Joe Fagan did a great job,' says Ian. 'He was a great coach and coaches sometimes find it difficult to make the transition to management, but Joe managed it with no problems at all. And he achieved something that Bob never did – a 'Treble' in his first season as boss.

'We had such a good team. If we scored three we wanted to score four. If we got four we wanted five. The whole team was hungry for success. Every player was in their prime and I was lucky enough to be in a goalscoring position so many times.'

Ian finished the season with a remarkable 48 goals in all competitions for Liverpool – and a whole host of personal accolades. Besides the PFA Player of the Year Award and the Golden Boot, he was also voted Footballer of the Year by the Football Writers' Association, and he finished second to Michel Platini in the World Soccer Player of the Year poll. 'But I'd say that the PFA Award meant most to me, because it was awarded by my fellow professionals – to be judged by your peers has to be the ultimate test.'

PAUL WALSH
LUTON TOWN

Paul Walsh had been a teenage sensation with his first club Charlton Athletic – a goalscoring front runner, as skilful as he was quick.

Born in Plumstead in October 1962, he became an apprentice at The Valley on leaving school. He turned professional at 17 and made his first team début soon afterwards, in a Charlton side destined for relegation to the Third Division in 1980. In the following season Walsh was outstanding, making 40 appearances and scoring 11 goals as the club bounced straight back to the Second Division.

The exciting young star attracted interest from all over the country, but Charlton resisted selling him until July 1982 when he moved to David Pleat's Luton Town, newly promoted to the First Division, for £352,000. At Kenilworth Road he formed a productive partnership with Brian Stein and in his first season with the club managed to notch three hat-tricks. His form in that campaign was enough to earn him a PFA Young Player Award nomination for the first time.

In June 1983 he was selected for England's three match tour of Australia and made his début as a substitute for Luther Blissett in the 0–0 draw in Sydney. In the second match in Brisbane, Walsh teamed up in what appeared to be a promising striking partnership with Trevor Francis. Twelve minutes into the second half with the scoreline still at 0–0, Walsh struck the only goal of the game when he connected with a cross from John Gregory. He also played in the last game of the tour, a 1–1 draw in Melbourne.

(Walsh would make just two further international appearances, against France and Wales in 1984.)

Paul was again in top form in the first half of the 1983–84 season, as Luton flitted in and out of the top six. By the end of January he had notched eight goals, including a hat-trick in a 4–2 away defeat of Stoke City. Again he was nominated for a Young Player Award, and this time he won it. The presentation was made by former PFA Chairman Steve Coppell.

From February to the end of the season, Luton's League challenge simply disintegrated. They won just two of the remaining eighteen matches and finished in 16th position. But Paul Walsh continued to impress, and that summer he moved on to Liverpool for £700,000. He had played 80 league games for the Hatters.

YOUNG PLAYER OF THE YEAR

1984

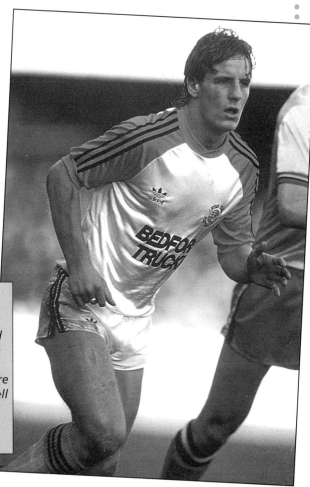

Paul Walsh scored after just 15 seconds on his Liverpool début against West Ham at Anfield. Although he won a Championship medal with the Reds in 1986, when he was again nominated for a PFA Young Player Award, much of his time with the club was spent on the injury list. He moved on again in February 1988, to Spurs where he stayed until June 1992. Then, after a loan spell at QPR, he became Portsmouth's most effective forward, before making a surprise return to the top flight with Manchester City in March 1994

BILL NICHOLSON

**MERIT
AWARD
WINNER**

1984

As the first manager to achieve the League and FA Cup 'Double' in the 20th century, Bill Nicholson has a special place in football folklore and is regarded with a godlike status in certain quarters of North London.

'Billy Nick' was a one-club-man throughout his playing career. Arriving at Tottenham in August 1938, after being spotted in his native Scarborough, he became a vital member of Arthur Rowe's famous 'push and run' team of the early-50s, with its emphasis on attack, economy of distribution and speed of movement.

'Make it simple, make it quick' was the basis of Rowe's supremely effective philosophy. His team which included Ted Ditchburn, Alf Ramsey, Ron Burgess, Eddie Bailey and Len Duquemin won promotion from the Second Division in 1950, and then took the First by storm, winning the 1950–51 Championship ahead of Manchester United and Blackpool. Nicholson fitted neatly into the scheme of things as an adaptable, hard-tackling, no-nonsense wing half. At the peak of his playing career in '51 he was selected just once for England, scoring a goal in the 5–2 win against Portugal at Goodison Park.

In 1955 Arthur Rowe was forced to retire through illness and was replaced at White Hart Lane by Jimmy Anderson, with Nicholson as his right-hand man. When Anderson moved on in October 1958, Bill (who had recently been coaching the England World Cup squad), took over the managerial reins and inherited a talented squad, which already included the mercurial Northern Irish genius Danny Blanchflower at right half and captain.

Maurice Norman, Peter Baker and Ron Henry were at the heart of the defence. The quicksilver Welsh winger Cliff Jones was accompanied in the forward line by Bobby Smith, Terry Dyson and Les Allen. Nicholson strengthened this formidable array of talent with the shrewd signings of three Scottish internationals: goalkeeper Bill Brown from Dundee, Dave Mackay, the brick wall wing half,

from Hearts, and playmaking inside forward John White from Falkirk. These players formed the core of Spurs' 1960–61 squad, destined to be remembered as one of the finest teams of all time.

The great adventure began on 20 August 1960 at White Hart Lane. The visitors were Everton. After a shaky start Tottenham finally got to grips with the match in the last five minutes when a goal apiece from Allen and Smith secured the points. Eight months later, on 17 April 1961, Les Allen struck the winner in a 2–1 victory over Sheffield Wednesday to clinch Tottenham's second League Championship. Between those dates football grounds up and down the country had been treated to some of the most devastating attacking football ever seen. Spurs lost just three away games, and scored four goals at Blackburn, Nottingham

Bill Nicholson played under Arthur Rowe in the fine Spurs' side of the early '50s. A decade later he produced an even better team at White Hart Lane

Forest, Newcastle and Wolves. At White Hart Lane they won fifteen and drew three, among the results at home Aston Villa were defeated 6–2, Birmingham City 6–0 and Preston 5–0.

Meanwhile, Nicholson's Spurs had already booked a place in the FA Cup Final after eliminating Charlton Athletic, Crewe Alexandra, Aston Villa, Sunderland and Burnley. They finished the job with a 2–0 win against Leicester City at Wembley. Both goals came late in the second half from Smith and Dyson, after Leicester had put up a spirited fight despite being virtually reduced to ten-men following an injury to Len Chalmers.

Bill Nicholson enjoyed further successes with Spurs – the FA Cup in 1962 and 1967, the League Cup in 1971 and 1973, the European Cup-Winners' Cup in 1963 and the UEFA Cup in 1972 – but he will always be remembered as the man who brought the 'Double' to Tottenham. He resigned in August 1974 against the wishes of everyone at White Hart Lane.

Above: Bill Nicholson holds the F.A. Cup in 1967, at Tottenham Town Hall

Left: Nicholson's Spurs complete the 1960–61 'Double' at Wembley

PETER REID
EVERTON

PLAYER OF THE YEAR

1985

When Peter Reid was presented with the 1985 PFA Player of the Year Award, by rock star and football aficionado Elton John, the cheers were loud and long. The membership and their guests were clearly appreciative of the never-say-die spirit and the sheer tenacity embodied within Everton's inspirational midfield general.

Peter was twenty-eight when he was voted top player by his peers in the game. Yet, a few years earlier, few would have backed him to one day win the Award. At that time he seemed destined to join that band of unfortunate footballers whose careers were cut short by injury – in Peter's case a whole string of them.

Born in Liverpool in June 1956, but brought up in nearby Huyton, Peter had been an England Schoolboys international and a prominent member of the Huyton Schoolboys' team which won the English Schools' Trophy in 1971, beating Stoke in the Final. Shortly afterwards he had signed as an apprentice for Second Division Bolton Wanderers. He turned professional in May 1974

and made his first team début that October as a substitute against Orient. He was soon a regular in the Wanderers' midfield and missed just a few games over the next three seasons. In April 1977 he made the breakthrough into the England Under–21 team and in the following season was a vital factor in Bolton's Second Division Championship-winning campaign.

'To know that your fellow professionals from all four divisions have voted for you is a tremendous feeling. I still get goose pimples thinking about it.'

Then came the first of those injuries – a broken left kneecap – sustained at the start of the 1978–79 season. He recovered and returned to action. By then Arsenal, Wolves and Everton were all keen to sign the talented terrier-like midfielder, and he was valued at around £600,000.

But, on New Year's Day 1979, in a match against Everton on a snowbound Burnden Park pitch, he collided with goalkeeper George Wood and consequently suffered torn ligaments in his right leg. 'Every day for a year I was in that Bolton treatment room,' recalls Peter. 'And every day the physio Jim Hedridge got the last bit out of me – he made me keep my body in perfect trim. He forced me not to swamp myself in self-pity when others were questioning whether I would ever play again after two serious injuries. It was a telling time in which the pressure built up. Only a player, and a good physio, really know how these pressures develop. All players worry. It's part of the job, an occupational hazard which causes sleepless nights.'

Of course, Peter did return to action, although he played only a handful of games due to a contractual dispute with the club. In 1981–82 the injury jinx returned, when he broke his right leg in a League match against Barnsley. Still he came back and in December 1982 Howard Kendall took him to Everton for just £60,000 – a gamble which eventually turned into one of the footballing bargains of the century.

Before that fact became apparent, however, injury was to strike Peter yet again, restricting him to ten appearances for Everton in 1982–83. He returned to the fray in September 1983, eventually playing in both the League Cup Final, losing 1–0 to Liverpool in a replay, and the FA Cup Final in which he collected a winners' medal in the 2–0 defeat of Watford.

'Everton really came to the forefront at that time,' he says, 'but in '84–85 we were even better. It was a fantastic season. We always had confidence in our ability even though we started off slowly and were beaten 4–1 in the first game at home against Spurs. They were a very talented side with Clive Allen up front and the likes of Chris Waddle, Graham Roberts and Glenn Hoddle. We went 1–0 up through a penalty by Adrian Heath, but after that they just sucked us in and hit us on the break. Then we lost 2–1 away at West Brom, but after winning the third game 1–0 at Chelsea we just went from strength to strength.

'Howard had built a strong side which could really play as well: it had strength in the likes of Andy Gray, Graeme Sharp, Kevin Ratcliffe and myself; it had tremendous ability in Kevin Sheedy, Trevor Steven and Adrian Heath – a complete mixture that worked. Then we had Neville Southall in goal. I've worked with Shilton, Woods, Flowers and Seaman – but in that season Neville Southall was the best goalkeeper I've ever seen. He went on to win the Footballer of the Year title from the Football Writers' and no one deserved it more.

'We also had something that all top sides need, strength in depth, with players like John Bailey, Alan Harper and Kevin Richardson waiting on the sidelines and playing their part whenever they were called on.'

In the 1985 close season, Peter Reid did not have much time to reflect on the glories of the past ten months. In June he got the call from Bobby Robson and joined in preparations for England's forthcoming tour of Mexico and California. He made his international début, as a substitute for Ray Wilkins in the second half of the game against Mexico in the Azteca Stadium. Mexico won 1–0 although England had justifiable claims against the result as Viv Anderson had headed an 'equaliser' which had been disallowed. 'It was the wrong result,' says Peter. 'But it marked the start of an England career which I thought had passed me by, what with my injuries and the amount of talented midfield players around at that time.'

Three days later he was in the starting line-up for the friendly encounter with West Germany who had only just arrived in Mexico City on a fact-finding mission ahead of the following year's World Cup Finals. The rarified conditions told against the German's who had had little chance to properly acclimatise and England won 3–0. Next stop was Los Angeles and another friendly, against the USA. This time Peter stepped in as a substitute for Bryan Robson as England romped to a crushing 5–0 victory.

1985–86 proved another good season for Peter, although it was an ultimately disappointing one for Everton who finished runners-up to Liverpool in both the League and the FA Cup. And in the aftermath of the terrible tragedy at Heysel they, along with other English clubs, had been excluded from European Competition.

In the summer Peter was again part of England's squad, this time for the 1986 World Cup Finals in Mexico. 'It was unfortunate for the likes of Ray Wilkins who got sent-off against Morocco, and for Bryan Robson who had shoulder problems, but I came into the team for the third game, against Poland, along with Steve Hodge, Trevor Steven and Peter Beardsley.'

Reid also played in the following games, against Paraguay and Argentina who eventually eliminated England from the tournament. 'The World Cup was a tremendous experience – right up to Maradona's 'hand of God' incident. I think we paid the Argentinians a bit too much respect on the day.'

Peter left Everton in February 1989, to join QPR. Ten months later he became player-coach (later player-manager) at Manchester City. He spent most of the 1994–95 season with Bury, before taking on the manager's job at troubled Sunderland

After the win against Chelsea at the end of August, Everton began to climb the table. Two months later they occupied top spot and, apart from a four match period which ironically began with a 4–3 defeat by Chelsea in December, they stayed there to bring an eighth Championship success to Goodison Park.

'And we were in with a chance of a "treble", having reached the Finals in both the FA Cup, against Manchester United, and the European Cup–Winners' Cup against Rapid Vienna in Rotterdam,' says Peter.

Everton were magnificent under the Rotterdam floodlights on 15 May, winning 3–1 with goals from Andy Gray, Trevor Steven and Kevin Sheedy, to bring home their first-ever European silverware. Could this brilliant run continue at Wembley on the 18th? 'Sadly not,' says Peter. 'The Cup Final was played on a baking hot day and we just didn't have enough left in the tank to play through two Finals of such importance within four days of each other. It was hard going, and to be fair to Manchester United they played well even though they had the boy Moran sent off for fouling me as I was going through.'

A solitary goal from Norman Whiteside put an end to Everton's 'Treble' hopes, but despite the disappointments of the day it had been a magnificent season for the Toffees – and for Peter Reid who considers that his PFA Award, together with his thirteen international caps, marks the pinnacle of his playing career. 'I know it's been said before, but to know that your fellow professionals from all four divisions have voted for you is a tremendous feeling. I still get goose pimples thinking about it.'

MARK HUGHES
MANCHESTER UNITED

After Mark Hughes' magnificent performance in Wales' 1–0 victory over Scotland, at Hampden Park in March 1985, Graeme Souness declared: 'Hughes may be an even better player than Ian Rush because he is *nastier*. He has a very determined streak which sees him win a lot of the ball.'

Ian Rush also heaped great praise on his Welsh team-mate: 'He's a strong lad with good ball control who is having a great season and deserves something for it. That's why I voted for him in the Young Player of the Year Award.'

Ron Atkinson, Mark's boss at Manchester United, said: 'He's the scoring sensation of the season … there is no limit to what he can achieve.'

Born in Wrexham in November 1963, Leslie Mark Hughes was a Welsh schoolboy international striker who had been snapped up by Manchester United, as an associated schoolboy, in March 1978. Two years later he progressed to an Old Trafford apprenticeship, and turned professional at seventeen. In 1982 he was a member of the Manchester United Youth team which lost the FA Youth Cup Final on a 7–6 aggregate to Watford.

Ron Atkinson gave him his first team début in October 1983, in a League Cup Second Round, second leg match against Port Vale: he came on as a substitute for Norman Whiteside as United recorded a 2–0 victory. A month later he was in United's starting line-up for the first time, in the Fourth Round of the same competition against Oxford United at the Manor Ground – and he scored his first senior goal in the 1–1 draw.

In January 1984 Mark experienced his first League action, once again as a substitute for Whiteside, in a 3–2 home win against Southampton. By the end of the season he had made eleven League appearances and had scored four League goals. He had also made his full debut for Wales, celebrating with a goal in a 1–0 victory over England in the last-ever Wales v England Home International. The victory was all the sweeter as the game was played in Wrexham, his hometown.

The youngster had impressed Atkinson in his brief first team outings – and when the 1984–85 campaign began he found himself pencilled in as United's first-choice striker, largely because of an injury to Frank Stapleton. Mark grabbed his chance, scoring in his third appearance of the season, a 1–1 draw with Ipswich Town at Portman Road. After that the goals seemed to flow from the strapping young striker. In late-September, in the League Cup Second Round, he struck a fine hat-trick in a 4–0 demolition of Burnley and, on New Year's Day 1985, he notched his tenth League goal of the season, against Sheffield Wednesday.

When the result of the PFA Young Player of the Year poll was announced on 24 March, it came as no surprise that Mark was the Award winner. By then his goals had helped United to a semi-finals berth in the FA Cup, and they were in with a chance of the League title.

In the event, they finished fourth in the table behind Everton, Liverpool and Spurs. But they did reach Wembley, thanks to Mark's winning goal against Liverpool in a semi-final replay at Maine Road. In the FA Cup Final they beat 'Double' hopefuls Everton 1–0, to give Hughes his second great honour of the season. In all competitions he had scored 25 goals. And, as the experts had predicted, there were many more to come in the future.

YOUNG PLAYER OF THE YEAR

1985

Mark Hughes' Young Player of the Year success in 1985 marked the beginning of a unique association with the PFA Awards

RON GREENWOOD CBE

When Don Revie 'defected' from his post as England's manager in the summer of 1977, to take up a lucrative contract in the Middle East, the FA decided to select a caretaker-manager as they had done prior to Revie's appointment. They chose West Ham United's Ron Greenwood, who had previously been in the running for the England managership in the early-60s when Alf Ramsey had so ably filled the vacancy.

Greenwood certainly had the pedigree for the job. Born in Worsthorne, near Burnley, in November 1921, his professional career had begun with Chelsea during the Second World War. In 1945 he returned north with Bradford Park Avenue where he developed into an intelligent and cultivated centre half. He joined Second Division Brentford in March 1949 staying for five seasons during which he won his only England honour, a 'B' cap against Holland. In October 1952 he returned to Stamford Bridge and was a member of Chelsea's League Championship-winning squad of 1954–55. His playing career ended with Fulham in 1956.

By then Ron had already decided that his future lay in coaching. Armed with his FA Certificate and Coaching badge, he became Chief Coach with both the Sussex FA and the Middlesex FA. He also managed non-league Eastbourne Town and coached the England Youth squad.

It was quickly apparent that here was a man of the future, a football thinker with a portfolio of new ideas. In December 1957 he was snapped up by Arsenal as assistant to Jack Crayston, while simultaneously stepping up to the job of coaching the England Under-23 squad. By 1961 he was ready for a club of his own, and was delighted to accept the challenge offered that spring by West Ham United.

Under Ron's thoughtful guidance West Ham became one of the more entertaining sides in the country and Upton Park became known as the 'football academy'.

Greenwood's first success as a manager came in the 1964 FA Cup Final, in which the Hammers beat Preston North End 3–2 in a close match. A year later he led the club on its first European adventure – and brought home the Cup-Winners' Cup after a 2–0 win over TSV Munich 1860 at Wembley.

Over the next decade West Ham remained a First Division mid-table club but were always a joy to watch. Their next success came in the 1975 FA Cup Final when they beat Fulham 2–0. By then John Lyall had taken over the running of the team, and Ron

Ron Greenwood, a fine football theorist whose 'temporary' appointment as England manager lasted five years

Greenwood was acting as general manager.

In 1977, he became the man England turned to in her hour of need. His temporary appointment was to cover only the next three matches in an attempt to rescue England's flagging World Cup hopes.

Unfortunately, a 0–0 draw with Switzerland and 2–0 victories over Luxembourg and Italy were not enough to take England to the 1978 Finals in Argentina. Nonetheless, the FA offered Ron the job on a permanent basis – much to the surprise of the Press who were convinced that the more flamboyant Brian Clough was the automatic choice (the other disappointed candidates were Bobby Robson and Lawrie McMenemy). The England players certainly seemed happy with the decision – perhaps skipper Emlyn Hughes best summed up their feelings: '[Greenwood] has got people believing in themselves and talking to each other.The family atmosphere had gone, but he has brought it back,' said Hughes.

Next on Greenwood's agenda was the 1980 European Championship to be held in Italy. England topped their qualifying group with just one point dropped. In the process they saw off Northern Ireland, the Republic of Ireland, Bulgaria, and Denmark. Now Greenwood was really into his stride and the squad he had assembled was regarded as England's finest since the 1966 World Cup Finals, harnessing as it did the combined talents of Phil Neal, Kevin Keegan, Trevor Brooking, Ray Wilkins, Tony Woodcock, Steve Coppell, Mick Mills and Ray Clemence among others.

But the Finals were to prove a bitter disappointment to Greenwood and his players, and were overshadowed by the spectre of hooliganism. In their opening game England drew 1–1 with Belgium in Turin. Next came a 1–0 defeat by Italy which effectively put England out of the competition, a blow only momentarily softened by a 2–1 victory over Spain before Greenwood's men caught the early flight home.

Greenwood's campaign to reach the 1982 World Cup Finals in Spain began well enough with a 4–0 thrashing of Norway at Wembley in September 1980. But there were fluctuating fortunes ahead for England. Defeats by Romania and Switzerland once again made qualification look more of a hope than a certainty.

The 2–1 defeat by Switzerland in Basle came as a shock to Greenwood and his players. With the Press baying for his resignation, he decided to call it a day after the next game against Hungary in Budapest. Despite the protestation of

the FA, his mind was made up.

At half-time against Hungary the score stood level at 1–1, England's goal coming when Trevor Brooking put the finishing touch to a fine move involving five of his team-mates. Then, after an unfortunate error by Ray Clemence had conceded the equaliser, Brooking became the hero of the hour when he fired England back into the lead with a left foot shot hit so hard that the ball wedged firmly in the stanchion at the back of the goal. Kevin Keegan rounded things off with a penalty conversion 16 minutes from time and England had recorded their first victory in Budapest since 1909.

On the flight home Greenwood announced his decision to quit his job. This brought a deputation from the shocked players, exhorting him to change his mind. 'We started this together – let's finish it together,' reasoned the captain Kevin Keegan, and by the time the team's luggage was circling the carousel at Luton Airport, Greenwood had reversed his decision.

Another shock defeat followed at the hands of Norway, in Oslo, leaving the fate of England's World Cup future in the hands of the other nations in the group. The cause was greatly helped, of course, by a 1–0 win over Hungary at Wembley in England's last match of the qualifying campaign and in the final analysis this proved enough to give England second place and a passage to Spain.

Following the relief of tension at actually qualifying, Greenwood's side, undergoing various phases of experiment, enjoyed a string of fine results in the build-up to the Finals; among them 4–0 against Northern Ireland and 4–1 against Finland.

The squad which eventually went to Spain was depleted soon after arriving in Bilbao, with injuries to key men Keegan and Brooking. Nonetheless, England's campaign got off to a flying start in the Spanish heat, with Bryan Robson's opening goal against France coming just 27 seconds after the kick-off (the quickest-ever World Cup Finals goal). They went on to win the game 3–1 with Robson and Paul Mariner supplying the remaining goals.

Further victories over Czechoslovakia and Kuwait took England through to the second phase, but two 0–0 draws against West Germany and Spain ensured they went no further.

Ron Greenwood resigned after the game against Spain in Madrid. 'It's the end of my career as a football manager,' he said. 'I don't think I would have been any prouder of my lads if we had won.'

GARY LINEKER
EVERTON

**PLAYER OF
THE YEAR**

1986

*'It is a bit
special isn't
it? It's the
big one to
win.'*

I n the summer of 1985 Gary Winston Lineker was the hottest property in British football. After seven seasons with Leicester City, a move to a bigger club had become inevitable for the likeable young striker who had scored 95 goals in 194 League games for the Foxes and had already played seven times for England.

Reigning League Champions Everton eventually secured his signature, paying £800,000 for the privilege on 23 July. Precisely one year later Gary would be on the move yet again, this time for more than double his original fee – and by then his name would be known across the world.

All of this was not at all bad for a footballer who admits, 'I was never a naturally gifted player. Certainly not in the way that Glenn Hoddle or Paul Gascoigne were gifted. I was more of a deliberate and methodical player who had to work at his craft.'

Nevertheless, he had always instinctively known the way to goal. In one season of schoolboy football in his native Leicester, he scored more than 160 times. Encouraged by his parents, who were well aware of his potential, Gary progressed through local boys' football and was eventually spotted by Leicester City scout Ray Shaw. He was invited to train twice a week at the club's Belvoir Road training ground, where he came under the influence of Youth team coach George Dewis, a former City striker.

'George was the perfect coach for a young striker,' recalls Gary. 'He devised training sessions for attacking players which invariably involved different kinds of finishing, be it crossing, shooting or heading, from every angle. This work undoubtedly had a big effect on polishing up my finishing.'

On leaving school Gary became a Filbert Street apprentice. He turned professional at eighteen and was given his Second Division

début by manager Jock Wallace, against Oldham Athletic on New Year's Day 1979. Three months later he struck his first League goal – the winner in an away match at Notts County.

In those early days Gary was considered a fairly ordinary player, living somewhat in the shadow of his multi-talented contemporary, Andy Peake. But the young Lineker was ambitious and with a single-mindedness of purpose he coolly dissected his own game. 'As I progressed as a young player I began to think long and hard,' he says. 'I analysed my strengths – pace and an undeniable instinct for goal – and I worked on improving them. I also considered my weaknesses and I worked on those too.'

The effect of all this positive thinking was to produce a potentially world-class striker – and the goals began to flow. Gary was the Second Division's top scorer with 26 goals in 1982–83, as Leicester returned to the First Division in the third promotion spot behind QPR and Wolves.

Gary's next two seasons in the top flight produced 46 goals and saw him hailed as the most exciting young striker in the country. His international début came in May 1984, against Scotland, and his first goal for his country was scored against The Republic of Ireland ten months later.

Then came that headline-grabbing transfer to Goodison Park, achieved after much haggling by both sides. Everton originally offered £400,000. Leicester's sights were set somewhat higher at £1.25 million. The off-again-on-again negotiations were eventually settled by an independent tribunal, at £800,000 (plus a percentage of any re-sale fee). Lineker was to prove himself worth every penny.

First he had to fill the boots of the departing Andy Gray who had been a Goodison Park folk hero since his arrival two years earlier, and had been a vital component in Everton's Championship winning campaign of 1984–85. 'Andy was as responsible as anyone for the club being as successful as it was,' says Gary. 'So I knew he was going to be a tough act to follow. I scored in my fourth game for Everton against Spurs, and followed up with a hat-trick at home against Birmingham. From then on I didn't look back. But it wasn't until after Christmas when I scored against Manchester United and then got two against Sheffield Wednesday, who were going well at the time, that I felt the fans truly accepted me.'

Two more Lineker hat-tricks, against Manchester City and Southampton, were to follow, and he scored two goals on six occasions

in the League. He ended the season as the First Division's top scorer with 30 goals, but like his team-mates he suffered the disappointment of finishing runners-up to Kenny Dalglish's Liverpool. For much of the season Everton had looked likely to win a second successive Championship, but a defeat by Oxford with just three games left to play, had let Liverpool in. (Even a 6–1 thrashing of Southampton at Goodison Park in the penultimate game was not enough.)

In the League Cup, in which Everton were eliminated by Chelsea in the Fourth Round, Gary scored three times. In the FA Cup he hit four goals on the way to Wembley, including arguably his best for Everton. 'It was the only goal of the game against Luton in the quarter-finals replay,' he recalls. 'It came from a long, high through-ball. The Luton defence had a head start on me and I got to the ball by pace alone. I hit it forward with my toe, got between Mal Donaghy and Steve Foster and then hit it on the volley. I wouldn't call it a great goal, I'd never been one for scoring spectacular twenty-five yarders. Nearly all my goals came from around the six-yard box.'

In the Final itself, against 'Double' chasing Liverpool, Lineker scored the opening goal in the 28th minute. Peter Reid took possession of the ball deep in the Everton half, then released a thirty-yard through pass to Lineker who outpaced Alan Hansen in the race towards goal. Bruce Grobbelaar parried his first shot, but Gary followed up to hit the ball home. Unfortunately for Everton, Liverpool replied with three second half goals to take the 'Double'.

Despite the twin disappointments, it had been a fabulous season for Gary, who acknowledges the service given to him throughout by his Everton team-mates. 'The likes of Trevor Steven, Kevin Sheedy and Gary Stevens were maginficent, they made things seem easy for me. And I had the perfect strike-partner up front in Graeme Sharp. We worked hard to develop our understanding and we seemed to improve with each game. He had a great first touch and was brilliant in the air – I got a lot of "flick-ons" from him. And remember he got over twenty goals himself that season.'

When the PFA's votes were counted in February, Gary came top in the Players' Player of the Year category and was duly invited to attend the presentation dinner, which for the first time would be held at the Grosvenor House Hotel on London's Park Lane, on Sunday 23 March. But on that date he was scheduled to be in Tbilisi

Soon after his double PFA and FWA Awards success, Gary Lineker was off to Mexico with England's 1986 World Cup Finals squad. After a somewhat shaky start for the team, he became the tournament's top scorer with six goals, a 'Golden Boot' statistic which made him world famous and which finally persuaded Terry Venables' Barcelona to pay Everton £4.2 million for his striking services.

Gary stayed at the Nou Camp for three seasons, in which he became a lifelong Catalan hero after scoring a hat-trick against rivals Real Madrid in January 1987. He also won a European Cup–Winners' Cup winners' medal in Barcelona's 2–0 victory over Sampdoria in 1989. Soon afterwards, following a failure to see eye-to-eye with new manager Johan Cruyff, Gary was reunited with Terry Venables at Tottenham with whom he would win the FA Cup in 1991.

His exceptional international career continued through the 1990 World Cup Finals in Italy, finally ending on a low note when he was substituted by Graham Taylor in the 1992 European Championship in Sweden. His international goals tally of 48 was agonisingly one short of Bobby Charlton's record for England.

Gary's playing career wound down with a two year stint at Nagoya Grampus 8 in Japan. He returned to England and a successful new career in the media in 1995

with the England squad, preparing for a friendly match with the USSR. However, the fixture was in some doubt because of complications with the squad's travel arrangements and the final decision would not be made until Friday the 21st. If the game was called off at the last minute then Gary would undoubtedly have been persuaded to attend the dinner.

If, however, the game was still on then a contingency plan was needed to ensure that pre-recorded television pictures of Gary receiving his Award would be available for showing at the Awards dinner. It was decided that, if necessary, Everton boss Howard Kendall would present the PFA Trophy to him in a surprise lunchtime ceremony at Goodison Park, after training on the Friday. The Player of the Year trophy, duly engraved and polished, was handed to Eric Woodward in Birmingham.

Depending on the decision on the match he would either transport the trophy to London for a normal presentation, or take it to PFA headquarters in Manchester and hand it to Gordon Taylor who would then take it to Goodison Park for the surprise event.

Word came through: the match was on, and 'plan B' was set in motion with Woodward setting off up the M6 at 8am on the Friday morning. But, unknown to him, the Queen was visiting Manchester that day and because of security arrangements traffic was at a virtual standstill as he approached the city centre. The handover to Gordon Taylor was made at 12.10. Her Majesty had left the city by then, and Gordon's journey to Goodison was reasonably quick.

Gary was disappointed to miss the PFA dinner at the Grosvenor House Hotel. 'Well, it is a bit special isn't it? It's the big one to win, and it would have been nice to have sampled the occasion and all that it stands for – though in truth, it was enough satisfaction to have won – and I can't think of a better reason for missing the night than playing for England.'

Within days of the season's end, Gary was also voted in as the Football Writers' Footballer of the Year, making him the fourth player to win both awards in the same season.

TONY COTTEE
WEST HAM UNITED

Tony Cottee didn't score until West Ham's seventh game of the 1985-86 League campaign. The goal came in a 2–2 draw with Sheffield Wednesday at Hillsborough on 7 September 1985. After that he could hardly stop scoring, as the Hammers enjoyed their best-ever League season, finishing in third place behind Liverpool and Everton.

By the time of the PFA Awards Dinner on 23 March 1986 Tony had hit no less than 17 goals in League and Cup competitions, and that gave him the edge when it came to the Young Player of the Year Award, which was presented to him by the 1976 senior Award winner, Pat Jennings.

An Eastender, born in July 1965, Tony Cottee had represented Essex Schools. He became a West Ham apprentice on leaving school and was selected for the England Youth team. His natural goalscoring abilities impressed Hammers' manager John Lyall who introduced him into the first team on New Year's Day 1983, against Spurs at Upton Park. Young Cottee repaid his manager's faith by scoring in the Hammer's 3–0 victory. He completed that season with five goals from eight games, coming on as a substitute in no less than five of them. For the next two seasons he was the club's top scorer and he received his first PFA Young Player Award nomination in 1984, after scoring four goals in a Milk Cup tie against Bury.

In the summer of 1985 West Ham signed Scottish striker Frank McAvennie from St Mirren for £340,000. Cottee and McAvennie gelled almost instantly and their partnership

added a new dimension to the Hammers' attack throughout the '85–86 season, earned Cottee his PFA Young Player Award and also saw McAvennie listed among the nominees for the senior Award.

The following season saw Cottee earn his first full international cap for England, when he came on as a substitute for Trevor Steven in a 1–0 defeat by Sweden in Stockholm. By the summer of 1988, the Hammers' striker was football's hottest property and a big money move became inevitable. He almost moved across London to join Arsenal, but eventually decided to go to Everton for a then-British transfer record of £2.2 million, in August 1988.

YOUNG PLAYER OF THE YEAR

1986

> *Two seasons after winning the PFA Young Player of the Year Award, Tony Cottee would become the most expensive player in the country when he moved from West Ham to Everton. Six years later he returned to Upton Park*

THE 1966 ENGLAND WORLD CUP TEAM SIR ALF RAMSEY AND HAROLD SHEPHERDSON

**MERIT
AWARD
WINNER**

1986

The greatest adventure in English football history began in February 1963 when ALF RAMSEY was appointed manager of the national team. An ex-Southampton, Spurs and England full back, he had gone into management with Ipswich Town in 1955 and within seven years had taken the East Anglian club from the relative obscurity of the old Third Division (South) to the hitherto undreamed-of heights of the League Championship.

Ramsey followed in the footsteps of Sir Walter Winterbottom who held the England managership for sixteen years, for most of that time enduring the vagaries of the so-called 'International Selection Committee'. This antiquated system of seemingly random selection meant that Winterbottom had little chance to build a consistent squad – yet it was he who suffered the brickbats whenever results went against the team. He had presided over some of England's worst moments – including the 1–0 defeat by the USA in the 1950 World Cup and the 6–3 'lesson' taught by Hungary at Wembley in 1953. He took the side to the Final stages of four World Cups, but never progressed beyond the quarter-finals. On the plus side he introduced a number of innovations to the international set-up, namely the Youth and Under–23 squads, and as the FA's Director of Coaching he initiated organised coaching at all levels throughout the game.

After the 1962 Finals in Chile, Winterbottom resigned. The FA's first choice as his replacement was Jimmy Adamson, the ex-Burnley star who had worked as Winterbottom's assistant. Adamson declined the offer and so Alf Ramsey was approached in the light of his brilliant success at Ipswich.

On accepting the job Alf Ramsey demanded, and was given, total control over team selection. He also prophesied that England would win the World Cup, due to be staged in England three years later. Yet his first three matches in charge – defeats by France and Scotland and a draw with Brazil – gave little indication that the prophecy would, or could, come true.

Then came a remarkable run of results beginning with a 4–2 win over Czechoslovakia in

Bratislava in May 1963. From then on, up to the moment when Bobby Moore lifted the Jules Rimet Trophy at Wembley on 30 July 1966, England lost only four of the 40 games played. Those results included an 8–1 away win against Switzerland, an 8–3 drubbing of Northern Ireland in which Jimmy Greaves scored four times, a 10–0 rout of the USA in New York in which Roger Hunt scored four and Fred Pickering three; and a 6–1 away win over Norway with Jimmy Greaves again finding the net four times.

Ironically, the quicksilver Greaves, arguably the finest goal-grabber of all time, would not be included in England's World Cup Final line-up against West Germany. He had picked up an injury in the First Round group match against Mexico and had been replaced by GEOFF HURST, for whom the Final marked only his eighth international appearance. In the event the young West Ham striker rose magnificently to the occasion to write his own special chapter in football history by becoming the first and, so far, only player to score a hat-trick in World Cup Final.

West Ham supplied two other members of the team that day. BOBBY MOORE skippered the side and displayed his usual precision and calm throughout. It was Moore's finely honed footballing instincts which led to England's early equaliser. His quickly taken free-kick travelled a full thirty yards to find Hurst who headed the ball home. Much later as extra time was running out Moore would send Hurst away with another superb long pass which led to the fourth goal.

The third 'Hammer' MARTIN PETERS scored England's second goal after collecting a deflected effort by Hurst in the 77th minute. Spearheading the attack, along with Hurst, was Liverpool's star striker ROGER HUNT.

Blackpool's ALAN BALL, the youngest player in the team, was a bundle of fierce and determined energy throughout the game. He supplied the cross from which Hurst scored England's third, and most controversial goal. The ball struck the underside of the crossbar and bounced in the goalmouth before being scrambled away by Weber. After consultation with his linesman, and much to the chagrin of the West Germans, the referee awarded the goal and England went 3–2 ahead.

Manchester United were represented by two players in the Final: NOBBY STILES, who so ably assisted Bobby Moore in repelling German attacks, will always be remembered for his happy, toothless grin of delight after the game; and the charismatic BOBBY CHARLTON, whose two goals in the semi-final against Portugal had sealed the Final berth for England.

Bobby's brother JACK CHARLTON, of Leeds United, performed magnificently in the centre of the defence. Something of a late-developer as far as international football was concerned, Jack did not win his first cap until April 1965, just a month before his 30th birthday. He experienced one nightmare moment in the Final. In the last minute of normal time, when England were 2–1 up, he was adjudged to have fouled Uwe Seeler. The referee awarded a free-kick after which Weber equalised to take the game into extra time.

Later Jack confessed that although he was entirely innocent of the misdemeanour, he still thinks back to that moment and shudders: 'I

might have been the one who lost the World Cup,' he says.

At 32, Everton's RAY WILSON may have been the oldest player in the England line-up but he was as solid and dependable as ever at left back – except for the one moment of misjudgement which led to Haller's opening goal for the Germans. Accompanying him at right back was the equally dependable GEORGE COHEN of Fulham.

Keeping goal was Leicester City's GORDON BANKS, for so long a vital factor in Alf Ramsey's plans. Gordon made several important saves in the World Cup Final and will always be remembered as one of the finest goalkeepers of all time.

HAROLD SHEPERDSON had been England's head trainer since October 1957, a job he shared with the coaching of Middlesbrough. Now he shared in the country's greatest triumph.

Twenty years later, the PFA marked the anniversary of England's greatest triumph with a Merit Award presented to the team by Sir Stanley Rous who had been President of FIFA in 1966.

CLIVE ALLEN
TOTTENHAM HOTSPUR

**PLAYER OF
THE YEAR**

1987

In May 1986 Tottenham Hotspur chose David Pleat as the man to replace Peter Shreeves in the White Hart Lane manager's chair. It was an appointment that would have a dramatic effect on the playing career of Clive Allen.

'I'd been with Spurs for two seasons,' he says. 'But in the first I had picked up a bad injury that kept me out for a whole year and needed a couple of operations. But I was fit again for the last eight or so League games of 1985–86.

'In the close season David Pleat spoke to me and established that I felt fine and was back from the injury. He told me he'd got a few new ideas that would suit both the way I play and the players he had at his disposal. He described it as a lone striker in front of a five-man midfield.'

Tottenham did not employ the new system straight away, but began the season using an orthodox two strikers, with Clive playing alongside Mark Falco.

Things started particularly well for Allen. In the first game of the season he struck a hat-trick in a 3–0 defeat of Aston Villa at Villa Park. This was followed by another goal in a 1–1 home draw with Newcastle. 'We really got off to a flyer and bagging four goals in the first two games gave me a great start,' says Clive. 'I was already designated as penalty taker and my fifth goal came from the spot against Chelsea.'

Spurs had completed fifteen League fixtures, and Mark Falco had moved on to Watford, before David Pleat finally opted to try his new system in November. 'Oxford, away, was the first time we used the five man midfield,' Clive recalls. 'David asked the players how they felt about it, and said he would take full responsibility – he wanted to see if it would actually work.'

By half time Spurs were leading 2–1, by the final whistle they had won 4–2 and Allen, the 'lone striker', had scored twice to take his League tally for the season to fourteen goals.

'The system worked straight away. Things fell into place right from that Oxford game, although some of the lads were a bit sceptical of playing that way. Ray Clemence in particular said that similar ideas had been tried at Liverpool but had never really worked. Personally I felt it worked because it tapped into the special abilities of Glenn Hoddle, Chris Waddle and Osvaldo Ardiles. Everybody fitted into the system – and that was all credit to the manager.

'David had considered the situation and he was using the players in the best way he could. That's his strength – he really is a great student of the game and his

knowledge is first class. He was definitely the key to *my* success that season.

'We played some great football. At times we let in more goals than we would have liked, but more often than not we were scoring more and entertaining the fans. We climbed from tenth up to third place where we eventually finished the season.'

The system also worked in the cup competitions. Spurs reached the semi-final of the League Cup before going out to Arsenal after two replays. In the process, Clive notched twelve goals – including a hat-trick against West Ham in the quarter-final replay – to set a new competition record. In the FA Cup they went all the way to Wembley.

Midway through the season the PFA membership had voted Clive their Player of the Year. 'Glenn Hoddle was also nominated and I thought he would win it. He was having a great year and probably made 80% of the goals we scored that season. He was the best provider of chances that I've ever played with, simply because of his sheer quality of passing. So, even though I was in the best form of my life, I didn't expect to win and it came as a total surprise when my name was announced. I think above all the Award reflected an appreciation of the kind of football we were playing at Tottenham.'

Clive was presented with his Player of the Year Award by the 1987 Merit Award recipient, Sir Stanley Matthews.

Two weeks before the FA Cup Final against Coventry City Clive was also voted the 1987 Footballer of the Year by the Football Writers' Association. 'I sat beside David Pleat at that ceremony and vividly remember saying to him that I hoped what had happened to Gary Lineker in the previous year wouldn't happen to me this time around. Gary had won both Awards in 1986, then scored the opening goal in the FA Cup Final – but he still ended up on the losing side.'

Such are the ironies of the game, that history did indeed repeat itself. Just two minutes into the Final Clive met an excellent cross from Chris Waddle to head the first goal of the game. Dave

Bennett equalised for Coventry seven minutes later. By half time Spurs were in the lead once again, after Gary Mabbutt had bundled the ball over the line following a free-kick.

Keith Houchen secured Coventry's second equaliser on 63 minutes, with a superb diving header still remembered as one of the most spectacular goals ever scored at Wembley. Six minutes of extra time had passed when a speculative cross from Lloyd McGrath struck Gary Mabbutt's knee and was deflected beyond Ray Clemence to give victory to Coventry.

Although it had ultimately been a frustrating season for Tottenham, it was one of personal triumph for Clive Allen. His Cup Final goal was his 49th of the season and still remains a club record.

Clive Allen was born on 20 May 1961, two weeks after his father, Les, had played for Tottenham in the FA Cup Final victory which secured the first 'Double' of the 20th century. His Uncle Dennis was also a professional player. So it is hardly surprising that Clive became a footballer, as did his younger brother Bradley and his cousins Martin and Paul.

As a boy he supported Tottenham, but watched most of his early football at Queens Park Rangers, where his father starred at centre-forward.

After representing England Schoolboys in 1975, Clive became an apprentice with QPR, eventually signing professional forms in 1978. Two years later he was transferred to Arsenal. In one of football's most bizarre episodes he was to stay at Highbury for just 63 days of the close season before being exchanged with Kenny Sansom at Crystal Palace. 'I felt like a pawn in the game,' he says. 'Arsenal's priority was to buy a full back, and as they already had Frank Stapleton and Alan Sunderland up front, I was the one who had to go.'

After precisely one year with Palace, Clive returned for a further three seasons at QPR, becoming an FA Cup finalist in 1982, in the first drawn Final against Tottenham. He missed the replay through injury and Spurs won 1–0. He played the first of his internationals for England in June 1984, as a substitute against Brazil. 'My one regret is that I never played at Wembley for England. My games were all abroad, and I never scored. I got one 'goal' in the European Championship qualifier against Turkey, but it was disallowed. Other than that it was a frustrating international career.'

Clive moved to Tottenham in August 1984. After his famous 49 goal haul in 1986–87 he enjoyed a season with Bordeaux, before returning to England with Manchester City in 1989. He later played for Chelsea, West Ham United and Millwall

TONY ADAMS
ARSENAL

Football was in the blood for Tony Adams. His father was an FA Coach and his cousin, Steve McKenzie, has played for Manchester City, West Bromwich Albion, Charlton Athletic, Sheffield Wednesday and Shrewsbury Town

Tony is a graduate of the Arsenal soccer academy. Born in Romford in October 1966, he first joined the Gunners as a schoolboy, and made his first team début shortly after his 17th birthday – standing in for David O'Leary in central defence for a First Division home game against Sunderland. His progress from then on was steady and sure: two more appearances in 1983–84, 16 in '84–85 and 10 in '85–86. He became an England Under–21 international in 1985 and was soon appointed captain of the squad.

When George Graham took the reins at Highbury in May 1986, he was already well-aware of Tony's talents, having observed him at close quarters during an FA coaching course at Lilleshall some years earlier. He remembered him as a 'natural leader' and praised his professional attitude.

Adams was ever-present in the heart of the Gunners' defence throughout Graham's first season in charge, not only in the League but in both Cup competitions as well. He scored his first goal for the club, against Liverpool at Anfield, and had added five more to his tally by the January. The following month brought his full international début, against Spain in Madrid and his first central defensive partnership with Terry Butcher. England won 4–2 with Gary Lineker notching all four goals. Of course, it was Lineker's match, but Robson also singled out Adams for praise, comparing him with Bobby Moore of old and predicting that he would one day captain England.

All of these factors were no doubt taken into account by the PFA membership who voted Tony their Young Player of the Year for 1987. The Award was presented to him by the legendary England defender of

the 1940s and '50s (and ex-Arsenal manager), Billy Wright. Tony was to finish the season with a Wembley appearance and a Cup winners' medal when Arsenal beat Liverpool 2–1 in the Littlewoods Cup Final.

> *Twenty-year-old Tony Adams showed remarkable consistency throughout the 1987–88 season and was highly praised by two of the game's top managers, George Graham and Bobby Robson. In 1994 he graduated to the captaincy of England, just as Bobby Robson had once predicted*

YOUNG PLAYER OF THE YEAR

1987

SIR STANLEY MATTHEWS

**MERIT
AWARD
WINNER**

1987

Stanley Matthews, 'the wizard of dribble' and arguably the finest exponent of wing artistry the English game has ever seen, was born in Hanley, Staffordshire, in 1915, the third in a family of four brothers. From his father, a formidable featherweight boxer, he inherited an almost fanatical dedication to fitness. As a boy he developed into an excellent sprinter, although it was as a footballer that he really stood out. He was a centre half, until a far-sighted schoolmaster recognised his potential as a right winger. It was an inspired move – young Stanley rose to the England Schoolboys' side and his local club Stoke City snapped him up as an apprentice at fifteen.

Two years later, in March 1932, he made his first-team début in a 1–0 victory at Bury. In 1932–33 he played fifteen times as Stoke won the Second Division Championship – and his uncanny ability to leave full backs floundering in his wake came under the close scrutiny of the England selectors. In September 1934 he won the first of his 54 international caps, in a 4–0 defeat of Wales in Cardiff. Just after half time he broke through the Welsh defence to fire England's third goal. Yet it wasn't until 1937–38

that he became a regular in the squad – from November '37 to the start of the war he missed just one international match. Among those he played in was the famous 6–3 drubbing of Germany in Berlin, in May 1938.

By that time Stan had requested a transfer from Stoke, following a dispute over bonus money. The news led to an outcry among the club's supporters and even began affecting production in the local potteries. When the owners called a public meeting to resolve the issue, over 3,000 people attended. Newcastle, Aston Villa, Everton and Manchester City were among the clubs reportedly wanting to buy Matthews, but the matter was eventually settled – with Stan staying on – when the club agreed to honour the original bonus arrangement.

He was called-up by the RAF in the Second World War, as a physical training instructor stationed near Blackpool and, like many of his footballing contemporaries, continued to play in regional games and unofficial internationals.

Injury forced Matthews to miss Stoke's opening games of the 1946–47 season, and when he recovered he was not automatically re-selected for the first team. Throughout the season it became apparent that an irreconcilable rift had developed between the player and his manager, Bob McGrory.

By then Stan and his family were settled in Blackpool where he owned an hotel and where he had been doing much of his training. At a time when most thirty-two year-old footballers would be contemplating retirement, Matthews knew that he still had a lot to give to the sport. And he was well aware that, beyond international stardom and a Second Division Championship medal, he had not achieved any tangible success with Stoke. When things came to a

Blackpool's Stanley Matthews – one of the greatest crowd-pullers in football history – gets his hands on the FA Cup at last, after one of the most celebrated Finals of all time

head he requested a transfer, insisting that he would only move to Blackpool (thereby ruling out any interest from other clubs). The deal was duly done and Matthews changed clubs in May 1947 for £11,500.

Apart from the Second Division Championship of 1929–30, Blackpool had still to achieve anything of true significance. So Stanley Matthews' arrival at Bloomfield Road brought renewed hope to club and player alike.

Under Joe Smith's management The Seasiders had a formidable, attack-minded team which included Matthews' England team-mates Harry Johnston at right half and Stan Mortensen – the quickest centre forward of the day.

Things went very well in Matthews' first season in the tangerine shirt. He was voted the first-ever Footballer of the Year by the Football Writers' Association – and Blackpool reached the FA Cup Final for the first time, meeting Manchester United at Wembley. The match, regarded as one of the all-time classic Cup Finals, ended in disappointment for Blackpool who were twice ahead, yet lost 4–2 following a fine comeback by United.

The 1950 World Cup tournament in Brazil promised another milestone in Matthews' career with England and the host nation expected to reach the Final in Rio de Janiero. But things did not go according to plan. Many believe the outcome would have been far different if Stan had been selected in the two early games, which included that humiliating 1–0 defeat by the USA. As it was he only appeared in the 1–0 defeat by Spain after which the English squad flew home.

Back on the domestic scene the possibility of FA Cup glory once more beckoned for Matthews when Blackpool met Newcastle United in the 1951 Final. Again the Saturday sports pages centred on Matthews' quest for a winners' medal, but again the *Sunday* papers reported his failure to fulfil the dream. Despite his superhuman efforts Blackpool did not score and the match belonged to Jackie Milburn who hit two second-half goals which took the Cup to St James' Park.

Two years later, aged thirty-eight, Stan was back at Wembley for a third attempt at an FA Cup winners' medal. This time Blackpool's opponents were Bolton Wanderers whose forward line was led by the 1953 Footballer of the Year, Nat Lofthouse. The stage was set for a classic Lancashire derby, but the sympathies of all neutral fans were with Stan and the Seasiders.

Two minutes after kick-off it looked as though Matthews' dream would again turn to

nightmare when a speculative shot from Lofthouse swerved unexpectedly and beat keeper George Farm to put Bolton ahead. Stan Mortensen equalised, but after 55 minutes Bolton were 3–1 up and Blackpool's cause seemed lost.

Matthews had been relatively quiet for most of the match. But when Bolton's left back Ralph Banks began suffering from cramp, Wanderers' manager Bill Ridding made the fatal error of not regrouping his defence to cope with the situation. Blackpool took advantage by bringing Stan back into the game with Jackie Mudie feeding him a string of passes. He began tormenting the Bolton defence and in the 70th minute put in a far post cross which was met by Mortensen for Blackpool's second goal.

Bolton held out until, with just two minutes remaining, Mortensen wrote himself into the history books by becoming the first man in the 20th century to score a hat-trick in an FA Cup Final. The goal came from a free-kick which found a gap in the Wanderers' defensive wall.

With the scoreline at 3–3 and the seconds ticking away, Matthews collected the ball some eighteen yards out, beat the unfortunate Banks yet again and took the ball further to the right. Then he dummied centre half Malcolm Barrass to reach the byline from where he hit a cross which bypassed Mortensen and reached South African left winger Bill Perry who buried the ball in the Bolton net. Blackpool had won, Stan had his medal at last and 'The Matthews Final' became part of football folklore.

His international career continued until 1957. He was 42 when he played his last game for England, a 4–1 win against Denmark in Copenhagen. He remained with Blackpool until October 1961, when he made a sensational return to Stoke, helping them gain promotion to the First Division in 1963. On 6 February 1965, five days after his fiftieth birthday he became the oldest player ever to play in the First Division. Stanley retired at the end of the season.

Matthews began and ended his career with Stoke City. In between he became a legend whose name was known all over the world. In 1956 he became the first European Footballer of the Year

JOHN BARNES
LIVERPOOL

**PLAYER OF
THE YEAR**

1988

An anonymous Watford supporter is to be credited with kick-starting John Barnes' professional football career. This far-sighted individual alerted the Vicarage Road scouts to the potential of the 17-year-old winger after seeing him perform for Sudbury Court in the Middlesex Senior League in 1980.

Eventually the Hornets' general manager Bertie Mee went to take a look for himself, and later said: 'I couldn't believe my eyes. How on earth could a player with such obvious qualities have been missed by the scouts?'

So impressed was Mee that he immediately contacted John's father, a military attaché based in London, to offer the youngster a place in his squad. However, it appeared that Barnes Snr was about to make a return to Jamaica and his son was scheduled to join him. But Bertie Mee persisted with his offer and invited the youngster to training sessions at the club. John was soon convinced that the life of a professional footballer would suit him well, and his father agreed that he should sign for Watford in July 1981.

Watford were a team on the rise. Thanks largely to the financial input of their pop star chairman Elton John, and the astute management of future England boss Graham Taylor who advocated the 'long ball' game, they had lifted themselves from the Fourth to the Second Division in the space of two seasons between 1977 and 1979 – and they were hungry for more success.

Two months after signing, John made his League debut for Watford, in a 1–1 draw with Oldham Athletic at Vicarage Road. He ended the season with thirteen goals in 36 League

appearances, and he won the hearts of the Vicarage Road fans who adored his extravagant skills. At the end of the season Watford were promoted to the First Division as runners-up to their local rivals Luton Town.

A year later Graham Taylor had steered them to the Championship runners-up spot behind Liverpool. Their top striker Luther Blissett was the League's leading scorer with 27 goals, while John, who was ever-present throughout the campaign, again reached double figures with ten goals. He also made his England debut that season, as a substitute for Blissett in a 0–0 draw with Northern Ireland.

In 1984 John was a prominent member of the Watford side which reached the FA Cup Final

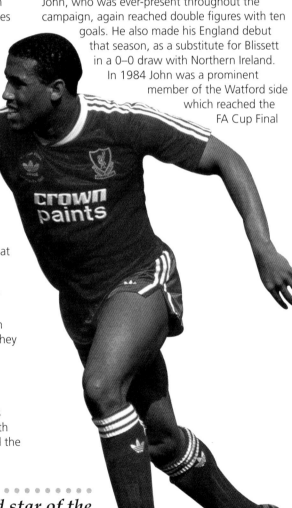

He became the undoubted star of the season as Liverpool embarked on a magnificent run.

after knocking-out Luton Town, Charlton Athletic, Brighton, Birmingham City and Plymouth Argyle. Watford met Everton (a club desperate for success) at Wembley, and John almost scored after 16 minutes – but Neville Southall dived bravely at his feet to spoil the chance. Everton's first goal came on 38 minutes, from Graeme Sharp; the second from Andy Gray on 51 minutes. John and his team-mates had to be content with losers' medals.

The other highlight of John Barnes' 1983–84 season came three weeks after his FA Cup Final appearance, when he scored his first goal for England – arguably the finest solo goal ever scored by anyone in an England shirt.

The opponents were the brilliant Brazilians; the setting was the vast Maracana Stadium in Rio de Janeiro. John was on top form and midway through the first half he gave warning of what was to come with a dazzling run through the Brazilian defence which was eventually halted. Then, shortly before half time, he collected the ball wide on the left before setting off on another mazy dribble to beat four defenders before slotting the ball home.

Even the Brazilians, used to seeing goals of quality, were astonished by Barnes' strike – they applauded his skill and considered it a goal worthy of the best of their countrymen. Later in the game John was involved in the move from which Mark Hateley headed a second goal to seal England's first ever victory in Brazil.

For the next three seasons John continued to impress with Watford as they maintained a mid-table position. In 1986 he was a member of England's World Cup squad in Mexico, although he only played in what proved to be England's last match of the campaign against Argentina. By the time he was brought on as a substitute for Trevor Steven, England were already 2–0 down – no thanks to the so-called "hand of god" goal and a magnificent individual strike by Maradona. John supplied the superb cross from which Gary Lineker scored England's only goal of the game.

At club level, Barnes was ambitious for true success – and when Graham Taylor moved on to the managership of Aston Villa in the summer of 1987, he also left Vicarage Road. Rumours of a move abroad, or to Rangers in Scotland, were soon quashed when he signed for Kenny Dalglish at Liverpool in a £900,000 transfer deal.

The move to Anfield presented him with a new challenge. Not only did he have to contend with the pressures of joining the most successful of clubs, but since he was Liverpool's first black player of true significance he also had to deal with the ugly spectre of racism. Both club and player received derogatory mail after the signing and John was even warned to stay away. He simply answered his critics in the best way possible, by getting on with his job – just as he had always done.

Kenny Dalglish had also strengthened his attack with the signing of Peter Beardsley from Newcastle United. Barnes and Beardsley, together with John Aldridge – who had arrived at Anfield in January 1987 as a replacement for the soon-to-depart Ian Rush – would soon form the most devastating strike force in the First Division.

Because of necessary repair work to the drainage system at Anfield, Liverpool were forced to play their opening games of the 1987–88 campaign away from home. John made his Liverpool debut in the first game of the season, a 2–1 win at Arsenal in which he and Peter Beardsley combined to create the chance from which John Aldridge scored the Reds' first goal. In the next match, at Coventry, he was prominent in Liverpool's 4–1 victory. In the third game, at West Ham, he was quite devastating as he created scoring opportunities from either wing. Nevertheless, the points were shared in a 1–1 draw.

The Anfield repair work was completed for the fourth game of the season, by which time the Liverpool faithful were desperate to see their favourites on home territory. The Reds did not disappoint the fans. John was man of the match and the new hero of The Kop, scoring his first goal for Liverpool in the 2–0 defeat of Oxford United. In fact, he became the undoubted star of the season as Liverpool embarked on a magnificent run. In their ninth League game they slaughtered leaders QPR 4–0 at Anfield to take over top spot; it was the fifth time they had notched four goals in the campaign. Yet again John Barnes was singled out as the most effective player in a superb Liverpool line-up.

By 20 March Liverpool remained unbeaten in 29 League games, thereby equalling Leeds United's record set in 1974. On that day they met Everton in a Merseyside derby at Goodison Park – and the Blues won 1–0 to prevent the Reds from breaking that particular record. But they were still on target for the title.

Everton had earlier knocked Liverpool out of the League Cup competition, with a 1–0 defeat in the Third Round. The two clubs had met again in the Fifth Round of the FA Cup – and this time the Reds won 1–0. Prior to that they had eliminated Stoke City and Aston Villa. In the Sixth Round Manchester City were destroyed in a 4–0 defeat at Maine Road, a result which took Liverpool to a semi-final encounter with Nottingham Forest at Hillsborough on 9 April. For the umpteenth time that season, John Barnes inspired a Liverpool victory and the Reds were through to Wembley where they would meet Wimbledon.

On the day after the semi-final triumph John attended the PFA's fifteenth Annual Awards presentation, at which he and three of his team-mates – Peter Beardsley, Alan Hansen and Steve McMahon – were among the nominees for the Players' Player of the Year title. But to all present, it came as no great surprise when John's name was read out by England manager Bobby Robson as the winner.

He was the first black player to win the Player of the Year Award and afterwards said: 'I welcome this, not just as a personal honour, but as encouragement to other black kids to believe they can reach the top in this game.'

A few weeks later John's brilliant season would also be recognised by the Footballer Writers' Association, who named him Footballer of the Year for 1988; he was the first black player to win that Award too.

Liverpool went on to clinch their seventeenth League title with four games left to play – thereby setting themselves up for a crack at a second 'Double'. That dream, however, was to be burst by Wimbledon who won 1–0 in one of the most famous FA Cup Finals upsets of all time. It was a rare disappointment in a magnificent season for John Barnes.

John Barnes, the 1988 PFA Players' Player of the Year, went on to collect more honours with Liverpool, including the Football Writers' Footballer of the Year title, for a second time, in 1990

PAUL GASCOIGNE
NEWCASTLE UNITED

In April 1988 'Gazza-Mania' was still a phenomenon of the future. Thanks to his brilliant displays in the Newcastle United midfield, the 20 year-old Paul Gascoigne *had* been getting his fair share of the headlines since 1985–86, and deservedly so – but they were hardly of the 'Princess Diana' proportions that were to follow.

The Gateshead-born star had first been spotted at thirteen by Middlesbrough who invited him to train at Ayresome Park. Southampton, Ipswich Town and Newcastle United also showed an interest and in 1984 he became a St James' Park apprentice. The club was then managed by Jack Charlton who brought Gascoigne on, for the last twenty minutes of the home game against Queens Park Rangers in April 1985. He was sub twice more that season, but his real moment of glory came when he captained Newcastle's Youth team in the two-legged FA Youth Cup Final against Watford. After a hard-fought 0–0 draw at St James' Park, the young Magpies put in a magnificent performance to win 4–1 at Vicarage Road. Gascoigne provided the inspiration, and one of the goals, to bring the Youth Cup to Newcastle for the first time. The club offered him professional terms very soon afterwards.

But these were troubled times for Newcastle United's first team and things came to a head that summer when Jack Charlton resigned. He was replaced by former Magpies' star Willie McFaul who gambled on plunging Gascoigne in at the deep end, playing him in midfield in the opening match of the 1985–86 season, away to Southampton – a game in which the youngster gave many hints of the glories to come, almost got his name on the scoresheet and received a standing ovation from the travelling fans.

He played in the next match, a 2–2 draw at home to Luton Town, and the next – a magnificent 1–0 home win over mighty Liverpool who were just starting out on the campaign that would bring them the 'Double'. His first League goal came in September 1985, in a 3–0 home win against Oxford United. He finished the season with 31 League appearances, nine goals and an endorsement from Newcastle legend Jackie Milburn who predicted that Paul Gascoigne would one day captain England.

A knee injury sustained on a pre-season tour hampered his start to the 1986–87 campaign and when he returned he found his growing reputation working against him – he became a marked man. And although he was gradually waking up to the realities of life in the First Division, the situation brought about a crisis of confidence, an inevitable loss of form and a spell in the reserves.

But, when he did get back into the first team in the latter stages of the season, the lessons had been well-learned. He was back to his mercurial best and his return to form was an important factor in Newcastle's climb out of the relegation zone.

That summer Paul realised another ambition when he was called up by Dave Sexton for the England Under-21 side in the Toulon tournament. In his début game against Morocco he made one goal and scored another.

The arrival at St James' Park in August 1987 of the Brazilian international Mirandinha would further stimulate Gascoigne's game. After seeing the youngster perform at the beginning of the 1987–88 season, Mirandinha pronounced him: 'One of the best players I've ever seen … he plays like a Brazilian'.

YOUNG PLAYER OF THE YEAR

1988

Paul went on to enjoy a stunning season, making 35 League appearances and scoring seven goals as Newcastle finished in 8th position, their best performance since returning to the top flight.

Mid-way through the campaign he had impressed England boss Bobby Robson with a bravura performance against Swindon Town in the Fourth Round of the FA Cup, and his name was pencilled in for future international consideration. Around the same time PFA members were casting their votes for the 1988 Awards. And on 11 April Paul stepped onto the stage at the Grosvenor House Hotel to collect the PFA Young Player of the Year Award from Bobby Charlton.

By then a transfer had become inevitable and in the summer of '88 Gascoigne joined Spurs for a British record £2 million. After the signing the young player went off with some of his friends to see the sights of London, hotly pursued by photographers who snapped him at Madam Tussaud's waxworks – where his own wax double would one day stand. Pictures of the grinning footballer duly appeared in the following day's newspapers. The media had discovered a new character and 'Gazza-Mania' was about to descend upon us…

The young Paul Gascoigne, who was about to fly south to Tottenham – thereby beginning a great adventure that would see him shed tears in a World Cup semi-final, earn his living in the land of the lira and live his life in the glare of publicity

BILLY BONDS *MBE*

Billy Bonds must be one of the best footballers never to play for England. He was called into the England squad by Ron Greenwood in May 1981, as a central defender, but an injury ruled him out of contention for the game against Brazil and he never again had the chance to prove himself at international level.

As a club player Bonds was quite superb. Born in Woolwich in September 1946, he would spend his entire playing career with London clubs, signing for Charlton Athletic as an 18-year-old where he attracted attention at right back. In May 1967, after two season at The Valley, he was transferred to West Ham United. The Hammers converted him into an effective midfielder playing under the captaincy of Bobby Moore who would continue to be an inspiration to him.

Such are the ironies of the game, that the two men would meet on opposite sides in the 1975 FA Cup Final. Moore had moved on to Fulham a year earlier, and had helped the Second Division side defy all the odds to make their first-ever Wembley appearance. By then Bonds had become captain of West Ham in succession to his great idol. Because of a groin injury he had painkilling injections before being able to play in the Final.

The match itself was hardly the 'Cockney Classic', that had been anticipated. Gradually, however, the Hammers took charge and two goals in five minutes by little Alan Taylor were enough to take the Cup to Upton Park.

Five years later Billy led West Ham, by then in the Second Division, to another all-London FA Cup Final, this time against Arsenal. As if to underline his versatility, he was back in the centre of the defence in a dominant partnership with Alvin Martin. Together they managed to subdue the Gunners' front runners Alan Sunderland and Frank Stapleton. The match, won by the rare sight of Trevor Brooking actually heading a goal, brought Bonds his second FA Cup winners' medal.

Billy's legendary fitness gave him a long career in the game. He was still playing first team football at the age of 41 in the 1987–88 season during which he announced his

retirement – after a club record of 663 League games.

The PFA honoured him with a Merit Award, presented by Ted Croker the Chief Executive and General Secretary of the FA, and the Queen honoured him with an MBE. He joined the Upton Park coaching staff and eventually succeeded Lou Macari as team manager, a job which he held until announcing his resignation in the summer of 1994.

MERIT AWARD WINNER

1988

The versatile Billy Bonds, a shy and thoughtful man who became West Ham's most faithful servant. He went on to manage the Hammers and steer them back into the top flight

MARK HUGHES
MANCHESTER UNITED

**PLAYER OF
THE YEAR**

1989

A great deal had happened to Mark Hughes in the four years since he won the 1985 PFA Young Player of the Year Award.

In 1985–86 he made 40 League appearances for Manchester United and was once again the club's top scorer, with 18 goals in all competitions. He was again among the six leading contenders for the PFA Young Player of the Year title (won by West Ham's Tony Cottee) and was a Divisional Award winner in the First Division 'team'. United had again finished fourth in the First Division. Their early title challenge, which saw them well ahead in the table by Christmas, was later to be seriously damaged by an injury crisis involving several key players.

On the international front Mark had now won twelve caps for Wales and had scored four times. The Welsh fans, like those of Manchester United, adored his voracious appetite for the game and his penchant for scoring spectacular goals.

But Mark Hughes' wasn't only a goalscorer. He was proving a magnificent team player whose great strength and determination enabled him to hold the ball up, to shield it and not release it until his fellow attackers had regrouped or found themselves a more advantageous position for his eventual pass.

It was this talent, allied of course to his goalscoring skills, that so attracted Terry Venables, the forward-thinking manager of Barcelona. Venables – a successful player

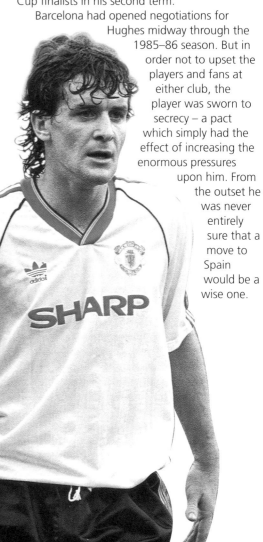

with four London clubs and at all levels with England – had joined the Spanish giants in 1984 after cutting his managerial teeth at Crystal Palace and QPR. With the help of former Spurs striker Steve Archibald, Barcelona had won the Spanish League Championship in Venables' first season at the Nou Camp, and were European Cup finalists in his second term.

Barcelona had opened negotiations for Hughes midway through the 1985–86 season. But in order not to upset the players and fans at either club, the player was sworn to secrecy – a pact which simply had the effect of increasing the enormous pressures upon him. From the outset he was never entirely sure that a move to Spain would be a wise one.

Secret pact or not, rumour soon had it that Mark would be going to Barcelona at the end of the season. The PFA's own Young Player nominee profile of Hughes in the brochure for the 1986 Awards dinner stated: " … it is reckoned to be football's most open secret that he is set to join Barcelona for £2 million in the summer". In fact, the eventual fee was in the region of £2.5 million. Before leaving Manchester United he signed off with a spectacular goal in the last game of the season against Watford at Vicarage Road.

Of course, Mark was not the only British player to join Barcelona that summer. Following the World Cup Finals in Mexico the club had signed the tournament's top scorer, England's Gary Lineker from Everton.

"Lineker and Hughes" had an exciting ring to it and Venables must have thought it a pairing made in football heaven. Both were brilliant goalscorers, and Lineker would no doubt benefit from Hughes' unmatched talent for shielding the ball and making space.

Unfortunately, Mark quickly discovered that his earlier fears were well founded; he was

unhappy in Spain. He found it difficult to adapt to life in Barcelona. He felt he was out of his depth and, to make matters worse, he was homesick and missing his girlfriend (later to become his wife). He also became sensitive to the political atmosphere surrounding the Nou Camp and to criticism, both within the club and in the vitriolic sporting press, launched directly at him for his distinctly physical style and his failure to find the net in his first five games for Barcelona.

Despite support and encouragement from both Venables and Lineker, things eventually came to a head when Barcelona cancelled Mark's Spanish League registration. While this meant a release of pressure for the Welshman and a probable return to Britain (Rangers, Spurs, Everton and Manchester United were all interested), such a move would not have been financially prudent at the time as Hughes had not been abroad long enough to avoid a large tax liability. To do so, he would have to spend another season on the continent.

On 15 April 1989, the day before the PFA's sixteenth Awards dinner, 95 people died and scores more were injured in the disaster which occurred prior to the kick-off of the Liverpool v Nottingham Forest FA Cup semi-final at Hillsborough.

Consequently the dinner began with a sombre announcement made by Chief Executive Gordon Taylor: 'Gentlemen. We are all aware that what was to be our normal evening of celebration has been overshadowed by the horrific tragedy at Hillsborough yesterday. We did have a difficult decision with regard to whether the dinner would continue to take place.

'We decided it should, as it was the first opportunity to pay our respects to those who have suffered and, furthermore, to offer practical support by way of a collection which we hope you will contribute to throughout the evening. Because of the sadness which must underline the occasion we have decided to omit the more light-hearted element of the programme.'

A minute's silence was observed, followed by a prayer read by Taylor, which concluded: '…and we hope that any lessons there are to be learned from the disaster are quickly enacted, to ensure that never again will we witness such scenes as we saw yesterday.'

Nine months later Lord Justice Taylor published his 104-page report on the tragedy. The document contained 76 recommendations to improve safety at leading sports venues, including the removal of perimeter fencing, the elimination of terracing and a review of crowd control by the police

In November 1987, Bayern Munich, the reigning Bundesliga Champions, stepped in to rescue the situation by taking Mark on loan from Barcelona. This time, under the management of World Cup winner Uli Hoeness, he found himself in a more conducive atmosphere and in a League more suited to his aggressive style. The goals began to come once more from Hughes' boots and by the time he was able to return to Britain, Bayern had joined the list of club's ready and willing to buy Mark Hughes from Barcelona.

In the end, persuaded by new Manchester United manager Alex Ferguson, he decided on a return to Old Trafford and the £1.5 million transfer deal was concluded in July 1988. United's fans, who had not wanted him to go in the first place, gave him a rapturous welcome in his re-appearance in the first home game of the 1988–89 season, a 0–0 draw with QPR.

Mark did not disappoint the Old Trafford faithful. Although his new striking partnership with Brian McClair took a while to click, Hughes would end the season as the club's top League scorer with 14 goals as United finished in a rather poor eleventh place. He also scored twice in the FA Cup campaign, which saw United eliminated in the Sixth Round by Nottingham Forest.

Mark's return to England, and his return

to top form – he scored in five consecutive League games in September and October and enjoyed a particularly purple patch around Christmas – was noted by his fellow professionals when they cast their votes for the 1989 PFA Awards.

Three Manchester United players – Bryan Robson, Brian McClair and Mark Hughes – were among the nominees for the Players' Player of the Year Award, but it was Mark who came top of the poll. The Award, presented to him by Denis Howell MP, was in recognition of a great comeback and a true fighting spirit.

The Award was in recognition of a great comeback and a true fighting spirit.

PAUL MERSON
ARSENAL

On Boxing Day 1988 Arsenal replaced Norwich City at the top of the First Division, with a 3–2 victory over Charlton Athletic at Selhurst Park. Brian Marwood scored two of the goals (one from the penalty spot), the other came from Paul Merson, the fastest rising young star in the League.

So far that season the 21-year–old forward had missed just one game in Arsenal's League campaign. He had struck up a fine attacking partnership with leading scorer Alan Smith and had notched five goals of his own. As Arsenal increased the pressure in the first three games of 1989, he scored three more.

It was this level of consistency which had earned Paul the Barclays Young Eagle Award for December, and which encouraged the PFA membership to elect him their Young Player of the Year for 1989, an Award presented by former Arsenal favourite and former PFA Chairman, Brian Talbot.

Born in Harlesden, north London, in March 1968, Paul had begun his rise through the Highbury ranks as an apprentice. He made his first League appearance as a substitute for Martin Hayes against Manchester City in November 1986. Later that season he picked up more valuable experience in seven matches spent on loan with Third Division Brentford, then he made a further six appearances in the Arsenal first team, scoring his first goal for the club in a 2–1 win over Wimbledon in April 1987.

After Charlie Nicholas' return to Scotland in 1988 and Arsenal's failure to sign striker Tony Cottee from West Ham, George Graham began utilising the talents of the young striker on a more regular basis.

Paul finished the 1988–89 League campaign with 37 appearances and ten goals. The most important of those strikes was Arsenal's second goal in a 2–2 draw at home to Wimbledon in the penultimate match of the season, on 17 May. The result kept them in with a slim chance of the title, although to win it they would have to beat fellow contenders Liverpool by at least two clear goals in the last match of the season, at Anfield.

That is precisely what happened, thanks to an Alan Smith goal in the 52nd minute and

Michael Thomas' last gasp strike which eventually took the trophy to Highbury. Paul Merson had played his part in the game, just as he had throughout that memorable season for The Gunners.

> The 1989 PFA Young Player of the Year Award made to Paul Merson was an honour eminently justified at the end of the season when he collected a Championship medal after Arsenal's nail-biting 2–0 win over Liverpool at Anfield, in the last match of the campaign. In 1994 Merson's life was plunged into despair when he admitted an addiction to drugs, alcohol and gambling. His rehabilitation was aided by the PFA – and he returned to the Arsenal line-up in February 1995

YOUNG PLAYER OF THE YEAR

1989

NAT LOFTHOUSE

**MERIT
AWARD
WINNER**

1989

Nathaniel Lofthouse was Bolton born and bred. He served Bolton Wanderers for fifteen seasons as a player, making 452 League appearance and scoring 255 League goals between 1946 and 1961. Later he continued to dedicate his time to the club, with two spells as manager and another as chief scout and administration manager. In 1986 he was made Club President.

A coalminer's son who followed his father into the pits, Lofthouse actually signed for the Trotters as a 17 year-old in 1942, although he continued to work at the coalface as a 'Bevin Boy' during the war. The heavy work toughened up an already formidable physique and when his professional career resumed in peacetime he became one of the most feared centre forwards in the game.

Lofthouse was also a national treasure. He had first been selected for England against Yugoslavia in November 1950 and had scored twice in the 2–2 draw. But it was the match against Austria in Vienna's Prater Stadium on 25 May 1952 that was to earn him everlasting fame. At the time Austria were considered the best attacking team in Europe, while England, despite being unbeaten in eight games, had been on the receiving end of some harsh criticism following a rather tame 1–1 draw with Italy seven days earlier.

Team manager Walter Winterbottom decided to concentrate on defence, hoping to score on the breakaway. That's precisely what happened when an Austrian attack broke down in the 21st minute. The ball was quickly fed to Lofthouse who then volleyed England's first goal. By half time the scoreline was 2–2 (Jackie Sewell had scored England's second).

Aggressive, physical and as tough as old boots, lion-hearted Nat Lofthouse usually took the direct route to goal. He was the First Division's leading scorer with 33 goals in 1955–56 and his name now stands equal-fourth in the list of England's top international goalscorers: with 30 successful strikes he is behind Bobby Charlton, Gary Lineker and Jimmy Greaves and on level terms with Tom Finney

But it was to be the second half that would go down in soccer history. Austria pressed for most of the time and the game became more physical. With eight minutes to go England were still holding on. Then goalkeeper Gil Merrick relieved the pressure of yet another attack, by throwing the ball out to Tom Finney who quickly realised that the Austrians had left themselves wide open at the back. He put the ball through to the lone figure of Lofthouse, while simultaneously drawing out the last defender.

Nat collected the ball inside the England half, then set off on a fifty yard run with only goalkeeper Musil to beat. The two players met in a bone-crunching collision during which Lofthouse managed to get a shot at goal. By the time the ball was nestling in the goal for what turned out to be England's winner, the brave centre forward was out cold. He later claimed, modestly: 'If the goalkeeper had not checked as he came, I'd never have scored.'

After treatment on the touchline, Nat returned to the fray, a hero to the 2,000 or so British servicemen in the crowd of 65,000. The next day's headlines proclaimed him 'The Lion of Vienna', a nickname by which he would be known forever after. He went on to collect 33 international caps and his 30 goals earned him equal-fourth place in the all-time England scoring chart.

Although Bolton were to remain a First Division club throughout Nat's playing career they never achieved true League success in that time, their best placing being 4th in 1958–59. The FA Cup told a different tale. In 1953 Bolton played Blackpool at Wembley in one of the most celebrated finals of all time. Lofthouse – already voted Footballer of the Year by the Football Writers – had scored in each round so far. Now he hit the opening goal in the second minute when his initial, poorly struck attempt somehow bamboozled Blackpool's keeper George Farm. From then on Bolton took command and with a 3–1 lead it seemed the trophy was bound for Burnden Park. But this was the 'Stanley Matthews Final' in which the mercurial winger inspired a marvellous comeback by Blackpool who eventually won 4–3. Five years later, in May 1958, Bolton were back at Wembley to face Manchester United who had reached the Final in spite of the tragic air-crash at Munich which had so cruelly decimated the 'Busby Babes' team three months earlier. All neutral support and sympathy was with United, and Bolton were again cast as underdogs.

Lofthouse, who had only recently recovered from a broken shoulder, opened the scoring in the third minute when he hit a deflected cross from Bryan Edwards past Harry Gregg.

Five minutes after the interval came the most controversial moment of the match. Lofthouse, full of his usual fire and enthusiasm, saw another opportunity to score when Gregg partially parried a shot from Dennis Stevens. The 'keeper caught the ball and had it cradled in his arms when Lofthouse barged him over the goal-line. Astonishingly, referee Sherlock awarded a goal and Bolton had the whip hand amid the protests. In fairness, Wanderers were the best team on the day. They did the professional thing in not relinquishing that two-goal lead. Nat Lofthouse had a winners' medal at last.

DAVID PLATT
ASTON VILLA

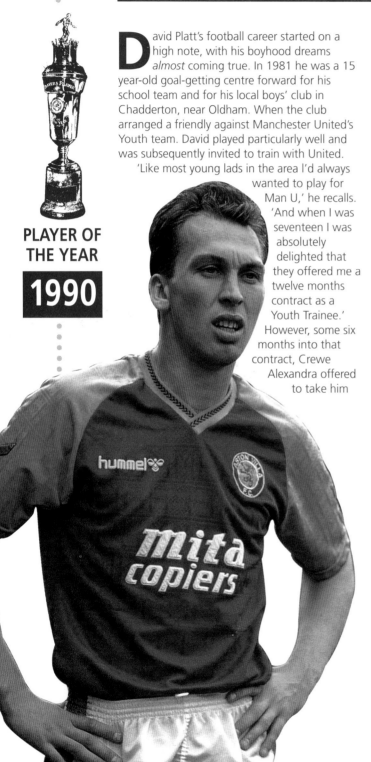

**PLAYER OF
THE YEAR**

1990

David Platt's football career started on a high note, with his boyhood dreams *almost* coming true. In 1981 he was a 15 year-old goal-getting centre forward for his school team and for his local boys' club in Chadderton, near Oldham. When the club arranged a friendly against Manchester United's Youth team. David played particularly well and was subsequently invited to train with United. 'Like most young lads in the area I'd always wanted to play for Man U,' he recalls. 'And when I was seventeen I was absolutely delighted that they offered me a twelve months contract as a Youth Trainee.' However, some six months into that contract, Crewe Alexandra offered to take him on loan. 'I went there for a month, then Dario Gradi said he wanted to sign me permanently. United's boss Ron Atkinson told me he was uncertain about renewing my contract and, even if he did, he explained that I was in line behind Norman Whiteside, Frank Stapleton, Alan Brazil, Mark Hughes and another young lad called Nicky Wood.'

Young Platt then made the first in a string of mature decisions which have helped shape one of the most illustrious careers in the modern game. He cut his losses with United and moved to Crewe on a free transfer in January 1985. 'I had to come to terms with the fact that the United dream had burst. But, even though I was taking a step down in the level of club, it was definitely a step up in the level of play. I'd been stuck in the third team at United, but I was playing Fourth Division football with Crewe.'

When Ron Atkinson was later asked how he managed to let such star potential slip through his fingers, he was ruefully adamant that Platt had seemed 'too shy... to make it in the jungle that is professional football'. Shy he may have been, but he was also determined to survive. He had adopted a positive approach to his own game and remains a self-confessed perfectionist. 'I was seeking perfection from a very early age,' he says. 'Of course, I knew I never would be perfect, I never could be. But with that aim in mind I knew I could always get better.'

David has nothing but praise for Dario Gradi, the man who did recognise his potential. 'Although his first priority was obviously the interests of Crewe Alexandra, Dario has a well deserved reputation for bringing on and coaching young players. My own success as well as that of Geoff Thomas and Rob Jones is proof of that,' says Platt.

Under Gradi's guidance David put in extra training to build himself up and add strength to

'I reckon it's one of the greatest Awards that any player can receive.'

his game. Consequently he developed into one of the most lethal strikers in the Fourth Division, scoring 55 goals in 134 League appearances between 1984 and 1988. Another piece in the jigsaw fell into place when Geoff Thomas was injured and David was moved into a midfield support role. 'I realised I could be more dangerous if I came in from the deep,' he said.

Other clubs began showing an interest. 'Dario recognised that I needed the challenge of going higher and he kept me fully informed about the situation regarding offers. Leicester City came in first with a £60,000 bid which they later increased, but it was still turned down. Hull City offered £100,000, followed by Hibernian at £125,000 which they raised by a further £25,000. Then Aston Villa came in at £150,000. They were top of the Second Division at the time and looked likely to go up, so I was definitely interested.'

Gradi re-negotiated with Villa boss Graham Taylor who revised his offer upwards to £200,000 and David Platt – then the most expensive player to come out of the Fourth Division – duly became an Aston Villa player in February 1988. 'It turned out to be a good time to make the move, settle in and get to know the other lads. There were twelve games left, so I played my part in winning promotion.' He scored on his début for the club, away at Blackburn. His next goal crowned an outstanding home début, as Villa thrashed Plymouth 5–2. He added three more to his tally that season as Villa finished runners-up to Millwall.

In the summer David made his England Under-21 début in a 2–1 win over Mexico in Toulon. He was ever present throughout Villa's First Division campaign in 1988–89, in which they finished in a disappointing 17th place. He continued to make inroads on the international front, playing three times for England's 'B' team.

It was in 1989–90 that David Platt really made his mark as Villa hit runners-up spot in the First Division, albeit ten points adrift of Champions Liverpool. He was the club's leading scorer with 19 League goals, he missed only the last match of the League programme and

impressed everyone with his determination, versatility and consistency – including England's manager Bobby Robson who brought him on in place of Peter Beardsley for the last 13 minutes of England's friendly against Italy in November 1989. He also impressed his fellow professionals who, in mid-season, voted him Player of the Year in the PFA poll.

David almost missed the Awards presentation. Earlier on 1 April, the day of the ceremony, he had played for Villa at home to Manchester City. 'We didn't play well at all and were beaten 2–1,' he recalls.

Indeed, that result and a defeat by Crystal Palace in the previous game had seriously dented Villa's hopes of the title. 'The Gaffer was less than pleased and he said we had to come in next morning and give up our day off. Although I was one of the contenders for Player of the Year, I didn't actually believe I had a chance winning it. I had intended to travel down in a min-bus with a few of the players and some friends, but Stuart Gray and I decided not to go as we'd have to come straight back again for the extra training next day.'

The rest of the party set off for London, while Stuart telephoned Gordon Taylor to tell him David was not going to the ceremony. 'But Gordon said we'd *got* to come because I'd won it. So we then phoned someone on the bus and asked them to wait for us at Watford Gap services where we eventually caught them up.

'We arrived at the Grosvenor House just in time. I can remember going up and being nervous when Jack Charlton handed me the trophy. But it didn't hit me until afterwards just what an honour it was to be voted Player of the Year by those you are competing against week in, week out. I reckon it's one of the greatest Awards that any player can receive.'

That summer as a member of the England squad at the Italia '90 World Cup Finals, David underlined just what an excellent choice the players' had made in voting for him. 'I didn't expect to play in the Finals, so I was absolutely delighted to be on the bench for the first game and to actually get on as sub against Holland was unbelievable. Then, all of a sudden, I came on again against Belgium, scored that goal and ensured my place right up to the semi-finals and the third place play-off.'

"*That goal*" was the most breathtaking of the entire tournament. It came in the last minute of extra time with the score deadlocked at 0–0 and the prospect of a penalty shoot-out looming. Paul Gascoigne was tripped and he quickly floated the resulting 35 yard free-kick into the Belgian penalty area. David timed his move to perfection. 'I slipped my marker, the ball passed over my shoulder and I was able to hook a volley past Michel Preud'homme. It's easy enough to describe how I scored the goal. But I find it impossible to describe how I *felt* at the time – whatever words I use can't do justice to that feeling.'

England were through to the quarter-finals, the goalscorer had written himself into football folklore and there was much, much more to come in the David Platt story, including three Italian clubs and the captaincy of England.

A season after playing in the World Cup Finals and winning the PFA Players' Player of the Year Award, David Platt was off to ambitious Bari in Italy, for £5.5 million. Although Bari were relegated in his first season, the transfer proved to be another shrewd career move. David notched 12 goals and had effectively put himself in the Serie A shop window. The top clubs were queuing for his signature and he decided on Juventus. 'In that year with Bari, I learned the language – so much so that when I did move to Juventus I was almost classed as an Italian rather than a foreigner. Without doubt, learning the language is essential for a player going abroad. Once you do that your whole life becomes much easier. Nothing phases you and you begin to enjoy your football.'
After spending too much time on the subs' bench with Juventus. David eventually settled with Sampdoria. 'I'm now enjoying my football more than at any time in my life' he said. 'When I first came to Italy I was certain I'd finish my career back home. Now it's less than 100%, although if I had to put a bet on it, I would still say I'll play in England again'

MATTHEW Le TISSIER
SOUTHAMPTON

Under Chris Nicholl's management, Southampton were enjoying one of their better League seasons at the turn of the 1990 New Year. They were laying in fourth place and had enjoyed some spectacular victories – 4–1 against QPR and Liverpool and 6–3 against Luton.

Prominent in the team was the twenty-one-year-old striker Matthew Le Tissier who had notched eleven League goals before New Year's Day and was being hailed as the most exciting young prospect in England that season. That opinion was endorsed by the PFA's membership who voted him their Young Player of the Year for 1990, an award presented by former Southampton favourite Terry Paine.

Born on Guernsey in October 1968, Matt made his League début for Southampton while still a Youth Trainee in August 1986, as a substitute for George Lawrence against Norwich at Carrow Road. (The Saints were 2–0 up at half time, but ended on the wrong end of a 4–3 scoreline). That October he signed professional forms and a few weeks later scored his first goal for the club, after coming on as a sub for Rod Wallace in the Littlewoods Cup Third Round replay against Manchester United at the Dell. Before the game ended he hit another as the Saints went through 4–1. He finished his first season with eight goals in all competitions.

The 1987–88 season was a barren one as far as Le Tissier League goals were concerned and he scored just two in the cup competitions, prompting cries of 'inconsistency' from the press – a label that would often be dragged out in Le Tissier stories. But he did receive international recognition when Graham Taylor included him in the England Under-20 tour of Brazil that summer.

The goal touch returned in 1988–89. As Southampton struggled to maintain a mid-table position, Matt was the club's second highest scorer with nine goals.

Then came those electrifying performances in the first half of 1989–90, followed by further international recognition in the England 'B' squad (thereby quelling speculation that he was eligible to play for France).

Southampton's form fell away somewhat in the second half of the season and they finished in 7th place. Le Tissier was top scorer with 24 goals. In the process of accumulating that tally he had notched two hat-tricks and also become the club's free kick expert and penalty-taker in chief.

Since becoming the 1990 PFA Young Player of the Year, Matt has continued to delight with a string of goals. He has assumed the captaincy at The Dell and has made the breakthrough at full international level.

YOUNG PLAYER OF THE YEAR

1990

Matt Le Tissier, the most exciting young player of 1990. Despite being labelled 'inconsistent' and 'prone to despondency' he continues to be one of football's great entertainers

PETER SHILTON *OBE MBE*

MERIT AWARD WINNER

1990

Twelve years after winning the Player of the Year Award, the remarkable Peter Shilton was still in contention for a PFA honour. By then he had graduated to 'Merit' status, an Award presented to him by the great Gordon Banks, his predecessor between the sticks at Leicester and Stoke and with England.

Since winning the 1978 top player title, Peter had collected a League Championship medal, a League Cup Winners' medal and two European Cup winners' medals with Nottingham Forest. He had then gone on to play for two more clubs – Southampton and Derby County – and was well on the way to a record 125 caps for England. He had also made ten appearances in the PFA's Divisional Awards.

Still to come was the 1990 World Cup Finals in Italy, in which he played his last international in the Third Place play-off against the hosts, the player-managership of Plymouth Argyle and spells as goalkeeping understudy with Wimbledon and Bolton.

Twelve years after his PFA Player of the Year Award, Peter Shilton was still going strong for Derby County and England

MARK HUGHES
MANCHESTER UNITED

In 1990–91 the Mark Hughes Story enjoyed the most satisfying of twists in the aftermath of his unfortunate experience with Barcelona. It was to be a real 'tale of the unexpected'.

After winning the PFA Players' Player of the Year Award in 1989, he had gone on to FA Cup Final success with Manchester United in 1990. In the first match against Crystal Palace he had first put United 2–1 ahead in the 62nd minute when he latched onto a rebounding ball in the penalty area and buried it in Nigel Martyn's net. Palace substitute Ian Wright then entered the fray and turned the match around first with an equaliser on 72 minutes, then with Palace's third goal just after the start of extra time.

With just seven minute to go, Mark rescued the game for United when he smashed home a Danny Wallace pass for the equaliser.

For the replay, at Wembley five days later, Alex Ferguson decided to drop goalkeeper Jim Leighton who had had a torrid time of things in the first game; he was replaced by Les Sealey who was on loan from Luton Town. This time the match was a much tighter, less exciting affair, in which Sealey pulled off a number of vital saves. The Cup was won by United in the 59th minute with a well-taken a goal by left back Lee Martin.

That goal earned Manchester United a place in the following season's European Cup-winners' Cup competition. It was the first time that English clubs would be re-admitted to the European tournaments following the UEFA ban imposed in 1985 after the Heysel riot – and it was fitting that Manchester United, the club which pioneered England's Euro efforts back in the 1950s, should be among those leading the return.

The FA Cup victory had also earned United a reprieve from a barren run which had

almost seen Alex Ferguson's demise as manager. And it marked the start of better days for the club.

Mark made 31 League appearances in 1990–91, but the top scoring honours were shared by Brian McClair and defender Steve Bruce who both scored 13 times. Defender Bruce achieved his relatively high total largely because he was the designated penalty-taker – seven of his goals came from the spot. Mark followed up in third place with 10 League goals, as United finished in sixth position.

In the League Cup he scored six times as United eliminated Halifax Town, Liverpool, Arsenal, Southampton and Leeds United to win through to a Wembley Final against Second Division Sheffield Wednesday, managed by former Old Trafford boss Ron Atkinson. In the Fifth Round replay against Southampton at Old Trafford Mark had emulated the Fourth Round feat of his team-mate Lee Sharpe, by notching a memorable hat-trick in United's 3–2 victory. In the Final, however, Ron Atkinson's side gained the upper-hand with a John Sheridan goal on 37 minutes. Wednesday held onto the lead for the remainder of the game.

PLAYER OF THE YEAR

1991

Mark Hughes scores against Barcelona

After achieving his unique personal 'PFA Double', Mark Hughes went on to become a vital factor in Manchester United's success in the coming seasons. He would add Premier League, FA Cup and League Cup medals to his collection

In the European Cup-winners' Cup Mark was a substitute for the opening game at Old Trafford against Pecsi Munkas, which marked Manchester United's first European tie in six years. United won 2–0, and took the second leg 1–0, to set up a Second Round clash with Mark's hometown team, Wrexham. He played in the home leg, a 3–0 win, but missed the away tie because of injury (United won the match 2–0).

The quarter-finals brought United's first real challenge of the tournament when they were drawn against Montpellier. In the first-leg, a 1–1 draw at Old Trafford, Mark found himself heavily marked by Pascal Baills who was sent-off after bundling him to the ground. Having received a hefty blow to the side of his face, Hughes had stayed down, and the French side unfairly branded him a cheat. They even said he should not play in the return fixture. The accusation merely had the effect of firing him up for the away leg, in which another Montpellier player was dismissed for spitting at Hughes. United won 2–0.

In the semi-finals United had arguably the best of the draw when they were scheduled to meet Polish side Legia Warsaw, leaving Juventus and Barcelona to settle the other tie. Mark scored United's second goal in the 3–1 away win which provided a good cushion for the meeting at Old Trafford. That game ended all-square at 1–1 and took Manchester United to their first European Final since 1968.

Meanwhile, Barcelona had scraped through the other semi-final against Juventus – which meant that Mark Hughes would line-up against the club that had discarded him as a flop three years earlier.

The showdown Final was played in the De Kuip Stadium in Rotterdam on 15 May. Mark was quite magnificent throughout the game. His goals – the first when he put the final touch to a Steve Bruce header; the second when he steered the ball wide of the keeper Busquets before hammering it into the net – won the game for United. Ronald Koeman pulled one back for Barcelona with a free-kick late in the game, but United held on for the 2–1 victory, largely thanks to a last-ditch clearance by Clayton Blackmore.

For Mark Hughes revenge was sweet indeed. Earlier in the season, on 24 March, he had achieved a unique personal niche in the history of the PFA Awards when he became the first player ever to win the Players' Player of the Year trophy for a second time. That was something else he could not have imagined three years earlier.

LEE SHARPE
MANCHESTER UNITED

On 28 November 1990 Manchester United's Lee Sharpe staked his claim as a PFA Young Player of the Year contender with a stunning display in a Rumbelows Cup Fourth Round tie against Arsenal at Highbury.

The 19-year-old was originally cultivated as a defensive midfielder by Alex Ferguson, but the wily manager had recently been playing him on the left wing where his pace and ability to run at defenders had already caused considerable havoc.

However, at that stage of the season United had leaked ten goals in seven away games, while the Gunners remained unbeaten at Highbury. It seemed a foregone conclusion that Arsenal would slip easily into the Fifth Round at United's expense.

Clayton Blackmore opened the scoring for United in the first minute of the match with a brilliant 25-yard free kick. On 44 minutes Mark Hughes hit the ball into the net while the Gunners' defence was appealing for an offside decision which never came. Just before half time, Lee Sharpe, moving in from the left, beat David Seaman with a superbly struck curling shot from all of 25-yards to put United 3–0 ahead.

Alan Smith pulled two back for the Gunners in the second half. But their dogged efforts to salvage the game was leaving their defence wide open. Lee was twice able to exploit the opportunities this created, first with a header and then with a low drive, to complete the first hat-trick of his career. Danny Wallace rounded off the scoreline at 6–2 to United.

Born in Halesowen in May 1971, Lee had been turned down as a youngster by local clubs Birmingham, Wolves and West Brom. Then, in May 1987, he joined Torquay United as a YTS Trainee. Six months later he made his League début as a substitute in a local derby against Exeter City. In the course of thirteen more appearances that season, he caught the eye of Manchester United and was duly signed for £125,000 in May 1988.

Despite being substituted in his Old Trafford début, against West Ham in September 1988, he put in a good performance which clearly demonstrated his defensive qualities. He was recognised at international level too, becoming – at 17 – the youngest-ever England Under-21 cap in February 1989. He scored his first goal for United seven months later in a 5–1 home win over Millwall.

Then came the 1990–91 season, that superb performance against Arsenal, followed by two more goals against Leeds in the Rumbelows Cup semi-final – one in the 2–1 first-leg victory and the only goal of the game in the second leg. All of which helped persuade the PFA membership to vote him their 1990 Young Player of the Year, an Award presented by former PFA Chairman Garth Crooks on 24 March.

Three days later, Lee won his first full England cap in the European Championship qualifier against The Republic of Ireland.

YOUNG PLAYER OF THE YEAR

1991

After being named 1991 Young Player of the Year, and winning his first full cap for England, Lee Sharpe was kept out of action by a groin injury followed by a bout of viral meningitis which threatened to end his career at the start of the 1992–93 season. Thankfully he pulled through and went on to win two Championship medals in successive seasons

TOMMY HUTCHISON

MERIT AWARD WINNER
1991

The 1991 Merit Award winner was another member of that elite band of footballers whose playing career extended beyond the age of 40. Indeed, on 13 September 1989, just a few days before his 42nd birthday, Tommy Hutchison set a record by becoming the oldest-ever débutant in a European competition, when he played in Swansea City's European Cup Winners' Cup clash with Panathinaikos in Athens. Swansea lost the game 3–2, and the tie 6–5, but Tommy's appearance on the wing in both matches was testament to his lifelong principles of fitness and dedication to his craft. And he was as enthusiastic as he'd ever been. Before the game in Athens he told reporters: 'I'm as excited at the thought of this chance as I was at the age of twenty-one when Blackpool brought me to England from Alloa.'

Tommy was born in Cardenden, Fife, in September 1947. While playing for local side Dundonald Bluebell he was given trials by Blackburn Rovers and Oldham Athletic, but neither club took him on. Eventually he went to Alloa where his skills flourished. He stayed for a season and a half at Recreation Park before Stan Mortensen paid £8,000 to secure his services for recently relegated Blackpool in February 1968.

Two seasons later he helped the Seasiders return to Division One, as runners-up to Huddersfield. When Blackpool went straight back down again in 1970–71 it became inevitable that the electrifying winger would move on and in October '72 Coventry City bought him for £145,000. Although he did not collect any medals in his eight seasons with the Sky Blues, he did gain international recognition making his Scottish début against Czechoslovakia in 1974 and going on to appear in that year's World Cup Finals in West Germany. Tommy supplied the pass from which Joe Jordan equalised for Scotland against Yugoslavia, but they did not progress beyond the First Round.

In October 1980 he was on the move again, this time to John Bond's Manchester City for £47,000. Seven months later he appeared at Wembley in the 100th FA Cup Final, against Spurs – and he played a most dramatic role in the game. With almost half an hour gone he launched into a spectacular diving header to meet a cross from Ray Ranson. The ball flew past Milija Aleksic in the Spurs goal and City were ahead.

With 80 minutes gone the scoreline remained 1–0 to City and the Cup looked to be on its way to Maine Road but then Spurs gained a free-kick on the edge of the area. Glenn Hoddle struck the ball in an attempt to beat the City wall, it struck Hutchison's shoulder and deflected past Joe Corrigan for Spurs' equaliser. After extra time the game was still drawn. Spurs won the replay 3–2 thanks largely to a stunning two-goal performance by Argentinian star Ricky Villa – and Tommy had to be content with a runners-up medal.

His Manchester City career ended in 1982 when he joined Bulova in Hong Kong, before returning to the Football League with Burnley in August 1983. Two years later came the final move of his career, to Swansea, and Tommy Hutchison's European adventure was yet to come…

Tommy Hutchison, the model professional whose skill and stamina were second to none. 'Blackpool manager Bob Stokoe instilled in me the qualities necessary for a long career,' Tommy said. 'He emphasised that you must do in training what you would do in a game – that there must be no slackening on the training pitch or else bad habits will overflow into the game situation'

GARY PALLISTER
MANCHESTER UNITED

I n 1987 when Alex Ferguson began laying the foundations of his Manchester United 'superteam' one of the first names on his shopping list was Middlesbrough's Gary Pallister. But negotiations broke down – the 6' 4" central defender remained at Ayresome Park and Ferguson's turned his attention to another outstanding defensive talent, Steve Bruce of Norwich City, who he signed for £800,000.

However, that was not the end of the Pallister–United affair. In August 1989 Ferguson finally got his man, although in the process he had to break the then-British transfer record by paying 'Boro a fee of £2.3 million.

Yet, the country's most expensive footballer, who was destined to play such a positive role in Manchester United's future, almost hadn't made it to the professional ranks at all. He was born in June 1965, in Ramsgate, where his father was working on a contract. Eight months later, when the work was finished, the family returned home to Billingham in North Yorkshire.

Gary developed into a promising young player who graduated through schools football to the ranks of the Northern League. 'In 1983 I was eighteen and playing for Billingham Town when I was first invited to Middlesbrough for a trial,' Gary recalls. 'Unfortunately I had a bad game and knew I'd flunked it.'

As Gary prepared to leave the dressing room and return home dejected, Middlesbrough's reserve team coach Willie Maddren cornered him and told him not to worry, there would always be another chance. The ex-Boro defender, a PFA Divisional Award winner in 1974, knew a potential professional when he saw one and promised to keep an eye on the youngster's progress. 'I thought he was just being polite. As soon as I was out the door I imagined he wouldn't think twice about me.'

But Maddren was true to his word. When he succeeded Malcolm Allison in the manager's chair at Ayresome Park in 1984, he invited Gary for a second trial. By then the strapping young defender had a good deal more Northern League experience under his belt. He had filled out physically and was a much tougher, far more

confident performer than he had been twelve months earlier. This time he played well in the trial and in November 1984 was offered professional terms by the Second Division club.

He made his first team début for 'Boro in a 3–0 defeat at Wimbledon in August 1985. After one more appearance, a 2–0 defeat by Mansfield Town in the League Cup, he went to Darlington on loan for seven games. On his return to Ayresome Park he completed a further 27 games in a team destined for the big drop into the Third Division.

By then Bruce Rioch (assisted by the 1975 PFA Player of the Year, Colin Todd), had succeeded Willie Maddren as manager.

PLAYER OF THE YEAR

1992

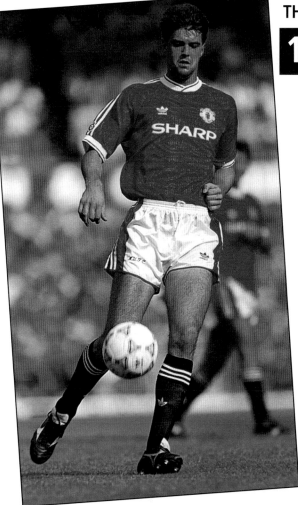

Under Rioch's guidance Middlesbrough bounced straight back into the Second Division as 1986–87 runners-up to Bournemouth. Wearing the No.6 shirt, Gary played in all but two of 'Boro's League games that season – and he notched his first goal for the club, against Carlisle United.

In 1987–88 he was ever-present in the Middlesbrough side which achieved promotion to the top flight after battling through the play-offs against Bradford City and Chelsea.

Although 'Boro were relegated in the following season, Pallister had emerged as one of the most effective central defenders in the country. By then he was also an England international, having received the call from Bobby Robson for the friendly against Hungary in Budapest, in April 1988. In the closing minutes he almost broke the 0–0 deadlock, but his header from a Chris Waddle corner went frustratingly wide and the match ended all-square.

Gary had played just three Second Division games for Middlesbrough in 1989–90, when the club finally agreed to his headline-making transfer to Manchester United on 28 August. He admits that the "Most-Expensive Player" tag was a quite a burden.

Two days after signing for United, the £2.3 million man was thrown in at the deep end in a home match against Norwich City, which turned into something of a personal disaster. Gary was the culprit who gave away a penalty from which Robert Fleck scored in the visitors' 2–0 victory.

As the season progressed Gary gradually began to establish an understanding with his central defensive partner Steve Bruce, but things did not improve much for the team as a whole. 'We had a terrible season, eventually finishing 13th in the table', says Gary. 'There was certainly a lot of bad press for the likes of myself and Paul Ince and the other lads who came to the club at the time.'

As the season drew to a close it appeared that Alex Ferguson's job was on the line. He had spent no less than £13 million on a talented squad which had failed to produce the kind of results warranted by such a large outlay. The last chance to salvage the situation was the FA Cup. United reached the Final against a Crystal Palace side playing at the top of their game. After 90 minutes the scoreline stood at 2–2. At the end of extra time it was 3–3, thanks to Mark Hughes snatching the late equaliser which saved United's season.

The replay five days later was devoid of the excitement of the first match. It was a far more physical affair won in the 59th minute when United's Lee Martin put the finishing touch to the best move of the game to beat Nigel Martyn in the Palace goal. It brought Gary Pallister his first major honour, 'And it was the turning point for Manchester United,' he says.

1990–91 bought further success to Old Trafford. Gary was right there in the thick of the action as United won the European Cup–Winners' Cup, beating Barcelona 2–1 in Rotterdam. He was in the side which lost the League Cup Final 1–0 to Ron Atkinson's Sheffield Wednesday, and he made 36 League appearances as United finished sixth, a vast improvement on the previous season.

At the start of the 1991–92 campaign he was troubled by a back problem which would recur on and off throughout the season. 'I was a substitute for the first game against Notts County, missed the second against Villa, and was sub again for the third against Everton. The defence wasn't conceding any goals and I was thinking I wasn't going to get back into the team. But I was in the starting line up for the fourth against Oldham – and I was just so pleased to get in.'

From those early games onwards it seemed that United were destined for their first Championship in twenty-five years. They alternated the lead with Leeds United for much of the season. But in the last stretch they flagged with a disastrous run of results, allowing Leeds to take the title for the first time since 1974.

'We ended the season with the best defensive record in the League,' says Gary ruefully. 'We were proud of what we'd done, but we obviously hadn't scored enough goals to win the Championship. In the end we just felt a great disappointment.'

Consolation for Gary came in the form of an England recall against Germany in September – and a League Cup winners' medal, won against Nottingham Forest on 12 April. Two weeks earlier he had also stepped onto the stage at Grosvenor House Hotel to collect the 1992 PFA Player of the Year Award from Trevor Brooking. His fellow professionals had voted him in for the sheer consistency of his performances for Manchester United.

'That is what's so pleasing about this award, the fact that you are voted for by the people you play against week in, week out,' says Gary. 'The utmost respect you can get is from your own peers. I'd say it's the ultimate individual accolade for a footballer.'

After collecting the 1992 PFA Player of the Year Award Gary Pallister's career went into overdrive. His defensive partnership with Steve Bruce became central to Manchester United's efforts in the first Premier League campaign. When those two performed well, the team performed well. By the end of the 1992–93 campaign United were Champions for the first time since 1966–67.

In the following season United did not do well in the European Cup, but they did lift the title again and they became only the sixth club to achieve the coveted 'Double' when they beat Chelsea 4–0 at Wembley. Gary had meanwhile established himself as a regular in the England defence

RYAN GIGGS
MANCHESTER UNITED

YOUNG PLAYER OF THE YEAR

1992

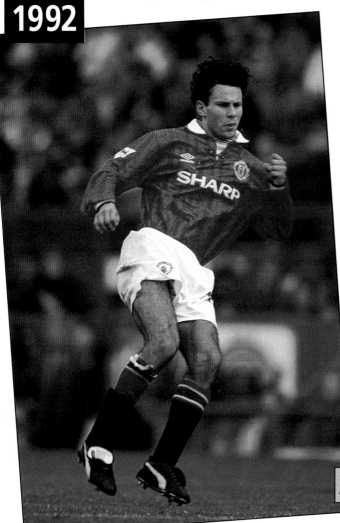

A s the young lad cracked in his sixth goal in a junior match for Manchester United, Bobby Charlton turned to Alex Ferguson and said 'Thank God we've got him'. The subject of the exchange was a certain Ryan Joseph Wilson.

The explosive young star might just as easily have become a Manchester City protégé – it was the Maine Road club who invited him to join their School of Excellence when he was 11-years-old. Soon afterwards he scored a hat-trick for Salford Boys in a trial game at Manchester United's training ground, The Cliff. As it happened City did not offer terms and so United were able to step in to make him an associated schoolboy in February 1988.

Ryan, born in Cardiff in November 1973, is the son of Danny Wilson who played rugby league for Swinton. When his parents' marriage broke up, young Ryan took his mother's maiden name – Giggs. And although he had already starred as captain of the England Schoolboys' Under-15 side, he declared himself to be 100% Welsh.

At sixteen he became a United trainee ('the best I have ever seen at his age' said Alex Ferguson) and rose quickly through the Old Trafford ranks, until Ferguson gave him his first team break, as a substitute for Bryan Robson in a League match against Everton in March 1991. Eight weeks later Ryan was in the starting line-up for the first time, in a local derby against City and he crowned the day by scoring the only goal of the game.

In 1991–92 he was fully involved in United's title chase, appearing 38 times, scoring four goals – and suffering the ultimate disappointment of finishing in runners-up spot behind Leeds United.

There were consolations though, he collected a League Cup winners' medal when United beat Nottingham Forest 1–0 in the Rumbelows Cup Final and he also became the youngest-ever débutante for Wales – at 17 years, 332 days, when he came on as a substitute against Germany in a European Championship qualifier in Nuremburg.

Ryan's electrifying performance on the flanks during the season had drawn almost-inevitable comparisons with former United wing legend, George Best. And his fellow professionals were in no doubt that the comparison held some merit, as they voted Ryan the PFA Young Player of the Year, an Award presented by his boss Alex Ferguson.

The rapid rise of Ryan Giggs brought comparisons with the great George Best

BRIAN CLOUGH OBE

**MERIT
AWARD
WINNER**

1992

Brian Howard Clough was born in Middlesbrough in March 1935, into a family of nine children. While still in short trousers, he boldly informed Middlesbrough FC coach Harold Shepherdson that he would play for the club one day. That prediction came true a few years later when, as a slightly-built teenager he arrived at Ayresome Park after impressing with local clubs Billingham Synthonia and Great Broughton. Following a spell in the Middlesbrough Juniors squad, he signed professional forms in May 1953.

National service in the RAF delayed Clough's first team début until the 1955–56 season. He soon made up for lost time and became the most talked about footballer on Teesside – a brave and skilful centre forward seemingly capable of scoring from anywhere in or around the penalty-area.

In 1956–57 he found the net 38 times and for the next three years was the Second Division's top striker – his total of 43 in 1958–59 made him that season's leading goalscorer in England. In October 1959 he was selected by Walter Winterbottom for his full England début.

Much to Clough's frustration Middlesbrough did not achieve promotion in his five seasons at Ayresome Park and in July 1961 the brash, ambitious young man transferred to Sunderland for £42,000, having been persuaded to make the move by manager Alan Brown who saw him as a vital factor in *his* promotion plans.

Clough continued scoring and Sunderland missed out on promotion by a single point in 1961–62. By Christmas-time 1962, they were going well again. Clough had already accumulated 28 goals in the '62–63 campaign, and in the process had earned the distinction of reaching the 250 goals mark in less games than anyone else in the history of English football. Then, on Boxing Day at Roker Park, he found himself chasing a ball into the muddy penalty area, with Bury keeper Chris Harker advancing towards him. Clough's right knee connected harshly with Harker's shoulder. Both men fell to the ground, but Clough was unable to stand up again. He had sustained a torn cruciate ligament, an inoperable condition in those days, and at

twenty-six his playing days were virtually over.

A new outlet was required for his volatile talents and as soon as he was given charge of the Sunderland Youth team in 1965, Clough knew he had found his metier. With a natural instinct he imparted his own hard-learned lessons to his young players and led them to the semi-final of the FA Youth Cup.

At thirty he became the Football League's youngest manager when he accepted the post at Fourth Division Hartlepools United. He also persuaded his good friend Peter Taylor, an ex-Middlesbrough goalkeeper with an uncanny knack for spotting potential stars, to join him in the venture.

In June 1967 Clough and Taylor moved on to Second Division Derby County, where they immediately strengthened the squad by signing John O'Hare from Sunderland.

They also swooped for central defender Roy McFarland from Tranmere Rovers, and left winger Alan Hinton from Nottingham Forest. Yet Derby finished the 1967–68 season in 18th position and it was obvious that more money needed to be spent on the squad.

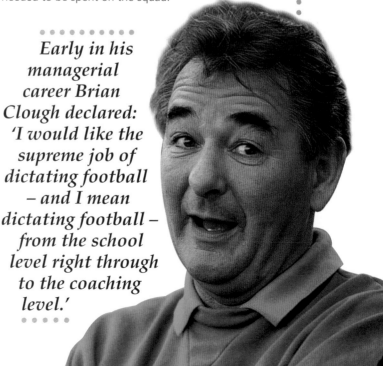

Early in his managerial career Brian Clough declared: 'I would like the supreme job of dictating football – and I mean dictating football – from the school level right through to the coaching level.'

In signing Scottish international and 'Double' winner Dave Mackay from Tottenham in July 1968, Clough pulled off what proved to be a major coup. Mackay was now aged 33, and had twice suffered a broken leg in recent seasons. Many had already written him off, yet Clough believed he was just the man to inspire Derby. Ten months later County finished as Second Division Champions – and captain Mackay, who had adapted brilliantly to his new role in the back four, was voted joint Footballer of the Year by the Football Writers.

In 1969–70 Derby underlined their new status as a First Division force by finishing fourth. Two seasons later, with a line-up which now included Archie Gemmill and Colin Todd (a former Sunderland Youth team player under Clough) – County completed their fixtures programme sitting on top of the First Division table with 58 points. However, they did not expect to win the title as fellow contenders Leeds and Liverpool both had a game in hand. To relieve the tension, Peter Taylor took the Derby team to Majorca while Clough and his wife went to the Scilly Isles. At those two destinations they heard the news that Leeds had lost to Wolves and Liverpool had drawn with Arsenal, leaving both on 57 points. Derby County were the 1971–72 Champions.

In the following season, bolstered by the then-record British signing of full back David Nish for £225,000 from Leicester, Derby, reached the semi-finals of the European Cup. They lost to Juventus by a 3–1 aggregate, and in dubious circumstances which raised Clough's hackles. Despite their anger and disappointment, Clough and Taylor had proved they were a match for the Europeans.

But Clough's and Derby County were about to part in bitterness and recrimination. Ever since he and Taylor had arrived at the Baseball Ground there had been tension between him and certain members of the board who now felt the young upstart was getting far too big for his boots. Things came to a head in October 1973 when chairman Sam Longson asked Clough to curb his television appearances and told him to seek the board's approval before publishing any more outspoken newspaper articles. Clough tendered his resignation and so did Taylor.

The news caused uproar among the Derby fans, who protested long and loud outside the stadium. The players were also incensed and sent a deputation asking the board to reinstate Clough and Taylor; but it was no use. Dave Mackay succeeded Clough in the hot seat and would lead the club a second League title in 1974–75.

In November 1973 Clough and Taylor moved south, to Third Division Brighton, but Clough's heart was not in the job and after eight months he left the Goldstone Ground to join reigning League Champions Leeds United in succession to Don Revie. Peter Taylor remained at Brighton.

Clough attempted to shake things up at Elland Road by bringing in John O'Hare and John McGovern from Derby and Duncan McKenzie from Nottingham Forest – but he succeeded only in alienating those Leeds regulars who had been schooled in the Revie way and who, in the recent past, had been on the wrong end of a few choice 'Cloughisms'. He departed after just 44 days in the job, describing his brief tenure as 'absolute agony'.

An upturn in his fortunes lay just a few miles down the M1. Nottingham Forest was a modest Second Division club when he was appointed manager in January 1975. It took him two and a half seasons to lift the club into the First Division, via the third promotion spot behind Wolves and

Love him or hate him, it is practically impossible to ignore Brian Clough – even in his 'retirement'. He was without doubt Britain's finest exponent of the dictatorial style of football management. No one did the job with more panache, and no one could match his gift for self-publicity. There was always a ready and apposite quip on his lips and he was a godsend for soccer scribes and radio and TV interviewers alike; they revelled in his unpredictability

Chelsea in 1976–77, a task achieved with the help of John O'Hare and John McGovern, who followed him from Leeds – and with Peter Taylor, who had agreed to resume the partnership in 1976. Viv Anderson, Martin O'Neill, Ian Bowyer, John Robertson, Tony Woodcock, Peter Withe and Larry Lloyd were among the other Forest players who would become stars under Brian Clough's guidance.

For the 1977–78 campaign Clough further strengthened his squad with the purchase of 'troublesome' central defender Kenny Burns from Birmingham, followed by Archie Gemmill from Derby and Peter Shilton from Stoke. But no one quite expected the effect that Forest would have in the coming months.

First they won the League Cup, beating holders Liverpool 1–0 in a replay at Old Trafford. Then they wrestled the Championship itself from Liverpool. Kenny Burns was voted 1978's Footballer of the Year by the Football Writers, Tony Woodcock was the PFA's Young Player of the Year and Brian Clough was the Manager of the Year. He was also the first team boss since Herbert Chapman in the 1930s to win the League Championship with two clubs.

Forest were set to take on the best in Europe, but they almost did so without their manager. If things had gone Clough's way he would have been managing the English national team. He certainly seemed the leading contender for the job when Ron Greenwood's brief period of caretakership drew to a close. In the event the FA was not prepared to appoint controversial Clough and chose the safer option of inviting Greenwood to continue on a permanent basis. It was a rejection which hurt Clough deeply.

Clough's Forest retained the League Cup, beating Southampton 3–2 in the Final and they finished in runners-up spot behind Liverpool in the League. But it was the European Cup which lit up the city of Nottingham. Forest reached the Final against Malmo in Munich on 30 May 1979.

Brian Clough's and Peter Taylor share the limelight after Nottingham Forest's first European Cup success in 1979. The brilliant partnership ended in 1982 and then turned to bitterness when Taylor took on the managership of Derby County

Trevor Francis – Britain's first £1 million player, signed from Birmingham City in February 1979 – was the hero of the night, heading the only goal of the game just before half-time.

The following May Forest were in the European Cup Final once more. This time they met SV Hamburg in Madrid. With European Footballer of the Year Kevin Keegan in their line-up, Hamburg were a much tougher proposition than Malmo had been twelve months earlier. In the event Forest won the encounter with the only goal, scored by John Robertson, and a performance of heroic proportions by Peter Shilton.

Two European Cup Final victories in successive seasons was a tremendous achievement for a club which only three years earlier had clawed its way out of the Second Division.

Brian Clough was to remain in charge of Nottingham Forest for the next thirteen years, twice more winning the League Cup (in 1989 and 1990) and reaching the FA Cup Final in 1991. In 1992 the PFA honoured his tenure with a Merit Award. A year later, when Forest were heading for what transpired to be temporary relegation, he announced his retirement.

PAUL McGRATH
ASTON VILLA

PLAYER OF THE YEAR

1993

Ron Atkinson called Paul McGrath 'The best central defender I have ever worked with. He ranks alongside Bryan Robson and Gordon Strachan in the top three players I have managed.'

Republic of Ireland boss Jack Charlton considered McGrath to be '… world class – no doubt about that. He has such pace, I don't think I've seen anyone get away from him. He's a tremendous tackler and in the air you know he will always win everything. Whatever I've asked him to do for us in midfield or defence he has done superbly.'

Shaun Teale, McGrath's central defensive partner for Villa throughout the 1992–93 season, endorsed both these views. 'Playing as close to Paul as I do, you realise just how hard he is to beat … He has a tremendous will to win.'

Each of those quotes was made prior to the 1993 PFA Awards ceremony, during a season in which the quietly-spoken McGrath had been outstanding for Villa as they challenged Manchester United for the first-ever Premier League

Championship. In the event Villa finished as runners-up, while Paul came top in the PFA poll.

'It was an honour in itself to be presented with the Award by Bobby Charlton – and it was great to be chosen by the players themselves, but I couldn't really understand why they picked me,' says Paul, with characteristic modesty. 'The presentation passed so quickly and I think I said about three words of thanks. I've got it on video but very rarely watch it because I just cringe when I see myself. The trophy itself, though, is the best thing I have in my house. It's the one that all pros want.'

Paul was born in Ealing, West London, in December 1959, but raised in three different Dublin orphanages, institutions which instilled within him a positive, never-say-die attitude. 'Life made me a winner,' he affirms. 'And I loved football from the time I was four or five. There were always plenty of lads to kick about with, we played three-and-in and all that – you had to fend for yourself. It was a good atmosphere to grow up in, but we lived a very "closed" existence and it wasn't until I started going to secondary school that I realised there were such things as organised "teams" who played against one another on a regular basis.'

Paul was spotted by the manager of a local boys' club who invited him to join his team. 'I said I couldn't because I had to go back to the orphanage after school every day and they were quite strict about who went where. He went straight down to the office and asked them if I could join and thankfully they agreed.'

'The PFA trophy is the best thing I have in my house. It's the one that all pros want.'

That was the start of Paul McGrath's rise in the game, although he confesses that it took him a while to grasp the concept of team work. 'I didn't have much of a clue at first and was hopelessly confused about positions and stuff like that. But once the penny dropped, I started studying techniques and tactics, especially those of Chelsea who appeared regularly on TV in Ireland. The Blues were always my team. I worshipped Charlie Cooke, Peter Osgood – and David Webb, scorer of the winning goal against Leeds United in the replayed 1970 FA Cup Final.'

By the age of 17 Paul had grown into a strapping young man and was a more than promising footballer. With the recommendation of his final institution, Racefield, he was signed by Dalkey United of the Leinster Senior League and quickly began to learn the tricks of the trade as they were doled out to him by wily older players. But, at 18, his progress was unexpectedly hampered by a depressive illness which lasted on and off for two years before he returned properly to football. (One positive aspect of the situation was a reunion with his mother and his family, who helped in his recovery.) Thankfully this enforced absence did little to impair his skill, or his enthusiasm for the game.

Eventually young McGrath joined League of Ireland side St Patrick's Athletic – a move that turned out to be a stepping-stone to Manchester United, who had been keeping a watchful eye on him for quite some time. 'By then I was 22. I was comfortable, set in my ways, and I wasn't really looking to leave St Pat's. I'd heard there were English clubs interested, but I never believed it – I'd heard it all before when I was younger.'

Nevertheless, he arrived at Old Trafford in April 1982 and found himself training alongside the likes of Steve Coppell, Bryan Robson, Gordon McQueen, Ray Wilkins and Frank Stapleton. 'I'd only seen them on TV before, and to be actually walking beside them was incredible.

'Ron Atkinson selected Paul for his first-team début, as a replacement for the injured Kevin Moran, in a League Cup Third Round tie against Bradford City at Valley Parade in November 1982. Three days later he was in the starting line-up again, in a 1–0 victory against Tottenham. By the end of the 1982–83 season he had 14 League appearances and three goals to his credit, as United finished in third place. He also stood on the sidelines as the club competed in both the League and FA Cup Finals at Wembley.

By the time United next reached Wembley, in May 1985, Paul was not only a fully-fledged Old Trafford favourite, but also a Republic of Ireland international, having won his first cap as a substitute against Italy that February.

He remembers the 1985 FA Cup Final against Everton, not only because it brought United's sixth success in the competition – and his first major honour in English football – but also for his weak backpass to Kevin Moran which was intercepted by PFA Player of the Year, Peter Reid. As Reid sped goalwards, Moran brought him down with a lunging tackle which caused a referee to wave a red card for the first time in FA Cup Final history. 'I still feel guilty about that pass,' says Paul.

Eighteen months later Ron Atkinson was sacked after United's poor start in the 1986–87 League campaign. He was succeeded by Alex Ferguson, an appointment that would ultimately bring the glory days back to Manchester United, but not to Paul McGrath.

McGrath, an easy-going, laid-back character, perceived Ferguson as a strict disciplinarian and their relationship was never an easy one. At the time Paul was also plagued with knee injuries which required a series of operations.

The situation between manager and player came to a head in the winter of 1988–89 when Paul was disciplined for breaching pre-match restrictions on the eve of an FA Cup tie – although he was under the impression that he had not been included in the squad for the match, nor did he feel fit enough to play because of his knee problems. The seriousness of his actions was brought home to him on the following Monday morning, by the presence at Old Trafford of the PFA's Chief Executive Gordon Taylor, who had the unenviable task of telling Paul that United wanted him to quit football

altogether in return for a pay-off and a testimonial match. After much consideration, and with Taylor's counsel, Paul decided not to accept the offer, preferring to stay in the game he loved, "dodgy knees" and all. 'Gordon discussed the situation with United and reported back to me. He was magnificent and helped persuade me to play on, as did my good friends at United, Bryan Robson, Norman Whiteside and Kevin Moran.'

Paul eventually left Old Trafford in August 1989, to join Graham Taylor's Aston Villa. He settled in quickly and Villa put in a bid for the 1989–90 title which ultimately went to Liverpool. 'My game improved with the move and my first season with Villa was one of my best-ever. I thoroughly enjoyed myself and was delighted when my team-mate David Platt, won the PFA Player of the Year title.'

That summer saw Paul wearing the No. 7 shirt for the Republic of Ireland in the Italia '90 World Cup tournament, appearing in all five games as they reached the quarter-finals. He had previously played in the 1988 European Championship Finals and has the highest regard for Jack Charlton, the man who breathed new life into Irish football. 'He's been a father-figure really. He talks sternly when he has to – and he's had to speak sternly to me on occasions, but he always lets it rest and doesn't hold any grudges.'

Back in England two disappointing seasons followed, with Villa finishing 17th in 1990–91 (under the Czech coach Dr Josef Venglos) and 7th in the 1991–92 campaign in which Paul found himself reunited with his first English manager, Ron Atkinson.

Then came the first Premier League campaign in which McGrath's outstanding consistency earned him the Player of the Year accolade from his fellow professionals.

In 1994 Paul collected a League Cup winners' medal with Aston Villa and appeared in all four of the Republic of Ireland's matches as they reached the Second Round of the World Cup Finals in the USA.

'I often wonder what would have become of me, if I'd taken Manchester United's pay-off in 1989,' he says. 'I certainly would not have become a PFA Player of the Year, I would have missed out on appearances in the finals stages of two World Cup tournaments and I would not have been part of Villa's League Cup success - against Manchester United.'

RYAN GIGGS
MANCHESTER UNITED

Twelve months after collecting his first PFA honour, Ryan Giggs again stepped onto the stage at the Grosvenor House Hotel, as the only player to twice win the Young Player of the Year Award. This time he received the trophy from the 1979 recipient, Cyrille Regis, who was still going strong with Aston Villa.

At the time of voting and the time of the presentation Manchester United were mounting a formidable challenge to both Aston Villa and Norwich City for the new Premier League title and Ryan had so far missed only one game in the campaign. Indeed, he was more than fulfilling the potential shown in the previous season.

Playing mainly on the right wing, as a compliment to Lee Sharpe on the left, Ryan gave United an added dimension. His pace and skill earned him headlines and plaudits in equal measure. His team-mate Mark Hughes said: 'Ryan's qualities are outstanding and because of his ability it's easy to forget that he's still only nineteen … [he] must be murder to play against'.

His current form even brought him to the attention of Italian giants AC Milan who reportedly offered £15 million for his services. But Alex Ferguson fended off the speculation by saying that Giggs was definitely not for sale.

By the season's end, Ryan had a Premier League Championship medal (they had won the race ten points ahead of Villa), marking Manchester United's first League success since 1967. He was also the Barclays Young Eagle of the Year, he collected the Bravo Award as the best young player in Europe – and all before his twentieth birthday.

YOUNG PLAYER OF THE YEAR

1993

In 1993 nineteen-year-old Ryan Giggs won a Premier League championship medal and became the first player to be twice voted PFA Young Player of the Year. In 1994 Ryan was also among the contenders for the senior Award which eventually went to his team-mate Eric Cantona

THE 1968 MANCHESTER UNITED TEAM

**MERIT
AWARD
WINNER**

1993

The 1993 Merit Award recalled a magic night twenty-five years earlier, when Manchester United became the first English club to win the European Cup. The team, assembled, encouraged, bullied and inspired by Matt Busby, had finally fulfilled the quest begun in 1956. Poignantly, the triumph came ten years after the tragic air crash in Munich which had destroyed the heart of Busby's great team of the 'fifties.

En route to the 1968 Final the Red Devils had dispatched mighty Real Madrid in a celebrated semi-final second-leg at the Bernabeau Stadium. After being 3–1 down at half-time, United fought back to level the score at 3–3 to add to their 1–0 win in the home leg. The Final was played at Wembley on 29 May 1968, against Portuguese giants Benfica, Eusebio and all, who had already won the trophy twice in four European Cup Final appearances.

Matt Busby regarded the signing of goalkeeper ALEX STEPNEY, for £50,000 from Chelsea in September 1966, as the turning point in his quest for European success. Indeed, Stepney's consistently brilliant form throughout the 1966–67 League campaign had proved a vital factor in United's Championship success which had opened the door to the 1968 European Cup campaign.

Right back SHAY BRENNAN had made a dramatic and emotional entry into Manchester United folklore as a member of the very first post-Munich team. As a 20-year-old accustomed to playing in the reserves, he was suddenly selected to play out of his normal position at outside-left in the 1958 FA Cup Fifth Round tie against Sheffield Wednesday. He rose to the challenge and scored twice in United's 3–0 victory.

Since then Shay had established himself in the heart of United's defence and was ever-present in the Championship-winning side of 1964–65, as was his full back partner and fellow Irish international, TONY DUNNE. It was fitting that these two United stalwarts should play in the club's finest hour.

Along with Alex Stepney (and because of the injury-enforced absence of Denis Law) PAT

CRERAND was one of only two big-money signings in the European Cup Final team. Busby had bought the Scottish international playmaker for £43,000 from Celtic in February 1963 to bolster United's half-back line.

At centre-half BILL FOULKES' first-team career had spanned both the pre- and post-Munich eras. One of the original 'Busby Babes' he had collected Championship medals in 1955–56 and 1956–57. He survived the 1958 air crash and was in that year's FA Cup Final line-up which lost to Bolton. Throughout the '60s he continued to serve United with consistency as he added to his personal collection of honours.

Recalled by Busby for his 29th European tie, against Real Madrid in the semi-final second-leg, Bill made a late and uncharacteristic surge into the Real penalty area and met a perfectly placed pass from George Best to side-foot the ball into the net. The goal, which levelled the score at 3–3, turned the aggregate in United's favour and booked a place in the Final.

Two years earlier NOBBY STILES had been a World Cup winner with England *(see 1986 Merit Award)*. Now he was back at Wembley in his familiar left half role for United.

GEORGE BEST had arrived at Old Trafford as a shy and diffident 15-year-old from Belfast – and was so overwhelmed by the experience that he turned around and went straight back home again. Thankfully, Matt Busby was able to persuade him to return, and so began one of the most electrifying careers in modern football history.

In 1968 George was at the top of his game – the single most exciting player of his day, blessed with fantastic skill, perfect balance, underlying strength and a touch of genius.

BRIAN KIDD was the baby of the side. Indeed, the day of the Final was also his 19th birthday. He had joined the club from school and was enjoying his first season in the first team.

Captaining the team was the redoubtable BOBBY CHARLTON *(see 1974 Merit Award)*, who had been with Matt Busby on every step of United's European quest.

DAVID SADLER was yet another home-grown talent who had established himself as an Old

Trafford favourite. He had replaced the injured Denis Law in the semi-final second-leg against Real Madrid and had scored United's second goal of the match. With Law still confined to a hospital bed, Sadler retained his place for the Final.

The line-up was completed by left-winger JOHN ASTON whose father had won an FA Cup winners' medal with United in 1948. He was to prove one of United's best players in the Final. Goalkeeper JIMMY RIMMER was named as substitute but was destined to sit out the match.

The first half was a typical European battle of wits and brawn, a somewhat dull affair which gave no clue to the excitement that would follow. George Best, in particular, was closely and harshly marked by Humberto and Cruz. After forty-five minutes, which saw no less than thirty fouls and a number of missed chances at both ends, the game was still ruled by stalemate.

In the interval Matt Busby calmed his disrupted team 'Don't let the crowd get hold of you,' he urged. 'Just keep playing your football.'

The advice was heeded. Soon after the restart Tony Dunne and David Sadler combined on the left before Sadler delivered a cross which was met perfectly by Bobby Charlton who later said the ball skidded off his balding head before glancing into Henrique's goal.

Although United's confidence grew, they were unable to penetrate convincingly. David Sadler came close but he fluffed a golden opportunity to put the result beyond doubt. Then, with nine minutes left and United resigned to holding on to that slender lead, Jaime Graca cracked home the equaliser for Benfica. In the dying minutes of normal time, Eusebio slipped

the attentions of Nobby Stiles and was through with a clear run on Alex Stepney's goal. But, instead of placing the ball past the keeper, who had advanced too far from goal, he went for a spectacular shot which Stepney was able to parry to take the match into extra time.

Once again Matt Busby cajoled and encouraged his wilting players who were sprawled, exhausted and drained, on the Wembley turf. 'You're throwing the game away with careless passing, instead of continuing with your football,' he told them. 'You must start to hold the ball and play again.'

After the break United's players seemed rejuvenated. Nobby Stiles later said the rest had been vital 'Just a few minutes more and I'm sure Benfica would have won'.

George Best sparked a United revival when in the second minute he lost his marker, Cruz, before jinking his way around the keeper Henrique to slip the ball into the back of the net. A minute later Brian Kidd rounded off his birthday by heading home United's third after his initial header rebounded off the crossbar. Bobby Charlton completed the rout when he met Kidd's cross from the right to make the score 4–1.

At last Manchester United were the Champions of Europe. After a long journey, begun twelve years earlier and tinged with tragedy and heartbreak, Matt Busby's dream had come true.

Fittingly, the 1993 PFA Merit Award was presented to the team by Eusebio, the man who had come so close to spoiling Manchester United's party at Wembley twenty-five years earlier.

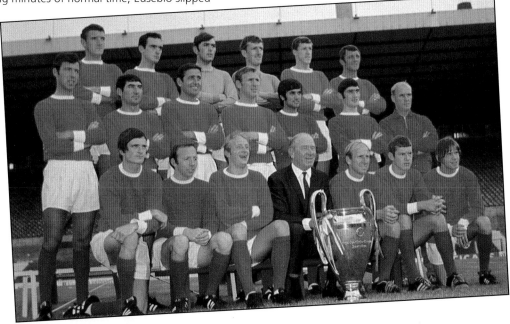

ERIC CANTONA
MANCHESTER UNITED

PLAYER OF THE YEAR

1994

The twenty-first PFA Player of the Year Award went to the flamboyant Frenchman Eric Cantona, of Manchester United, the first foreign player ever to lift the title.

At the time of the Awards ceremony Eric had been in England for just twenty-six months, and every football fan and every player in the country was by then well aware of his prodigious talents. Here was a footballing genius – in the mould of his great hero Maradona – with a brilliant footballing brain, sublime control, a whole repertoire of tricks and a talent for the unexpected. And with a certain nonchalance, a posture aided by the casually upturned collar and the look of seeming disinterest on his face, he was fast becoming one of the great characters of the English game.

On the flip side, we had also become aware of his fiery, explosive temperament, and of his turbulent history spent with half a dozen French clubs.

In 1987, while with Auxerre, he had been fined for striking his own goalkeeper ... In 1988 he was banned from the French national side after insulting coach Henri Michel ... In 1989 he was suspended for kicking the ball into a stand and throwing his shirt at the referee after being substituted by Marseille ... In 1990 he had been banned for ten days after a clash with a Montpellier team-mate ... 1991 he threw a ball at a referee and then lost his temper at the resulting disciplinary hearing ... In January 1992 he had 'vanished' after walking out on his club, Nimes.

' ... I would like to thank other people from football in England, even the player who did not vote for me.'

When he reappeared again, it was at Hillsborough, where it was announced that was about to sign for Sheffield Wednesday who were then vying for a top three spot in the First Division. However, when manager Trevor Francis suggested a week's trial period so that he could further assess the formidable French star, M. Cantona declined, reportedly saying: 'A player like me does not need testing.'

Within days he was a Leeds United player, under Howard Wilkinson. Within weeks he was the darling of the Elland Road faithful as Leeds challenged Manchester United for the 1991–92 First Division Championship.

Cantona's first goal in English League football came in his second appearance, a 2–0 home win over Luton Town. His best that season was a splendid endorsement of his prodigious talents – in the 3–0 victory over Chelsea on 11 April, he first cushioned the ball on his chest and then beat two defenders before firing home from an awkward angle. In all, Eric played fifteen games in the run-in to the season's end – a tally which earned him a Championship medal as Leeds pipped Manchester United at the post.

In November 1992 after a further 13 appearances for Leeds in the new Premier League Cantona was on the move once again, apparently piqued at not commanding an automatic first team place in Howard Wilkinson's set-up. This time Manchester United paid £1.2 million to bring him to Old Trafford.

Alex Ferguson's team, packed with frustrated talent chomping at the bit for League success, were determined to wipe out the 'so near, yet so far' experience of the previous season and were already challenging for the lead when Cantona arrived.

It was quickly apparent that the Frenchman's sublime creativity and his ability to produce the unexpected gave an extra edge, a sense of completeness to the side. He appeared in all but three of the remaining twenty-five games and ended the season as the club's joint-second top goalscorer, with nine goals. Manchester United took the 1992–93 Premiership title ten points ahead of Aston Villa and Eric became the first player to win successive titles with two different clubs.

Things got even better for United in 1993–94. Five victories and a draw in the first six games of the League campaign put them in top spot and by Christmas they were 14 points ahead of Blackburn Rovers. A setback occurred in March when they lost the League Cup Final 3–1 to Ron Atkinson's Aston Villa, but they

quickly put the result behind them, by beating Liverpool 1–0 in the League three days later.

There were other splendid individual performers in the first half of the 1993–94 Premiership campaign – Peter Beardsley, Ryan Giggs, Paul Ince, Andy Cole and Alan Shearer were the other main contenders for the Player of the Year title – but none quite captured the imagination in the way that Cantona had done. Despite further disciplinary problems – in a European Cup encounter with Galatasaray – he was the undisputed star of the season and was duly voted in as the PFA Player of the Year. The Award was presented to him by England coach Terry Venables, at The Grosvenor House Hotel, on 10 April.

Cantona's confidence that he would win the top player title was underlined by his acceptance speech in which he quipped: ' ... I would like to thank other people from football in England, even the player who did not vote for me.'

In the normal course of events, Cantona would have played for Manchester United against Oldham Athletic in the FA Cup semi-final at Wembley earlier on the day of the PFA Awards dinner. The match ended in a 1–1 draw thanks to a late equaliser scored by Mark Hughes. But Cantona took no part – he was under suspension following two sendings-off in the space of four days in March, and would also miss the replay against Oldham at Maine Road (which United won 4–1 to take them into the Final).

Cantona returned to action for the last five games of the League campaign, in which United secured their second consecutive Championship, finishing eight points ahead of Blackburn and with a new Premiership record of 92 points. He was the club's top League scorer with 18 goals, two of them from the penalty-spot.

He was also eligible for the FA Cup Final against Chelsea on 14 May. The Blues had been the only side to have twice beaten United in the League campaign, and in the first half of the Final they looked the most likely to score, especially when Gavin Peacock latched onto a poor backpass – only to see his shot rebound off the crossbar. Then United were awarded a penalty, on the hour, when Eddie Newton upended Denis Irwin. Cantona, United's spot-kick specialist, took the kick and sent Dmitri Kharine the wrong way to give United the lead.

Five minutes later United had a second penalty when Andrei Kanchelskis was brought down by Frank Sinclair on the edge of the area. The Chelsea players hotly-disputed the decision, claiming that the incident had occurred outside the area. But referee David Elleray was adamant and Cantona stepped up to score his second goal of the game, again sending Kharine diving in the wrong direction.

United stepped up the pressure and Mark Hughes and Brian McClair both added to their tally (and Cantona almost completed his hat-trick) to record a 4–0 victory and secure only the fourth 'Double' of the twentieth century.

Eric Cantona had been a vital component in Manchester United's magnificent success story.

In 1994–95 Manchester United were challenging for a third successive League Championship in a neck-and-neck race with Blackburn Rovers. On Wednesday 25 January they were lying in second place and would occupy top spot if they could beat Crystal Palace at Selhurst Park. In fact the match was drawn 1–1, but the result seemed secondary to the incident which dominated the game.

Eric Cantona was having a rough ride in the game. Early in the second half a tackle by Richard Shaw caught him from behind and shortly afterwards, when the two players challenged for a high clearance from Peter Schmeichel, Cantona's legendary short temper flared into retaliation. Referee Alan Wilkie issued the Frenchman's fifth sending-off in sixteen months, and the player trudged dejectedly along the touchline.

As he proceeded towards the dressing room, a spectator came forward in the stand, shouting and gesturing towards Cantona. Suddenly, in an action which would reverberate around the world, Cantona leapt across the barrier at the fan. Feet and fists flew, before police and stewards could separate the two men.

Cantona was immediately disciplined by Manchester United who fined him two weeks wages and imposed a suspension for the remainder of the season – a subsequent FA inquiry extended the ban until the following October and the French Football Federation stripped him of the captaincy of the national side.

When the dust had settled a cold analysis of the 'Cantona Affair' underlined the immense pressure under which professional players increasingly find themselves

ANDY COLE
NEWCASTLE UNITED

In his first full season with Newcastle United Andy Cole became the Premiership's top scorer with 34 goals. He also smashed the club record (previously held jointly by Hughie Gallacher in 1926–27 and George Robledo in 1951–52) of 39 goals in a season. In fact, he finished the 1993–94 campaign with a phenomenal 41 goals in all competitions and a special place in the affections of the 'Toon Army'.

Andy was already well on the way to top scorer status when the PFA membership voted him their Young Player of the Year for 1994.

Yet, there was a time when the young Nottingham-born striker must have doubted that he would make it at the top level. Born in October 1971, he started out as an associated schoolboy with Arsenal in 1985, graduating to a Traineeship at Highbury two-and-a-half years later. But there, he found himself in a similar situation to that recently experienced by David Platt at Manchester United. He stood in line behind a number of more experienced strikers – Niall Quinn, Alan Smith and Paul Merson – and therefore his chances of first team selection were severely limited. Unlike Platt, however, Andy Cole did make a League appearance with his first club, as a sub in a 4–1 win over Sheffield United in December 1990.

With such an abundance of riches in the striking department plus the imminent arrival of Ian Wright, George Graham reluctantly loaned Andy to Fulham in September 1991, and at the tail end of the '91–92 season, to Bristol City where he hit top form, scoring eight goals in twelve games and helping City climb out of the Second Division relegation zone.

That summer Andy made three appearances for England's Under-21 side in the Toulon tournament, scoring one goal in a 2–2 draw with Hungary. On his return to England Bristol City made the arrangement a permanent one by paying £500,000 for his striking services. The investment proved a sound one, the goals kept coming – twelve in 29 league games in 1992–93 – and in March 1993 City realised a £1.25 million profit on the player when he moved on to Kevin Keegan's Newcastle United for £1.75 million (thereby setting transfer records at both clubs).

Andy slotted perfectly into the scheme of things at St James' Park. A dozen more Cole goals followed in as many matches, making him the club's joint second top scorer of the season, as Newcastle continued their march into the Premiership.

That summer Keegan completed another piece of the Magpies' jigsaw with the surprise signing of former Newcastle favourite Peter Beardsley, from Everton. It proved to be one of the shrewdest deals of the year as Beardsley and Cole formed a near-perfect partnership up front for the Magpies.

As Newcastle proceeded to score more goals then any other Premiership team in 1993–94, eventually finishing in third place behind Manchester United and Blackburn Rovers, Kevin Keegan declared himself delighted with Andy Cole's progress. 'The remarkable thing about him is that he's not just scoring, but creating three or four good chances in every match … that's incredible.'

YOUNG PLAYER OF THE YEAR

1994

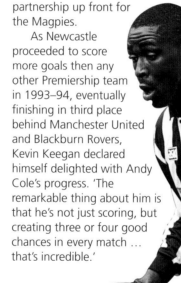

Less than twelve months after winning the PFA Young Player of the Year Award, Andy Cole became Britain's most expensive footballer in a sensational £7 million move to Manchester United. In March 1995, he made his full England début against Uruguay

BILLY BINGHAM *MBE*

**MERIT
AWARD
WINNER**

1994

Born in August 1931, Billy Bingham once played football in the same Belfast streets as the Blanchflower brothers, Danny and Jackie, and like them he rose to international prominence with Northern Ireland.

Billy's playing career got off to a flying start with Irish League side Glentoran. His abundant talents as a right winger first came to the notice of English clubs in an Irish League v Football League representative match, and Sunderland obtained his signature in November 1950. But the 'fifties were undistinguished days for the slumbering north-east giants and when the club was relegated in 1957–58, Bingham moved on in a £15,000 transfer deal to Luton Town.

Shortly before the move he had returned from World Cup action in Sweden, where Northern Ireland had reached the last eight before elimination by France. Perhaps the inspirational international managership of Peter Doherty instilled a similar ambition in the 26-year-old winger.

Although Billy didn't win any top honours with Luton, he did come close with a losers' medal in the 1959 FA Cup Final against Nottingham Forest. *En route* to the Final he scored in every round, helping the Hatters to reach Wembley for the first time in their history. Perhaps the most important of these strikes was the winner against Third Division 'giant-killers' Norwich City in the semi-final replay at St Andrews, Birmingham. The Final itself was marred by injury to Forest's Roy Dwight who broke his leg in a collision with Brendan McNally. Dwight had already scored the opening goal, and Tommy Wilson had added a second before the accident. The ten-men of Nottingham Forest gamely held on for the rest of the match. David Pacey pulled one back for the Hatters in the second half but they never looked likely to save the match

The following season saw Luton's descent into the Second Division and early in the 1960–61 season Bingham found himself on the move yet again. Everton were the buyers, at £20,000 plus two players. At Goodison Park his talents were at last rewarded with a League Championship medal in 1962–63.

Bingham's playing days ended after he broke a leg in the 1964–65 season while playing for Third Division Port Vale. He then cut his managerial teeth with Southport, taking them to the Fifth Round of the 1966 FA Cup and into the Third Division in 1967. In 1968 he moved south to manage Plymouth Argyle. That year also saw him in charge of the Northern Ireland team for the first time. Next came a spell as coach to the Greek national team before Bingham accepted the plum job of succeeding his old boss Harry Catterick at Everton in 1973.

However, success was to elude the Toffees in Bingham's three year tenure at Goodison Park and in January 1977 he was replaced by Gordon Lee. Three months later he was back in Greece in charge of PAOK Salonika. A third spell in Football League management came with Mansfield Town in 1978.

Then, in 1980, Bingham was re-appointed manager of Northern Ireland. This time his methods would meet with more success. Two years later his squad – which included the likes

A gifted winger, Billy Bingham was a star turn for Sunderland, Luton Town, Everton, Port Vale and Northern Ireland. As manager of Northern Ireland he worked miracles with limited resources by twice winning the (now defunct) Home International Championship and taking his country to the last stages of two World Cup Finals

of Pat Jennings, Jimmy Nicholl, Mal Donaghy, Martin O'Neill, Sammy McIlroy, David McCreery and Gerry Armstrong – had won its way to the last sixteen in the World Cup Finals in Spain, having beaten the hosts 1–0 along the way with a famous Gerry Armstrong goal. Unfortunately, just as they had done twenty-four years earlier when Bingham had been a player, France put a stop to any further progress, this time with a 4–1 win in the second stage.

In 1986 Bingham's boys were back again, in the Mexico World Cup Finals. Once again they were drawn in the same group as Spain, whose 2–1 victory exacted revenge for the defeat in 1982. Another defeat, by Brazil, and a draw with Algeria meant that Northern Ireland caught the early flight home.

In the 1990 World Cup qualifying tournament Spain again proved to be something of a thorn in Billy's side. A 4–0 defeat in Seville was followed by a 2–0 defeat in Belfast. The

Republic of Ireland were no help either, handing out a 3–0 defeat in Dublin which virtually sealed their neighbours' fate.

Spain and the Republic of Ireland were again drawn in Northern Ireland's group for the 1994 qualifiers. And although Bingham's side put in a much better showing than in the previous tournament they still missed out. Following their elimination, Billy announced his retirement.

On 10 April 1994 the PFA recognised his achievement in bringing the belief back into Northern Irish football, when Bryan Hamilton, his successor in the job, presented him with a well-deserved Merit Award.

ALAN SHEARER
BLACKBURN ROVERS

PLAYER OF THE YEAR

1995

When Blackburn Rovers' manager Kenny Dalglish opened the envelope and read out Alan Shearer's name as the winner of the 1995 PFA Players' Player of the Year Award, the announcement was met with thunderous applause.

The positive mood of the PFA membership – a reaction perhaps to modern football's worst-ever season of allegations, 'sleaze' and scandal – was clearly reflected in Shearer's articulate acceptance speech. 'I think it's fair to say that the image of football has suffered a bit this season. I think I'm speaking for the 99% of players in England who with a little bit of hard work and a little bit of help will try to succeed and put a little bit of pride back into the national game.'

Talking to the Press later, he added: 'Ninety-nine percent of people in football are honest and good. It's been a difficult year but we are only human, we make mistakes, we can't change what's happened. But what we have to try to do is learn from where certain people have gone wrong.'

'To add my name to the names of the previous PFA Winners is a tremendous honour.'

The sentiments were met with universal approval – and a quiet sense of relief on the part of the game's administrators.

Alan had won the Player of the Year trophy following a magnificent season up front for Blackburn. By the time of the presentation ceremony on 9 April, Rovers appeared to be edging ahead of Manchester United in the title race and Shearer's contribution to the cause so far had been 31 Premiership goals, a collection which included strikes from all angles and distances, spectacular goals and easy ones. 'It doesn't matter if they're from three yards or thirty yards, so long as they go in,' he says. 'At the end of the day it's points for Blackburn that count more than any individual achievement.'

Alan had also become the first player since Jimmy Greaves in the '60s, to hit the 30-League goals mark in consecutive seasons – and he had recently notched the 100th League goal of his career. It came in a 2–1 victory over Chelsea at Ewood Park. 'That was quite a milestone for me, but I hadn't realised it was coming up until someone reminded me that I was on 97 or 98.'

Alan was born in Newcastle in August 1970, which rather begs the question: How does a young Geordie start his career on the south coast with Southampton? 'That's something I've never been able to answer fully,' he says. 'I suppose it was just a gut feeling. I'd been playing for a couple of schoolboy sides – Wallsend Boys' Club and Cramlington Juniors – and I'd had trials with Manchester City, West Brom and Newcastle United (they were my favourite club, I used to watch them whenever I could). But it was a scout called Jack Hickson who took me down to Southampton when I was twelve or thirteen. They had a great record for bringing youth players through, and of course that was one of the main reasons for me going down there. I signed as a schoolboy when Lawrie McMenemy was the manager, and as a trainee at sixteen when Chris Nicholl was in charge.'

It was Nicholl who gave the young Shearer his first team début in March 1988, as a substitute for Danny Wallace in a First Division game against Chelsea at Stamford Bridge. He missed the next match against Wimbledon, but was again a substitute for Wallace in the following 0–0 draw with Oxford United.

Then, on 9 April, he found himself in the Saints' starting line-up for the first time, although he wasn't aware of his selection until 90 minutes before the start of the game. The opponents were Arsenal, who were about to become the first club to experience the striking power of Alan Shearer. His first League goal came within five minutes of the kick-off – a powerful header from five yards. By half time Southampton were 3–1 ahead, and Shearer had supplied another headed goal on 33 minutes. Four minutes into the second half and his name was on the scoresheet again – after his initial strike hit the crossbar, he hammered home the rebound to beat John Lukic for the third time. Southampton won 4–2, and at 17 years 240 days Alan had just beaten Jimmy Greaves' record, set in 1957, to become the youngest-ever player to score three goals in a First Division match.

Injury kept Shearer out of contention for a regular first team place during the first half of the 1988–89 campaign. In all he made just 10 League appearances that season, yet he netted nine goals and was the club's second top scorer. A goal-drought seemed to afflict him in 1989–90 when he scored just three times in 26 outings as the Saints finished in seventh position. Just four League goals followed in 1990–91 along with eight in the Cup competitions. In 1991–92 his striking form returned and he was the club's top scorer for the first time with 13 goals.

By then Alan had made the breakthrough into the full England side, after impressing with 13 goals in 11 Under-21 appearances. Graham Taylor selected him for the friendly with France in February 1992, a dress rehearsal for that summer's European Championship Finals. Shortly before half time, a Nigel Clough corner was flicked on by Mark Wright. Shearer, finding himself unmarked, spun to hit the ball into the back of the net. England won 2–1, the other goal coming from Gary Lineker midway through the second half.

Alan Shearer is an 'old-fashioned centre-forward' in the best English tradition. Like some of the great goalscorers of the past – Nat Lofthouse, Tommy Lawton, Bobby Smith, Malcolm Macdonald et al – he is strong, brave, good in the air, adept at shielding the ball when necessary and a master of banging the ball into the back of the net.

But Alan is loathe to analyse just what it is that makes a successful striker. 'People often ask me "what's the secret of goalscoring?" But I honestly don't know why I score so many goals. It's an instinctive thing, a habit ... being in the right place at the right time. It's also about team work – the Blackburn lads often make it easy for me. Sometimes the performance of a striker will overshadow the work done by the rest of the team – and that's wrong. Sometimes others don't get the credit they deserve.'

Shearer's bright start for England earned him a place in the European Championship squad and selection as Gary Lineker's striking partner for England's second game of the finals, against France in Malmo. This time a diving header from Shearer almost broke the deadlock, but the game ended in a 0–0 stalemate.

Shortly after his return to England, Alan joined Blackburn Rovers for a then-club record £3.3 million. Other clubs, notably Manchester United and Marseille, were reportedly interested in capturing his signature, but he is adamant that, 'Blackburn were the only club to make

Southampton an offer and they were the only club I spoke to. I came to Ewood Park to win things and I've never regretted the move. Kenny Dalglish is a brilliant manager and you can't help but learn from him – or from his assistant, Ray Harford.'

The famous Lancashire club – six times FA Cup winners and twice League Champions in the distant past – had faded somewhat since the mid-1960s, when they had dropped out of the First Division. But, under the recent patronage of millionaire Jack Walker and the astute management of Kenny Dalglish, Rovers had returned to the top flight, the brand new Premier League, via the play-offs.

True to tradition Alan scored on his début for Blackburn, in a 3–3 draw at Crystal Palace on the opening day of the 1992–93 season. He went on to play in the next 20 League games, scoring 16 goals in the campaign and helping Rovers to maintain a top three spot. He also scored six times in the League Cup. But on Boxing Day he injured a knee, yet still scored twice in a 3–1 victory over Leeds at Ewood Park. The injury was later diagnosed as a ruptured cruciate ligament, which required surgery in order for him to play again. Alan accepted that it would be a long time before he was fit for action and with characteristic determination he set his mind to a positive recovery. The fact that he took no further part in the remainder of Rovers' season had a detrimental effect on the team and they eventually finished fourth.

Alan returned to the first team as a substitute for several games at the beginning of the 1993–94 campaign, but was soon back to his scoring ways. He ended the season with 31 goals, was the Premiership's second top scorer and found himself voted Footballer of the Year by the Football Writers. Blackburn finished runners-up to Manchester United – and with a determination to do even better in 1994–95.

A new club record was set with the signing of Chris Sutton from Norwich City for £5 million in the summer of 1994. Sutton teamed up with Shearer – in a partnership dubbed 'The SAS' – and the goals continued to flow as Rovers challenged for, and won, the Premiership title.

Alan was voted the 1995 PFA Player of the Year ahead of his old Southampton team-mate Matthew Le Tissier and Spurs' brilliant German import Jurgen Klinsmann. 'This was my third nomination for the Player of the Year Award, along with one for the Young Player title,' says Alan. 'And to add my name to the names of the previous PFA winners is a tremendous honour.'

ROBBIE FOWLER
LIVERPOOL

O n 9 April 1995, Robbie Fowler enjoyed his twentieth birthday, and he completed the day's celebrations by receiving the PFA's Young Player of the Year Award from QPR manager Ray Wilkins.

At that time the young Liverpool striker had scored 23 League goals in the 1994–95 season, and was second in the Premiership scoring stakes behind Blackburn's Alan Shearer. He had also notched four in the League Cup and, only a week before the Awards ceremony, had collected his first major honour when the Reds beat Bolton Wanderers 2–1 in the Coca-Cola Cup Final at Wembley – thereby booking a UEFA Cup berth in 1995-96.

In total, Robbie had amassed an amazing 46 goals in all competitions in just eighteen months as a professional player and was considered Liverpool's best striking prospect since the emergence of Ian Rush in the early-80s.

Liverpool-born, Robbie had started out as an Anfield trainee, and it was apparent right from the start that he had that instinctive feel for goal, referred to earlier by Alan Shearer, which is common to all great strikers. He was a star turn for the England Under–18s team in November 1992 when he scored a hat-trick in a 7–2 victory over Switzerland.

He made his first team début for Liverpool in September 1993 in a 1–0 defeat by Chelsea at Stamford Bridge. His first League goal came in a 2–1 victory over Oldham Athletic at Anfield, his third appearance. Two games later he hit his first hat-trick, in Liverpool's 4–2 defeat of Southampton, also at Anfield.

Despite a six week lay-off through injury in January and February, he still finished as the club's second top scorer with 12 League goals. In 1994–95 he finished top of the list.with 25 goals.

YOUNG PLAYER OF THE YEAR

1995

In a 1994–95 pre-season interview Robbie said he would be happy if he scored ten goals in the new campaign. In the event he reached that target within the first three months of the season and went on to become Liverpool's top scorer and the recipient of the PFA Young Player of the Year Award

GORDON STRACHAN MBE

MERIT AWARD WINNER

1995

It was hard to believe that Gordon Strachan was going to retire at the end of the 1994–95 season. The little Scot, once dubbed 'The Peter Pan of Football' by Andy Roxburgh, somehow seemed likely to go on playing forever. But it was true enough. The 37-year-old Leeds United and Scotland midfield motor was calling it a day, adamantly declaring that he had run himself 'to a standstill.'

Gordon Strachan had been tirelessly running over endless acres of football pitch ever since his schooldays in Edinburgh – and he had always run flat out, unable as Roxburgh said 'to go at half pace.'

He had always been the most competitive of professionals too. Howard Wilkinson, his boss at Leeds United said: 'You could video him and sell it as what you expect from a player – the control, the passing, the will to take responsibility, to work and retrieve situations. [He] defends better than some people twice as big as him, twice as strong and twice as athletic'.

Strachan's football career began at fifteen, with an apprenticeship at Dundee where he supplemented his earnings with a summertime job in the dispatch department of the Timex watch factory. He made his first team début in 1974–75 and became a Dens Park regular over the next two seasons. Despite his slight 5'6" frame, his tenacious, battling qualities, allied to great skill and stamina, brought favourable comparisons with former Scottish internationals Dave Mackay and Billy Bremner. He also possessed an instinctive footballing brain.

Gordon made a £50,000 move to Aberdeen in November 1977, seven months before the appointment of Alex Ferguson as manager. Their partnership, which was never an easy one and occasionally flared into open argument, lasted for six seasons and through the most glorious spell in the Dons' history in which the club challenged the domination of the two Glasgow giants. In his time at Pittodrie, Strachan collected two Premier League Championship medals and three Scottish Cup winners' medals. He was the also the chief architect of Aberdeen's European Cup–Winners' Cup Final triumph

Gordon Strachan was the architect of many goals for Dundee, Aberdeen, Manchester United, Leeds United and Scotland. In common with other PFA Merit Award winners who enjoyed careers of great longevity, Strachan was at pains to look after his health and fitness throughout the long seasons. He is an example to all aspiring professionals

over Real Madrid in Gothenburg, in 1983. He made his international début in May 1980, against Northern Ireland, and would go on to win 50 caps for Scotland.

In August 1984, after being courted by numerous European clubs, he said goodbye to the Scottish League and crossed the border to sign for Ron Atkinson's Manchester United in a £500,000 transfer deal. He merged well into the side, alongside the likes of Bryan Robson, Mark Hughes, Norman Whiteside, Paul McGrath, Kevin Moran and fellow new-signee Jesper Olsen from Ajax.

In his first season at Old Trafford Gordon missed just one League game as United finished fourth behind Everton, Liverpool and Spurs. He was the club's second top scorer in the League and was also at the heart of the dramatic FA Cup Final victory, which called a halt to Everton's 'Double' hopes in May 1985.

A shoulder injury kept him out for several games of the 1985–86 season, in which United again finished fourth. But changes were just around the corner. The 1986–87 campaign began disastrously for United with a single victory in the first nine matches of the League campaign, and a place deep in the drop zone. Ron Atkinson was replaced – by none other than Strachan's former Aberdeen boss, Alex Ferguson, who gradually effected a climb to mid-table safety.

The uneasy peace between Strachan and his 'new-old' manager continued throughout the following season, in which United finished as runners-up to Liverpool. That summer Gordon almost moved to Lens in France, but changed his mind at the eleventh hour and played a further 21 League games for Manchester United in the 1988–89 campaign before making a transfer deadline day move to Howard Wilkinson's Leeds United in March 1989.

He found that the challenge of Second Division football had a rejuvenating effect on his game. All his old enthusiasm returned – and he was greatly appreciated by the Elland Road fans. In 1989–90 Wilkinson's faith in the Scottish warhorse was more than repaid as Strachan became a vital factor in Leeds' return to the top flight, as Second Division Champions.

A year later Leeds finished fourth in the First Division and, at the age of 34, Gordon Strachan found himself voted the Football Writers' Footballer of the Year for 1991.

In 1991–92 things got even better for Leeds and for Strachan. Under his captaincy they won the Championship in a neck-and-neck race with Alex Ferguson's Manchester United. Elland Road had not seen anything like it since the Revie-inspired days of Billy Bremner, Johnny Giles, Paul Madeley – and the first-ever PFA Player of the Year, Norman Hunter.

Gordon Strachan kept running for three more seasons – until towards the end of the 1994–95 campaign, and a few months after announcing his retirement, he left Elland Road to join Coventry City as assistant to manager Ron Atkinson. But even then the running didn't stop, as he was on standby to play in the Sky Blues' final matches of the season.

No one was more deserving of the 1995 PFA Merit Award, which was presented to Gordon by another legendary Scot, Denis Law.

PFA DIVISIONAL AWARD WINNERS 1974–1995

1974

Division One	Division Two	Division Three	Division Four
Pat Jennings (Tottenham Hotspur)	Bryan King (Millwall)	Roger Jones (Blackburn Rovers)	Steve Death (Reading)
Paul Madeley (Leeds United)	John Craggs (Middlesbrough)	Ian Wood (Oldham Athletic)	Ian Branfoot (Lincoln City)
Roy McFarland (Derby County)	Dave Watson (Sunderland)	Mel Machin (Bournemouth)	Jimmy Giles (Exeter City)
Norman Hunter (Leeds United)	Willie Maddren (Middlesbrough)	Barry Swallow (York City)	John Hulme (Reading)
Colin Todd (Derby County)	John Gorman (Carlisle United)	Colin Sullivan (Plymouth Argyle)	David Peach (Gillingham)
Billy Bremner (Leeds United)	Bruce Rioch (Aston Villa)	Ernie Machin (Plymouth Argyle)	Freddie Hill (Peterborough United)
Tony Currie (Sheffield United)	Don Masson (Notts County)	Barry Lyons (York City)	Brian Godfrey (Newport County)
Johnny Giles (Leeds United)	Asa Hartford (West Bromwich Albion)	Alan Durban (Shrewsbury Town)	Paul Walker (Peterborough United)
Mick Channon (Southampton)	Dennis Tueart (Sunderland)	Bruce Bannister (Bristol Rovers)	Fred Binney (Exeter City)
Malcolm Macdonald (Newcastle United)	Duncan McKenzie (Nottingham Forest)	Alan Warboys (Bristol Rovers)	Jim Hall (Peterborough United)
Allan Clarke (Leeds United)	Don Rogers (Crystal Palace)	Phil Boyer (Bournemouth)	Brian Yeo (Gillingham)

1975

Division One	Division Two	Division Three	Division Four
Peter Shilton (Stoke City)	Bryan King (Millwall)	Roger Jones (Blackburn Rovers)	Peter Grotier (Lincoln City)
Paul Madeley (Leeds United)	John Gidman (Aston Villa)	Andy Burgin (Blackburn Rovers)	Sandy Pate (Mansfield Town)
Kevin Beattie (Ipswich Town)	Stewart Houston (Manchester United)	Phil Burrows (Plymouth Argyle)	John Breckin (Rotherham United)
Billy Bonds (West Ham United)	Len Cantello (West Bromwich Albion)	Chris Turner (Peterborough United)	Bobby Doyle (Barnsley)
Gordon McQueen (Leeds United)	Dave Watson (Sunderland)	Graham Hawkins (Blackburn Rovers)	Jimmy Giles (Exeter City)
Colin Todd (Derby County)	Martin Buchan (Manchester United)	Derek Jeffries (Crystal Palace)	Trevor Storton (Chester)
Duncan McKenzie (Leeds United)	Ray Graydon (Aston Villa)	Arfon Griffiths (Wrexham)	Alan Durban (Shrewsbury Town)
Colin Bell (Manchester City)	Mick Channon (Southampton)	Peter Eastoe (Swindon Town)	Derek Draper (Chester)
Bob Latchford (Everton)	Stuart Pearson (Manchester United)	Bill Rafferty (Plymouth Argyle)	Ray Clarke (Mansfield Town)
Alan Hudson (Stoke City)	Phil Boyer (Norwich City)	Alan Buckley (Walsall)	Gordon Hodgson (Mansfield Town)
Leighton James (Burnley)	Billy Hughes (Sunderland)	Peter Taylor (Crystal Palace)	Paul Stratford (Northampton Town)

1976

Division One	Division Two	Division Three	Division Four
Pat Jennings *(Tottenham Hotspur)*	Jim Montgomery *(Sunderland)*	Eric Steele *(Peterborough United)*	Peter Grotier *(Lincoln City)*
Paul Madeley *(Leeds United)*	Gary Locke *(Chelsea)*	Ray Evans *(Millwall)*	Ian Branfoot *(Lincoln City)*
Kevin Beattie *(Ipswich Town)*	John Gorman *(Carlisle United)*	Clive Charles *(Cardiff City)*	Ken Sandercock *(Torquay United)*
Don Masson *(Queens Park Rangers)*	Tony Towers *(Sunderland)*	Dennis Burnett *(Brighton & Hove Albion)*	Geoff Hutt *(Huddersfield Town)*
Roy McFarland *(Derby County)*	Paul Jones *(Bolton Wanderers)*	Ian Evans *(Crystal Palace)*	Sam Ellis *(Lincoln City)*
Colin Todd *(Derby County)*	Geoff Merrick *(Bristol City)*	Derek Jeffries *(Crystal Palace)*	Terry Cooper *(Lincoln City)*
Kevin Keegan *(Liverpool)*	Bobby Kerr *(Sunderland)*	Peter O'Sullivan *(Brighton & Hove Albion)*	Ian Miller *(Doncaster Rovers)*
Alan Hudson *(Stoke City)*	Mick Channon *(Southampton)*	David Gregory *(Peterborough United)*	John Ward *(Lincoln City)*
Duncan McKenzie *(Leeds United)*	Paul Cheesley *(Bristol City)*	Dixie McNeil *(Hereford United)*	Ron Moore *(Tranmere Rovers)*
John Toshack *(Liverpool)*	Johnny Giles *(West Bromwich Albion)*	Alan Buckley *(Walsall)*	Peter Kitchen *(Doncaster Rovers)*
Dennis Tueart *(Manchester City)*	Peter Thompson *(Bolton Wanderers)*	Peter Taylor *(Crystal Palace)*	Tony Whelan *(Rochdale)*

1977

Division One	Division Two	Division Three	Division Four
Ray Clemence *(Liverpool)*	George Wood *(Blackpool)*	Jim McDonagh *(Rotherham United)*	Terry Poole *(Huddersfield Town)*
John Gidman *(Aston Villa)*	Gary Locke *(Chelsea)*	John McMahon *(Preston North End)*	Brendon Batson *(Cambridge United)*
Mick Mills *(Ipswich Town)*	David Peach *(Southampton)*	Kenny Sansom *(Crystal Palace)*	Andy Ford *(Southend United)*
Brian Talbot *(Ipswich Town)*	Garry Stanley *(Chelsea)*	Brian Horton *(Brighton & Hove Albion)*	Dennis Bond *(Watford)*
Roy McFarland *(Derby County)*	Paul Jones *(Bolton Wanderers)*	Ian Evans *(Crystal Palace)*	Lindsay Smith *(Colchester United)*
Kevin Beattie *(Ipswich Town)*	Paul Futcher *(Luton Town)*	Graham Cross *(Brighton & Hove Albion)*	Barry Dominey *(Colchester United)*
Kevin Keegan *(Liverpool)*	George Best *(Fulham)*	Arfon Griffiths *(Wrexham)*	Ian Miller *(Doncaster Rovers)*
Trevor Francis *(Birmingham City)*	Ray Wilkins *(Chelsea)*	Peter Ward *(Brighton & Hove Albion)*	Alan Curtis *(Swansea City)*
Andy Gray *(Aston Villa)*	John Richards *(Wolves)*	Billy Ashcroft *(Wrexham)*	Brian Joicey *(Barnsley)*
Trevor Brooking *(West Ham United)*	Mick Channon *(Southampton)*	Alan Buckley *(Walsall)*	Peter Kitchen *(Doncaster Rovers)*
Dennis Tueart *(Manchester City)*	John Robertson *(Nottingham Forest)*	Alan Crawford *(Rotherham United)*	Don Hutchins *(Bradford City)*

1978

Division One	Division Two	Division Three	Division Four
Peter Shilton (Nottingham Forest)	Barry Daines (Tottenham Hotspur)	Dai Davies (Wrexham)	Peter Springett (Barnsley)
John Gidman (Aston Villa)	Terry Naylor (Tottenham Hotspur)	Brendon Batson (Cambridge United)	Chris Lawler (Stockport County)
Derek Statham (West Bromwich Albion)	Kenny Sansom (Crystal Palace)	Keith Kennedy (Bury)	Keith Pritchett (Watford)
Liam Brady (Arsenal)	Glenn Hoddle (Tottenham Hotspur)	Ian Ross (Peterborough United)	Roger Joslyn (Watford)
Gordon McQueen (Manchester United)	Paul Jones (Bolton Wanderers)	Chris Turner (Peterborough United)	Sam Ellis (Watford)
Martin Buchan (Manchester United)	Paul Futcher (Luton Town)	Mickey Thomas (Wrexham)	Mick McCarthy (Barnsley)
Steve Coppell (Manchester United)	Alan Ball (Southampton)	Bobby Shinton (Wrexham)	Ian Miller (Doncaster Rovers)
Trevor Francis (Birmingham City)	Peter Ward (Brighton & Hove Albion)	Alan Buckley (Walsall)	Robbie James (Swansea City)
Joe Jordan (Manchester United)	John Duncan (Tottenham Hotspur)	Dixie McNeil (Wrexham)	Alan Curtis (Swansea City)
Trevor Brooking (West Ham United)	Peter Reid (Bolton Wanderers)	David Kemp (Portsmouth)	Brendan O'Callaghan (Doncaster Rovers)
John Robertson (Nottingham Forest)	Peter Taylor (Tottenham Hotspur)	David Moss (Swindon Town)	Alan Mayes (Watford)

1979

Division One	Division Two	Division Three	Division Four
Peter Shilton (Nottingham Forest)	Mark Wallington (Leicester City)	Chris Turner (Sheffield Wednesday)	Steve Death (Reading)
Viv Anderson (Nottingham Forest)	Kevin Hird (Blackburn Rovers)	John Stirk (Watford)	Gary Peters (Reading)
David O'Leary (Arsenal)	Mark Lawrenson (Brighton & Hove Albion)	Steve Sims (Watford)	Steve Foster (Portsmouth)
Dave Watson (Manchester City)	Mike Doyle (Stoke City)	Ian McDonald* (Carlisle United)	Mick McCarthy (Barnsley)
Derek Statham (West Bromwich Albion)	Kenny Sansom (Crystal Palace)	Trevor Storton* (Chester)	Kevin Moore (Grimsby Town)
Liam Brady (Arsenal)	Trevor Brooking (West Ham United)	John Breckin (Rotherham United)	Joe Waters (Grimsby Town)
Tony Currie (Leeds United)	Howard Kendall (Stoke City)	Brian Hornsby (Sheffield Wednesday)	Richie Bowman (Reading)
Osvaldo Ardiles (Tottenham Hotspur)	Brian Horton (Brighton & Hove Albion)	Ray McHale (Swindon Town)	Alan Little (Barnsley)
Cyrille Regis (West Bromwich Albion)	Bryan Robson (West Ham United)	Ian Callaghan (Swansea City)	Alan Cork (Wimbledon)
Kenny Dalglish (Liverpool)	Mike Flanagan (Charlton Athletic)	Luther Blissett (Watford)	Les Bradd (Stockport County)
Laurie Cunningham (West Bromwich Albion)	Peter Withe (Newcastle United)	Ross Jenkins (Watford)	Allan Clarke (Barnsley)
		Alan Curtis (Swansea City) *tied votes	

1980

Division One	Division Two	Division Three	Division Four
Peter Shilton *(Nottingham Forest)*	Phil Parkes *(West Ham United)*	John Jackson *(Millwall)*	John Turner *(Torquay United)*
Viv Anderson *(Nottingham Forest)*	Kirk Stephens *(Luton Town)*	Gerry Forrest *(Rotherham United)*	Malcolm Brown *(Huddersfield Town)*
Dave Watson *(Southampton)*	Colin Todd *(Birmingham City)*	Bill Green *(Chesterfield)*	Keith Oakes *(Newport County)*
David O'Leary *(Arsenal)*	Billy Bonds *(West Ham United)*	Mark Smith *(Sheffield Wednesday)*	Stephen Baines *(Bradford City)*
Kenny Sansom *(Crystal Palace)*	Mark Dennis *(Birmingham City)*	Kevin Moore *(Grimsby Town)*	Joe Hinnigan *(Wigan Athletic)*
Terry McDermott *(Liverpool)*	Archie Gemmill *(Birmingham City)*	Alex Sabella *(Sheffield United)*	Joe Laidlaw *(Portsmouth)*
Liam Brady *(Arsenal)*	Trevor Brooking *(West Ham United)*	Joe Waters *(Grimsby Town)*	Murray Brodie *(Aldershot)*
Glenn Hoddle *(Tottenham Hotspur)*	Alan Devonshire *(West Ham United)*	Ray McHale *(Swindon Town)*	Terry Brisley *(Portsmouth)*
Kenny Dalglish *(Liverpool)*	Clive Allen *(Queens Park Rangers)*	Andy Rowland *(Swindon Town)*	Alan Buckley *(Walsall)*
David Johnson *(Liverpool)*	Peter Withe *(Newcastle United)*	Alan Mayes *(Swindon Town)*	Don Penn *(Walsall)*
Garry Birtles *(Nottingham Forest)*	David Moss *(Luton Town)*	Terry Curran *(Sheffield Wednesday)*	Ian Robins *(Huddersfield Town)*

1981

Division One	Division Two	Division Three	Division Four
Peter Shilton *(Nottingham Forest)*	Phil Parkes *(West Ham United)*	Nicky Johns *(Charlton Athletic)*	Mervyn Cawston *(Southend United)*
Kenny Swain *(Aston Villa)*	Ray Stewart *(West Ham United)*	Malcolm Brown *(Huddersfield Town)*	Cec Podd *(Bradford City)*
Russell Osman *(Ipswich Town)*	Alvin Martin *(West Ham United)*	John Breckin *(Rotherham United)*	Steve Sherlock *(Stockport County)*
Allan Evans *(Aston Villa)*	Billy Bonds *(West Ham United)*	Ian Evans *(Barnsley)*	Trevor Peake *(Lincoln City)*
Kenny Sansom *(Arsenal)*	Ray O'Brien *(Notts County)*	Mick McCarthy *(Barnsley)*	Dave Cusack *(Southend United)*
Frans Thijssen *(Ipswich Town)*	Trevor Brooking *(West Ham United)*	Ronnie Glavin *(Barnsley)*	Billy Kellock *(Peterborough United)*
John Wark *(Ipswich Town)*	Tony Currie *(Queens Park Rangers)*	Alan Birch *(Chesterfield)*	Alan Little *(Doncaster Rovers)*
Graeme Souness *(Liverpool)*	Alan Devonshire *(West Ham United)*	Danny Wilson *(Chesterfield)*	Anton Otulakowski *(Southend United)*
Paul Mariner *(Ipswich Town)*	Paul Goddard *(West Ham United)*	David Kemp *(Plymouth Argyle)*	Robbie Cooke *(Peterborough United)*
Kenny Dalglish *(Liverpool)*	David Cross *(West Ham United)*	Derek Hales *(Charlton Athletic)*	Derek Spence *(Southend United)*
Gary Shaw *(Aston Villa)*	Terry Curran *(Sheffield Wednesday)*	Tony Kellow *(Exeter City)*	Steve Phillips *(Northampton Town)*

1982

Division One	Division Two	Division Three	Division Four
Peter Shilton (Nottingham Forest)	Mark Wallington (Leicester City)	Gerry Peyton (Fulham)	Keith Waugh (Sheffield United)
Kenny Swain (Aston Villa)	Kirk Stephens (Luton Town)	Malcolm Brown (Huddersfield Town)	Cec Podd (Bradford City)
David O'Leary (Arsenal)	Mick McCarthy (Barnsley)	Tony Gale (Fulham)	Paul Hilton (Bury)
Alan Hansen (Liverpool)	Glenn Roeder (Queens Park Rangers)	Martin Dobson (Burnley)	Colin Methven (Wigan Athletic)
Kenny Sansom (Arsenal)	Steve Buckley (Derby County)	Dave Rushbury (Carlisle United)	Steve Sherlock (Stockport County)
Graeme Souness (Liverpool)	Ricky Hill (Luton Town)	Phil Bonnyman (Chesterfield)	Billy Kellock (Peterborough United)
Glenn Hoddle (Tottenham Hotspur)	Ian Banks (Barnsley)	Danny Wilson (Chesterfield)	Roger Osborne (Colchester United)
Bryan Robson (Manchester United)	Brian Horton (Luton Town)	Dick Tydeman (Gillingham)	Micky Gynn (Peterborough United)
Trevor Francis (Manchester City)	David Moss (Luton Town)	Gordon Davies (Fulham)	Bobby Campbell (Bradford City)
Kevin Keegan (Southampton)	Simon Stainrod (Queens Park Rangers)	Keith Cassells (Oxford United)	Mark Chamberlain (Port Vale)
Cyrille Regis (West Bromwich Albion)	Paul Walsh (Charlton Athletic)	Tony Kellow (Exeter City)	Craig Madden (Bury)

1983

Division One	Division Two	Division Three	Division Four
Peter Shilton (Southampton)	John Burridge (Wolves)	David Felgate (Lincoln City)	Iain Hesford (Blackpool)
Danny Thomas (Coventry City)	John Humphrey (Wolves)	Malcolm Brown (Huddersfield Town)	Chris Price (Hereford United)
Mark Lawrenson (Liverpool)	Mick McCarthy (Barnsley)	Trevor Peake (Lincoln City)	Paul Hilton (Bury)
Alan Hansen (Liverpool)	Tony Gale (Fulham)	Steve Bruce (Gillingham)	Phil Sproson (Port Vale)
Kenny Sansom (Arsenal)	John Ryan (Oldham Athletic)	Micky Adams (Gillingham)	Russell Bromage (Port Vale)
Bryan Robson (Manchester United)	Kenny Hibbitt (Wolves)	Neil Webb (Portsmouth)	Micky Gynn (Peterborough United)
Graeme Souness (Liverpool)	Ray Houghton (Fulham)	David Williams (Bristol Rovers)	Gary Emmanuel (Swindon Town)
Sammy Lee (Liverpool)	Ronnie Glavin (Barnsley)	Bobby Doyle (Portsmouth)	Geoff Hunter (Port Vale)
Ian Rush (Liverpool)	Kevin Keegan (Newcastle United)	Kerry Dixon (Reading)	Les Mutrie (Hull City)
Kenny Dalglish (Liverpool)	Andy Gray (Wolves)	Alan Biley (Portsmouth)	Paul Rideout (Swindon Town)
Steve Coppell (Manchester United)	Gordon Davies (Fulham)	Glenn Cockerill (Lincoln City)	Steve Fox (Port Vale)

1984

Division One	Division Two	Division Three	Division Four
Peter Shilton *(Southampton)*	Alex Williams *(Manchester City)*	David Felgate *(Lincoln City)*	Roger Jones *(York City)*
Mike Duxbury *(Manchester United)*	Mel Sterland *(Sheffield Wednesday)*	Gordon Nisbet *(Plymouth Argyle)*	Chris Price *(Hereford United)*
Mark Lawrenson *(Liverpool)*	Mick McCarthy *(Manchester City)*	Steve Bruce *(Gillingham)*	Colin Greenall *(Blackpool)*
Alan Hansen *(Liverpool)*	Mick Lyons *(Sheffield Wednesday)*	Malcolm Shotton *(Oxford United)*	John MacPhail *(York City)*
Kenny Sansom *(Arsenal)*	Joey Jones *(Chelsea)*	Bobby McDonald *(Oxford United)*	Steve Richardson *(Reading)*
Bryan Robson *(Manchester United)*	Gary Megson *(Sheffield Wednesday)*	Trevor Hebberd *(Oxford United)*	Ian Snodin *(Doncaster Rovers)*
Graeme Souness *(Liverpool)*	Jimmy Case *(Brighton & Hove Albion)*	Kevin Brock *(Oxford United)*	Jimmy Harvey *(Hereford United)*
Glenn Hoddle *(Tottenham Hotspur)*	Tony Grealish *(Brighton & Hove Albion)*	Brian Flynn *(Burnley)*	Trevor Quow *(Peterborough United)*
Ian Rush *(Liverpool)*	Kerry Dixon *(Chelsea)*	Keith Edwards *(Sheffield United)*	Trevor Senior *(Reading)*
Kenny Dalglish *(Liverpool)*	Kevin Keegan *(Newcastle United)*	Billy Hamilton *(Burnley)*	John Byrne *(York City)*
Frank Stapleton *(Manchester United)*	Mark Hateley *(Portsmouth)*	Colin Morris *(Sheffield United)*	Keith Walwyn *(York City)*

1985

Division One	Division Two	Division Three	Division Four
Peter Shilton *(Southampton)*	Terry Gennoe *(Blackburn Rovers)*	Tony Norman *(Hull City)*	Fred Barber *(Darlington)*
Gary Stevens *(Everton)*	Paul Parker *(Fulham)*	Gerry Forrest *(Rotherham United)*	Chris Price *(Hereford United)*
Mark Lawrenson *(Liverpool)*	Mick McCarthy *(Manchester City)*	Peter Skipper *(Hull City)*	Martin Dobson *(Bury)*
Kevin Ratcliffe *(Everton)*	Billy Gilbert *(Portsmouth)*	David Cusack *(Millwall)*	Steve Hetzke *(Blackpool)*
Kenny Sansom *(Arsenal)*	Bobby McDonald *(Oxford United)*	Kenny Mower *(Walsall)*	Russell Bromage *(Port Vale)*
Bryan Robson *(Manchester United)*	Neil Webb *(Portsmouth)*	Ian Snodin *(Doncaster Rovers)*	Jimmy Harvey *(Hereford United)*
Peter Reid *(Everton)*	Clive Wilson *(Manchester City)*	Stuart McCall *(Bradford City)*	Joe Jakub *(Bury)*
Kevin Sheedy *(Everton)*	Danny Wilson *(Brighton & Hove Albion)*	David Williams *(Bristol Rovers)*	Trevor Quow *(Peterborough United)*
Ian Rush *(Liverpool)*	John Aldridge *(Oxford United)*	Tony Cascarino *(Gillingham)*	Tony Adcock *(Colchester United)*
Chris Waddle *(Newcastle United)*	Billy Hamilton *(Oxford United)*	Bobby Campbell *(Bradford City)*	Stewart Phillips *(Hereford United)*
Kerry Dixon *(Chelsea)*	Paul Wilkinson *(Grimsby Town)*	Bobby Davison *(Derby County)*	John Clayton *(Tranmere Rovers)*

1986

Division One	Division Two	Division Three	Division Four
Peter Shilton *(Southampton)*	Chris Woods *(Norwich City)*	Mark Wallington *(Derby County)*	Mike Salmon *(Stockport County)*
Gary Stevens *(Everton)*	Paul Parker *(Fulham)*	Gordon Nisbet *(Plymouth Argyle)*	Chris Price *(Hereford United)*
Kenny Sansom *(Arsenal)*	Mark Reid *(Charlton Athletic)*	Steve Buckley *(Derby County)*	Martin Pike *(Peterborough United)*
Mark Lawrenson *(Liverpool)*	Steve Bruce *(Norwich City)*	Ross MacLaren *(Derby County)*	George Foster *(Mansfield Town)*
Paul McGrath *(Manchester United)*	Dave Watson *(Norwich City)*	Terry Boyle *(Newport County)*	Phil Sproson *(Port Vale)*
Glenn Hoddle *(Tottenham Hotspur)*	Danny Wilson *(Brighton & Hove Albion)*	John Gregory *(Derby County)*	Jimmy Harvey *(Hereford United)*
Bryan Robson *(Manchester United)*	Ian Snodin *(Leeds United)*	Terry Hurlock *(Reading)*	Kevin Hird *(Burnley)*
Stewart Robson *(Arsenal)*	Mark Aizlewood *(Charlton Athletic)*	Bobby Hutchinson *(Bristol City)*	Trevor Quow *(Peterborough United)*
Gary Lineker *(Everton)*	Kevin Drinkell *(Norwich City)*	Bobby Davison *(Derby County)*	Stuart Rimmer *(Chester City)*
Mark Hughes *(Manchester United)*	Vince Hilaire *(Portsmouth)*	Trevor Senior *(Reading)*	Frank Worthington *(Tranmere Rovers)*
Paul Walsh *(Liverpool)*	Keith Bertschin *(Stoke City)*	Tony Cascarino *(Gillingham)*	Richard Cadette *(Southend United)*

1987

Division One	Division Two	Division Three	Division Four
Neville Southall *(Everton)*	Andy Goram *(Oldham Athletic)*	Gerry Peyton *(Bournemouth)*	Jim Stannard *(Southend United)*
Viv Anderson *(Arsenal)*	Lee Dixon *(Stoke City)*	Paul Parker *(Fulham)*	Alan Paris *(Peterborough United)*
Alan Hansen *(Liverpool)*	Larry May *(Barnsley)*	Colin Greenall *(Gillingham)*	Keith McPherson *(Northampton Town)*
Tony Adams *(Arsenal)*	Noel Blake *(Portsmouth)*	Gary Pallister *(Middlesbrough)*	Sam Allardyce *(Preston North End)*
Kenny Sansom *(Arsenal)*	Julian Dicks *(Birmingham City)*	Kenny Mower *(Walsall)*	Terry Phelan *(Swansea City)*
Glenn Hoddle *(Tottenham Hotspur)*	John Sheridan *(Leeds United)*	Brian Laws *(Middlesbrough)*	Richard Hill *(Northampton Town)*
Kevin Sheedy *(Everton)*	John Gregory *(Derby County)*	Asa Hartford *(Bolton Wanderers)*	Jimmy Harvey *(Hereford United)*
David Rocastle *(Arsenal)*	Stuart McCall *(Bradford City)*	Bobby Hutchinson *(Walsall)*	Tommy Hutchison *(Swansea City)*
Ian Rush *(Liverpool)*	Bobby Davison *(Derby County)*	David Kelly *(Walsall)*	Richard Cadette *(Southend United)*
Clive Allen *(Tottenham Hotspur)*	Micky Quinn *(Portsmouth)*	Ian McParland *(Notts County)*	Trevor Morley *(Northampton Town)*
Peter Beardsley *(Newcastle United)*	John Hendrie *(Bradford City)*	Tony Cascarino *(Gillingham)*	Colin Pascoe *(Swansea City)*

1988

Division One	Division Two	Division Three	Division Four
Neville Southall *(Everton)*	Nigel Spink *(Aston Villa)*	Kevin Hitchcock *(Mansfield Town)*	Mark Kendall *(Wolves)*
Gary Stevens *(Everton)*	Chris Price *(Blackburn Rovers)*	Roger Joseph *(Brentford)*	Phil Brown *(Halifax Town)*
Alan Hansen *(Liverpool)*	Gary Pallister *(Middlesbrough)*	Gary Bennett *(Sunderland)*	Terry Boyle *(Cardiff City)*
Gary Gillespie *(Liverpool)*	Tony Mowbray *(Middlesbrough)*	Dean Yates *(Notts County)*	Keith Day *(Leyton Orient)*
Stuart Pearce *(Nottingham Forest)*	Andy Hinchcliffe *(Manchester City)*	Keith Dublin *(Brighton & Hove Albion)*	Kevin Dickenson *(Leyton Orient)*
Steve McMahon *(Liverpool)*	Stuart McCall *(Bradford City)*	Ray Walker *(Port Vale)*	Mick Gooding *(Peterborough United)*
Peter Reid *(Everton)*	Andy Gray *(Aston Villa)*	Geoff Pike *(Notts County)*	Alan Davies *(Swansea City)*
Paul Gascoigne *(Newcastle United)*	John Sheridan *(Leeds United)*	Andy Williams *(Rotherham United)*	Paul Wimbleton *(Cardiff City)*
John Barnes *(Liverpool)*	Paul Stewart *(Manchester City)*	Gary Nelson *(Brighton & Hove Albion)*	Steve Bull *(Wolves)*
Peter Beardsley *(Liverpool)*	Mark Bright *(Crystal Palace)*	Leroy Rosenior *(Fulham)*	David Currie *(Darlington)*
Graeme Sharp *(Everton)*	John Hendrie *(Bradford City)*	Ian McParland *(Notts County)*	Andy Mutch *(Wolves)*

1989

Division One	Division Two	Division Three	Division Four
Neville Southall *(Everton)*	Tony Coton *(Watford)*	Nigel Martyn *(Bristol Rovers)*	Eric Nixon *(Tranmere Rovers)*
Steve Nicol *(Liverpool)*	David Bardsley *(Oxford United)*	Phil Brown *(Bolton Wanderers)*	Billy Russell *(Rotherham United)*
Des Walker *(Nottingham Forest)*	Graham Roberts *(Chelsea)*	Dean Yates *(Notts County)*	Joey Jones *(Wrexham)*
Paul Parker *(Queens Park Rangers)*	Colin Hendry *(Blackburn Rovers)*	Rob Newman *(Bristol City)*	Shaun Taylor *(Exeter City)*
Stuart Pearce *(Nottingham Forest)*	Tony Dorigo *(Chelsea)*	Chris Coleman *(Swansea City)*	Neil Thompson *(Scarborough)*
Bryan Robson *(Manchester United)*	Neil McNab *(Manchester City)*	Ray Walker *(Port Vale)*	Jimmy Harvey *(Tranmere Rovers)*
David Rocastle *(Arsenal)*	Gary McAllister *(Leicester City)*	Brian Mooney *(Preston North End)*	Tony Grealish *(Rotherham United)*
Andy Townsend *(Norwich City)*	John Sheridan *(Leeds United)*	Sammy McIlroy *(Bury)*	Paul Ward *(Leyton Orient)*
Mark Hughes *(Manchester United)*	Gordon Durie *(Chelsea)*	Steve Bull *(Wolves)*	Phil Stant *(Hereford United)*
Alan Smith *(Arsenal)*	Ian Wright *(Crystal Palace)*	Andy Mutch *(Wolves)*	Ian Muir *(Tranmere Rovers)*
Chris Waddle *(Tottenham Hotspur)*	David Currie *(Barnsley)*	Tony Agana *(Sheffield United)*	Kevin Russell *(Wrexham)*

1990

Division One	Division Two	Division Three	Division Four
Neville Southall *(Everton)*	Tony Coton *(Watford)*	Eric Nixon *(Tranmere Rovers)*	Chris Marples *(York City)*
Lee Dixon *(Arsenal)*	Denis Irwin *(Oldham Athletic)*	Phil Brown *(Bolton Wanderers)*	Scott Hiley *(Exeter City)*
Des Walker *(Nottingham Forest)*	Chris Fairclough *(Leeds United)*	Rob Newman *(Bristol City)*	Shaun Taylor *(Exeter City)*
Alan Hansen *(Liverpool)*	Earl Barrett *(Oldham Athletic)*	Dean Yates *(Notts County)*	Paul Fitzpatrick *(Carlisle United)*
Stuart Pearce *(Nottingham Forest)*	Julian Dicks *(West Ham United)*	Paul Edwards *(Crewe Alexandra)*	Rob McKinnon *(Hartlepool United)*
David Platt *(Aston Villa)*	Gordon Strachan *(Leeds United)*	Jimmy Harvey *(Tranmere Rovers)*	Mick Halsall *(Peterborough United)*
Steve Hodge *(Nottingham Forest)*	Gary McAllister *(Leicester City)*	Shaun Goodwin *(Rotherham United)*	Steve Spooner *(York City)*
Steve McMahon *(Liverpool)*	Scott Sellars *(Blackburn Rovers)*	Steve Thompson *(Bolton Wanderers)*	Danny Bailey *(Exeter City)*
John Barnes *(Liverpool)*	Andy Ritchie *(Oldham Athletic)*	Bobby Williamson *(Rotherham United)*	Darren Rowbotham *(Exeter City)*
Peter Beardsley *(Liverpool)*	Micky Quinn *(Newcastle United)*	Ian Muir *(Tranmere Rovers)*	David Crown *(Southend United)*
Gary Lineker *(Tottenham Hotspur)*	Steve Bull *(Wolves)*	David Lee *(Bury)*	Steve Neville *(Exeter City)*

1991

Division One	Division Two	Division Three	Division Four
David Seaman *(Arsenal)*	Ludek Miklosko *(West Ham United)*	Eric Nixon *(Tranmere Rovers)*	Keith Welch *(Rochdale)*
Lee Dixon *(Arsenal)*	David Kerslake *(Swindon Town)*	Phil Brown *(Bolton Wanderers)*	Malcolm Brown *(Stockport County)*
Des Walker *(Nottingham Forest)*	Earl Barrett *(Oldham Athletic)*	Lee Sinnott *(Bradford City)*	Steve Davis *(Burnley)*
Mark Wright *(Derby County)*	Nigel Pearson *(Sheffield Wednesday)*	Peter Atherton *(Wigan Athletic)*	Brendan Ormsby *(Doncaster Rovers)*
Stuart Pearce *(Nottingham Forest)*	Paul Bodin *(Swindon Town)*	Chris Coleman *(Swansea City)*	Rufus Brevett *(Doncaster Rovers)*
Gordon Strachan *(Leeds United)*	Ian Bishop *(West Ham United)*	Neil McNab *(Tranmere Rovers)*	Gary Gill *(Darlington)*
Paul Gascoigne *(Tottenham Hotspur)*	John Sheridan *(Sheffield Wednesday)*	Steve Castle *(Leyton Orient)*	David Frain *(Stockport County)*
Andy Townsend *(Chelsea)*	Carlton Palmer *(Sheffield Wednesday)*	Keith Jones *(Brentford)*	Mick Halsall *(Peterborough United)*
Mark Hughes *(Manchester United)*	David Hirst *(Sheffield Wednesday)*	Brett Angell *(Southend United)*	Stuart Rimmer *(Walsall)*
John Barnes *(Liverpool)*	Steve Bull *(Wolves)*	Tony Philliskirk *(Bolton Wanderers)*	Joe Allon *(Hartlepool United)*
Ian Rush *(Liverpool)*	Trevor Morley *(West Ham United)*	Wayne Biggins *(Stoke City)*	Steve Butler *(Maidstone United)*

1992

Division One	Division Two	Division Three	Division Four
Tony Coton *(Manchester City)*	David James *(Watford)*	Chris Turner *(Leyton Orient)*	Kelham O'Hanlon *(Carlisle United)*
Rob Jones *(Liverpool)*	David Kerslake *(Swindon Town)*	Scott Hiley *(Exeter City)*	Paul Fleming *(Mansfield Town)*
Stuart Pearce *(Nottingham Forest)*	John Beresford *(Portsmouth)*	Simon Charlton *(Huddersfield Town)*	Phil Hardy *(Wrexham)*
Gary Pallister *(Manchester United)*	David Linighan *(Ipswich Town)*	Terry Evans *(Brentford)*	Steve Davis *(Burnley)*
Des Walker *(Nottingham Forest)*	Colin Calderwood *(Swindon Town)*	Vince Overson *(Stoke City)*	Alan Walker *(Gillingham)*
Ray Houghton *(Liverpool)*	Micky Hazard *(Swindon Town)*	Chris Marsden *(Huddersfield Town)*	Shaun Goodwin *(Rotherham United)*
Gary McAllister *(Leeds United)*	Gordon Cowans *(Blackburn Rovers)*	Tony Kelly *(Bolton Wanderers)*	Paul Groves *(Blackpool)*
Andy Townsend *(Chelsea)*	Scott Sellars *(Blackburn Rovers)*	Nigel Gleghorn *(Birmingham City)*	Kenny Lowe *(Barnet)*
Gary Lineker *(Tottenham Hotspur)*	Duncan Shearer *(Swindon Town)*	Wayne Biggins *(Stoke City)*	Gary Bull *(Barnet)*
Alan Shearer *(Southampton)*	John Aldridge *(Tranmere Rovers)*	Dean Holdsworth *(Brentford)*	Dave Bamber *(Blackpool)*
Mark Hughes *(Manchester United)*	David Speedie *(Blackburn Rovers)*	Iwan Roberts *(Huddersfield Town)*	Phil Stant *(Mansfield Town)*

1993

Premier	Division One	Division Two	Division Three
Peter Schmeichel *(Manchester United)*	Ludek Miklosko *(West Ham United)*	Marlon Beresford *(Burnley)*	Mark Prudhoe *(Darlington)*
David Bardsley *(Queens Park Rangers)*	David Kerslake *(Swindon Town)*	Scott Hiley *(Exeter City)*	Andy McMillan *(York City)*
Paul McGrath *(Aston Villa)*	Craig Short *(Derby County)*	Vince Overson *(Stoke City)*	Paul Stancliffe *(York City)*
Gary Pallister *(Manchester United)*	Colin Cooper *(Millwall)*	Peter Swan *(Port Vale)*	Matthew Elliott *(Scunthorpe United)*
Tony Dorigo *(Leeds United)*	John Beresford *(Newcastle United)*	Simon Charlton *(Huddersfield Town)*	Damon Searle *(Cardiff City)*
Paul Ince *(Manchester United)*	Lee Clark *(Newcastle United)*	Ray Walker *(Port Vale)*	Kenny Lowe *(Barnet)*
Gary Speed *(Leeds United)*	Micky Hazard *(Swindon Town)*	Ian Taylor *(Port Vale)*	Derek Payne *(Barnet)*
Roy Keane *(Nottingham Forest)*	Martin Allen *(West Ham United)*	Darren Bradley *(West Bromwich Albion)*	Gareth Owen *(Wrexham)*
Alan Shearer *(Blackburn Rovers)*	John Aldridge *(Tranmere Rovers)*	Mark Stein *(Stoke City)*	Gary Bull *(Barnet)*
Ian Wright *(Arsenal)*	Guy Whittingham *(Portsmouth)*	Andy Walker *(Bolton Wanderers)*	Darren Foreman *(Scarborough)*
Ryan Giggs *(Manchester United)*	Gavin Peacock *(Newcastle United)*	Bob Taylor *(West Bromwich Albion)*	Carl Griffiths *(Shrewsbury Town)*

1994

Premier	Division One	Division Two	Division Three
Tim Flowers	Nigel Martyn	Marlon Beresford	Martin Hodge
(Blackburn Rovers)	(Crystal Palace)	(Burnley)	(Rochdale)
Gary Kelly	Gary Charles	Neil Aspin	Jason Cousins
(Leeds United)	(Derby County)	(Port Vale)	(Wycombe Wanderers)
Gary Pallister	Colin Cooper	Adrian Williams	Terry Evans
(Manchester United)	(Nottingham Forest)	(Reading)	(Wycombe Wanderers)
Tony Adams	Eric Young	Dean Glover	Alan Reeves
(Arsenal)	(Crystal Palace)	(Port Vale)	(Rochdale)
Denis Irwin	Scott Minto	Dylan Kerr	Roger Stanislaus
(Manchester United)	(Charlton Athletic)	(Reading)	(Bury)
Paul Ince	Jason McAteer	Steve Castle	Steve Guppy
(Manchester United)	(Bolton Wanderers)	(Plymouth Argyle)	(Wycombe Wanderers)
Gary McAllister	Mark Draper	Ian Taylor	Tony Rigby
(Leeds United)	(Notts County)	(Port Vale)	(Bury)
David Batty	Scot Gemmill	Ian Bogie	Neil Lennon
(Blackburn Rovers)	(Nottingham Forest)	(Leyton Orient)	(Crewe Alexandra)
Alan Shearer	Stan Collymore	Jimmy Quinn	Tony Ellis
(Blackburn Rovers)	(Nottingham Forest)	(Reading)	(Preston North End)
Eric Cantona	Paul Walsh	Andy Preece	Dean Spink
(Manchester United)	(Portsmouth)	(Stockport County)	(Shrewsbury Town)
Peter Beardsley	Chris Armstrong	Dean Windass	David Reeves
(Newcastle United)	(Crystal Palace)	(Hull City)	(Carlisle United)

1995

Premier	Division One	Division Two	Division Three
Tim Flowers	Shaka Hislop	Ian Bennett	Gary Kelly
(Blackburn Rovers)	(Reading)	(Birmingham City)	(Bury)
Rob Jones	Neil Cox	Gary Poole	Duncan Jupp
(Liverpool)	(Middlesbrough)	(Birmingham City)	(Fulham)
Gary Pallister	Alan Stubbs	Liam Daish	Dean Walling
(Manchester United)	(Bolton Wanderers)	(Birmingham City)	(Carlisle United)
Colin Hendry	Craig Short	Dean Richards	Russell Wilcox
(Blackburn Rovers)	(Derby County)	(Bradford City)	(Doncaster Rovers)
Graeme Le Saux	Ben Thatcher	Tom Cowan	Tony Gallimore
(Blackburn Rovers)	(Millwall)	(Huddersfield Town)	(Carlisle United)
Paul Ince	Jason McAteer	John Cornforth	Martyn O'Connor
(Manchester United)	(Bolton Wanderers)	(Swansea City)	(Walsall)
Matthew Le Tissier	Alex Rae	Mark Ward	Paul Holland
(Southampton)	(Millwall)	(Birmingham City)	(Mansfield Town)
Tim Sherwood	Jamie Pollock	Neil Lennon	Wayne Bullimore
(Blackburn Rovers)	(Middlesbrough)	(Crewe Alexandra)	(Scunthorpe United)
Alan Shearer	Jan-Aage Fjortoft	Gary Bennett	David Reeves
(Blackburn Rovers)	(Middlesbrough)	(Wrexham)	(Carlisle United)
Jurgen Klinsmann	John Hendrie	Andrew Booth	Doug Freedman
(Tottenham Hotspur)	(Middlesbrough)	(Huddersfield Town)	(Barnet)
Chris Sutton	John Aldridge	Nick Forster	Kyle Lightbourne
(Blackburn Rovers)	(Tranmere Rovers)	(Brentford)	(Walsall)

PFA AWARD WINNERS' CAREER FACTS

Note: International appearances up to 29.3.95

1974

NORMAN HUNTER

Born: Gateshead, 29 October 1943
Position: Central defender

Clubs	Seasons
Leeds United	1962–63 – 1976–77
Bristol City	1976–77 – 1978–79
Barnsley	1979–80 – 1982–83

Honours: League Championship 1969, 1974
FA Cup winner 1972
League Cup winner 1968
Inter Cities Fairs Cup winner 1968, 1971
PFA Player of the Year 1974

International: England – 28 caps

KEVIN BEATTIE

Born: Carlisle, 18 December 1953
Position: Central defender

Clubs	Seasons
Ipswich Town	1972–73 – 1980–81
Colchester United	1982–83 –
Middlesbrough	1982–83

Honours: FA Cup winner 1978
PFA Young Player of the Year 1974

International: England – 9 caps

SIR BOBBY CHARLTON CBE OBE

Born: Ashington, 11 October 1937
Position: Inside forward

Clubs	Seasons
Manchester United	1956–57 – 1972–73
Preston North End	1974–75

Honours: World Cup winner 1966
League Championship 1957, 1965, 1967
FA Cup winner 1963
European Cup winner 1968
FWA Footballer of the Year 1966
European Footballer of the Year 1966
PFA Merit Award 1974, 1986, 1993

International: England – 106 caps

CLIFF LLOYD OBE

Born: Ellesmere Port, 14 November 1916
Position: Left back

Clubs	Seasons
Wrexham	1937–38 – 1938–39
Fulham	1946–47 –
Bristol Rovers	1950–51

Honours: PFA Merit Award 1974

1975

COLIN TODD

Born: Chester–le–Street, 12 December 1948
Position: Central defender

Clubs	Seasons
Sunderland	1966–67 – 1970–71
Derby County	1970–71 – 1978–79
Everton	1978–79 – 1979–80
Birmingham City	1979–80 – 1981–82
Nottingham Forest	1982–83 – 1983–84
Oxford United	1983–84 –
(Vancouver Whitecaps – Canada)	
Luton Town	1984–85

Honours: League Championship 1972, 1975
PFA Player of the Year 1975

International: England – 27 caps

MERVYN DAY

Born: Chelmsford, 26 June 1955
Position: Goalkeeper

Clubs	Seasons
West Ham United	1973–74 – 1978–79
Leyton Orient	1979–80 – 1982–83
Aston Villa	1983–84 – 1984–85
Leeds United	1984–85 – 1989–90
Luton Town	1991–92 loan
Sheffield United	1991–92 loan

Honours: FA Cup winner 1975
PFA Young Player of the Year 1975

DENIS LAW

Born: Aberdeen, 24 February 1940
Position: Inside forward

Clubs	Seasons
Huddersfield Town	1956–57 – 1959–60
Manchester City	1959–60 – 1960–61
(Torino – Italy)	
Manchester United	1962–63 – 1972–73
Manchester City	1973–74

Honours: League Championship 1965, 1967
FA Cup winner 1963
European Footballer of the Year 1964
PFA Merit Award 1975

International: Scotland – 55 caps

1976

PAT JENNINGS MBE OBE

Born: Newry, 12 June 1945
Position: Goalkeeper

Clubs	Seasons
Watford	1962–63 – 1963–64
Tottenham Hotspur	1964–65 – 1976–77
Arsenal	1977–78 – 1984–85

Honours: FA Cup winner 1967, 1979
League Cup winner 1971, 1973
UEFA Cup winner 1972
FWA Footballer of the Year 1973
PFA Player of the Year 1976

International: Northern Ireland – 119 caps

PETER BARNES

Born: Manchester, 10 June 1957
Position: Winger

Clubs	Seasons
Manchester City	1974–75 – 1978–79
West Bromwich Albion	1979–80 – 1980–81
Leeds United	1981–82 –
(Real Betis – Spain)	
Leeds United	1983–84 –
Coventry City	1984–85 –
Manchester Utd	1985–86 – 1986–87
Manchester City	1986–87 –
Bolton Wanderers	1987–88 loan
Port Vale	1987–88 loan
Hull City	1987–88 –
(Farense – Portugal)	
Bolton Wanderers	1988–89 –
Sunderland	1988–89

Honours: League Cup winner 1976
PFA Young Player of the Year 1976

International: England – 22 caps

GEORGE EASTHAM OBE

Born: Blackpool, 23 September 1936
Position: Inside forward

Clubs	Seasons
(Ards – N Ireland)	
Newcastle United	1956–57 – 1959–60
Arsenal	1960–61 – 1965–66
Stoke City	1966–67 – 1973–74

Honours: League Cup winner 1972
PFA Merit Award 1976

International: England – 19 caps

1977

ANDY GRAY

Born: Glasgow, 30 November 1955
Position: Centre Forward

Clubs	Seasons
Dundee United	1973–74 – 1975–76
Aston Villa	1975–76 – 1978–79
Wolves	1979–80 – 1983–84
Everton	1983–84 – 1984–85
Aston Villa	1985–86 – 1986–87
Notts County	1987–88 loan
West Bromwich Albion	1987–88 – 1988–89
Rangers	1988–89

Honours: League Championship 1985
FA Cup winner 1984
League Cup winner 1977, 1980
Scottish League Championship 1989
European Cup–Winners' Cup winner 1985
PFA Player of the Year 1977
PFA Young Player of the Year 1977

International: Scotland – 20 caps

JACK TAYLOR OBE

Honours: PFA Merit Award 1977

1978

PETER SHILTON OBE MBE

Born: Leicester, 18 September 1949
Position: Goalkeeper

Clubs	Seasons
Leicester City	1965–66 – 1974–75
Stoke City	1974–75 – 1977–78
Nottingham Forest	1977–78 – 1981–82
Southampton	1982–83 – 1986–87
Derby County	1987–88 – 1991–92
Plymouth Argyle	1991–92 – 1994–95
Wimbledon	1994–95 –

Honours: League Championship 1978
League Cup winner 1979
European Cup winner 1979, 1980
PFA Player of the Year 1978
PFA Merit Award 1990

International: England – 125 caps

TONY WOODCOCK

Born: Eastwood, 6 December 1955
Position: Forward

Clubs	Seasons
Nottingham Forest	1973–74 – 1979–80
Lincoln City	1975–76 loan
Doncaster Rovers	1976–77 loan
(FC Cologne – West Germany)	
Arsenal	1982–83 – 1985–86
(FC Cologne, Fortuna Dusseldorf – West Germany)	

Honours: League Championship 1978
League Cup winner 1978, 1979
European Cup winner 1979
PFA Young Player of the Year 1978

International: England – 42 caps

BILL SHANKLY OBE

Born: Glenbuck, 2 September 1913. Died 1981
Position: Wing Half

Clubs	Seasons
Carlisle United	1932–33
Preston North End	1933–34 – 1948–49

Honours: (as player) FA Cup winner 1938
(as manager) League Championship 1964, 1966, 1973
FA Cup winner 1965, 1974
UEFA Cup winner 1973
PFA Merit Award 1978

International: Scotland – 5 caps

1979

LIAM BRADY

Born: Dublin, 13 February 1956
Position: Midfielder

Clubs	Seasons
Arsenal	1973–74 – 1979–80
(Juventus, Sampdoria, Inter Milan, Ascoli – Italy)	
West Ham United	1986–87 – 1989–90

Honours: FA Cup winner 1979
PFA Player of the Year 1979

International: Republic of Ireland – 72 caps

CYRILLE REGIS

Born: French Guyana, 9 February 1958
Position: Forward

Clubs	Seasons
West Bromwich Albion	1977–78 – 1984–85
Coventry City	1984–85 – 1990–91
Aston Villa	1991–92 – 1992–93
Wolves	1993–94 –
Wycombe Wanderers	1994–95 –

Honours: FA Cup winner 1987
PFA Young Player of the Year 1979

International: England – 5 caps

TOM FINNEY OBE

Born: Preston, 5 April 1922
Position: Forward

Clubs	Seasons
Preston North End	1946–47 – 1959–60

Honours: FWA Footballer of the Year 1954, 1957
PFA Merit Award 1979

International: England – 76 caps

1980

TERRY McDERMOTT

Born: Kirkby, 8 December 1951
Position: Midfielder

Clubs	Seasons
Bury	1969–70 – 1972–73
Newcastle United	1972–73 – 1974–75
Liverpool	1974–75 – 1982–83
Newcastle United	1982–83 – 1983–84

Honours: League Championship 1977, 1979, 1980
League Cup winner 1981, 1982
European Cup winner 1977, 1978, 1981
FWA Footballer of the Year 1980
PFA Player of the Year 1980

International: England – 25 caps

GLENN HODDLE

Born: Hayes, 27 October 1957
Position: Midfielder

Clubs	Seasons
Tottenham Hotspur	1975–76 – 1986–87
(AS Monaco – France)	
Swindon Town	1991–92 – 1992–93
Chelsea	1993–94 –1994-95

Honours: FA Cup winner 1981, 1982
PFA Young Player of the Year 1980

International: England – 53 caps

SIR MATT BUSBY CBE

Born: Orbiston, 26 May 1909. Died 1994
Position: Right half

Clubs	Seasons
Manchester City	1928–29 – 1935–36
Liverpool	1936–37 – 1945–46

Honours: (as player) FA Cup winner 1934
(as manager) League Championship 1952,1956,1957,1965, 1967
FA Cup winner 1948, 1963
European Cup winner 1968
PFA Merit Award 1980, 1993

International: Scotland – 1 cap

1981

JOHN WARK

Born: Glasgow, 4 August 1957
Position: Midfielder

Clubs	Seasons
Ipswich Town	1974–75 – 1983–84
Liverpool	1983–84 – 1987–88
Ipswich Town	1987–88 – 1989–90
Middlesbrough	1990–91 –
Ipswich Town	1991–92 –

Honours: FA Cup winner 1978
UEFA Cup winner 1981
PFA Player of the Year 1981

International: Scotland – 29 caps

GARY SHAW

Born: Birmingham, 21 January 1961
Position: Forward

Clubs	Seasons
Aston Villa	1978–79 – 1987–88
Blackpool	1987–88 loan
(Klagenfurt – Austria)	
Walsall	1989–90 –
(Kilmarnock – Scotland)	
Shrewsbury Town	1990–91

Honours: League Championship 1981
European Cup winner 1982
PFA Young Player of the Year 1981

JOHN TROLLOPE MBE

Born: Wroughton, 14 June 1943
Position: Left Back

Clubs	Seasons
Swindon Town	1960–61 – 1980–81

Honours: League Cup winner 1969
PFA Merit Award 1981

1982

KEVIN KEEGAN OBE

Born: Doncaster, 14 February 1951
Position: Forward

Clubs	Seasons
Scunthorpe United	1968–69 – 1970–71
Liverpool	1971–72 – 1976–77
(SV Hamburg – West Germany)	
Southampton	1980–81 – 1981–82
Newcastle United	1982–83 – 1983–84

Honours: League Championship 1973, 1976, 1977
FA Cup winner 1974
Bundesliga Championship 1979
European Cup winner 1977
UEFA Cup winner 1973, 1976
European Footballer of the Year 1978, 1979
FWA Footballer of the Year 1976
PFA Player of the Year 1982

International: England – 63 caps

STEVE MORAN

Born: Croydon, 10 January 1961
Position: Forward

Clubs	Seasons
Southampton	1979–80 – 1985–86
Leicester City	1986–87 – 1987–88
Reading	1987–88 – 1990–91
Exeter City	1991–92 – 1992–93
Hull City	1993–94 –

Honours: PFA Young Player of the Year 1982

JOE MERCER OBE

Born: Ellesmere Port, 9 August 1914. Died 1990
Position: Wing half

Clubs	Seasons
Everton	1932–33 – 1946–47
Arsenal	1946–47 – 1953–54

Honours: (as player) League Championship 1939, 1948, 1953
FA Cup winner 1950
(as manager) League Championship 1968
FA Cup winner 1969
League Cup winner 1961, 1970
European Cup Winners–Cup winner 1970
FWA Footballer ofthe Year 1950
PFA Merit Award 1982

International: England – 5 caps

1983

KENNY DALGLISH MBE

Born: Glasgow, 4 March 1951
Position: Forward

Clubs	Seasons
Celtic	1967–68 – 1976–77
Liverpool	1977–78 – 1989–90

Honours: (as player) Scottish League
Championship 1972, 1973,
1974, 1977
Scottish Cup winner 1972, 1974,
1975, 1977
Scottish League Cup winner 1975
League Championship 1979, 1980,
1982, 1983, 1984,
League Cup winner 1981, 1982,
1983, 1984
European Cup winner 1978, 1981,
1984
FWA Footballer of the Year 1979,
1983
PFA Player of the Year 1983
(as manager) League
Championship 1986, 1988, 1990,1995
FA Cup winner 1986, 1989

International: Scotland – 102 caps

IAN RUSH

Born: St. Asaph, 20 October 1961
Position: Forward

Clubs	Seasons
Chester City	1978–79 – 1979–80
Liverpool	1980–81 – 1986–87
(Juventus – Italy)	
Liverpool	1988–89 –

Honours: League Championship 1982, 1983,
1984, 1986, 1990
FA Cup winner 1986, 1989, 1992
League Cup winner 1981, 1982,
1983, 1984, 1995
European Cup winner 1984
FWA Footballer of the Year 1984
PFA Young Player of the Year 1983
PFA Player of the Year 1984

International: Wales – 69 caps

BOB PAISLEY OBE

Born: Hetton-le-Hole, 23 January 1919
Position: Wing half

Club	Seasons
Liverpool	1946–47 – 1953–54

Honours: (as player) League Championship
1947
(as manager) League Championship
1976, 1977, 1979, 1980, 1982, 1983
League Cup winner 1981, 1982,
1983
European Cup winner 1977, 1978,
1981
UEFA Cup winner 1976
PFA Merit Award 1983

1984

IAN RUSH

(see 1983)

PAUL WALSH

Born: Plumstead, 1 October 1962
Position: Forward

Clubs	Seasons
Charlton Athletic	1979–80 – 1981–82
Luton Town	1982–83 – 1983–84
Liverpool	1984–85 – 1987–88
Tottenham Hotspur	1987–88 – 1991–92
QPR	1991–92 loan
Portsmouth	1992–93 – 1993–94
Manchester City	1993–94 –

Honours: League Championship 1986
PFA Young Player of the Year 1984

International: England – 5 caps

BILL NICHOLSON

Born: Scarborough, 26 January 1919
Position: Wing half

Club	Seasons
Tottenham Hotspur	1938–39 – 1954–55

Honours: (as player) League Championship
1951
(as manager) League Championship
1961
FA Cup winner 1961, 1962, 1967
League Cup winner 1971, 1973
European Cup–Winners' Cup winner
1963
UEFA Cup winner 1972
PFA Merit Award 1984

International: England – 1 cap

1985

PETER REID

Born: Liverpool, 20 June 1956
Position: Midfielder

Clubs	Seasons
Bolton Wanderers	1974–75 – 1982–83
Everton	1982–83 – 1988–89
QPR	1988–89 – 1989–90
Manchester City	1989–90 – 1993–94
	(as player/coach)
Southampton	1993–94
Notts County	1993–94
Bury	1994–95 –

Honours: League Championship 1985, 1987
FA Cup winner 1984
European Cup–Winners' Cup winner
1985
PFA Player of the Year 1985

International: England – 13 caps

MARK HUGHES

Born: Wrexham, 1 November 1963
Position: Forward

Clubs	Seasons
Manchester United	1983–84 – 1985–86
(Barcelona – Spain, Bayern Munich –	
Germany loan)	
Manchester United	1988–89 –

Honours: Premier League Championship 1993,
1994
FA Cup winner 1985, 1990, 1994
League Cup winner 1992
European Cup–Winners' Cup winner
1991
PFA Young Player of the Year 1985
PFA Player of the Year 1989, 1991

International: Wales – 55 caps

RON GREENWOOD CBE

Born: Burnley, 11 November 1921
Position: Centre Half

Clubs	Seasons
Chelsea	1940–45
Bradford Park Avenue	1946–47 – 1947–48
Brentford	1948–49 – 1952–53
Chelsea	1952–53 – 1954–55
Fulham	1954–55 – 1955–56

Honours: (as player) League Championship
1955
(as manager) FA Cup winner 1964
European Cup–Winners' Cup winner
1965
PFA Merit Award 1985

1986

GARY LINEKER OBE

Born: Leicester, 30 November 1960
Position: Forward

Clubs	Seasons
Leicester City	1978–79 – 1984–85
Everton	1985–86
(Barcelona – Spain)	
Tottenham Hotspur	1989–90 – 1991–92
(Grampus Eight – Japan)	

Honours: FA Cup winner 1991
European Cup–Winners' Cup winner 1989
FWA Footballer of the Year 1986, 1992
PFA Player of the Year 1986

International: England – 80 caps

TONY COTTEE

Born: West Ham, 11 July 1965
Position: Forward

Clubs	Seasons
West Ham United	1982–83 – 1987–88
Everton	1988–89 – 1994–95
West Ham United	1994–95 –

Honours: PFA Young Player of the Year 1986

International: England – 7 caps

THE 1966 ENGLAND WORLD CUP TEAM

ALAN BALL

Born: Farnworth, 12 May 1945
Position: Midfielder

Clubs	Seasons
Blackpool	1962–63 – 1965–66
Everton	1966–67 – 1971–72
Arsenal	1971–72 – 1976–77
Southampton	1976–77 – 1979–80
(Vancouver – Canada)	
Blackpool	1980–81
Southampton	1980–81 – 1982–83
(Hong Kong)	
Bristol Rovers	1982–83

Honours: World Cup winner 1966
League Championship 1970
PFA Merit Award 1986

International: England – 72 caps

GORDON BANKS

Born: Sheffield, 20 December 1937
Position: Goalkeeper

Clubs	Seasons
Chesterfield	1958–59
Leicester City	1959–60 – 1966–67
Stoke City	1966–67 – 1972–73

Honours: World Cup winner 1966
League Cup winner 1964, 1972
FWA Footballer of the Year 1972
PFA Merit Award 1986

International: England – 73 caps

JACK CHARLTON OBE

Born: Ashington, 8 May 1935
Position: Centre Half

Club	Seasons
Leeds United	1952–53 – 1972–73

Honours: World Cup winner 1966
League Championship 1969
Inter Cities Fairs Cup winner 1968, 1971
FA Cup winner 1972
FWA Footballer of the Year 1967
PFA Merit Award 1986

International: England – 35 caps

SIR BOBBY CHARLTON CBE OBE

(see 1974)

GEORGE COHEN

Born: Kensington, 22 October 1939
Position: Right back

Club	Seasons
Fulham	1956–57 – 1968–69

Honours: World Cup winner 1966
PFA Merit Award 1986

International: England – 37 caps

ROGER HUNT

Born: Golborne, 20 July 1938
Position: Forward

Clubs	Seasons
Liverpool	1959–60 – 1969–70
Bolton Wanderers	1969–70 – 1971–72

Honours: World Cup winner 1966
League Championship 1964, 1966
FA Cup winner 1965
PFA Merit Award 1986

International: England – 34 caps

GEOFF HURST MBE

Born: Ashton–under–Lyne, 8 December 1941
Position: Forward

Clubs	Seasons
West Ham United	1959–60 – 1971–72
Stoke City	1972–73 – 1974–75
West Bromwich Albion	1975–76

Honours: World Cup winner 1966
FA Cup winner 1964
European Cup–Winners' Cup winner 1965
PFA Merit Award 1986

International: England – 49 caps

BOBBY MOORE OBE

Born: Barking, 12 April 1941. Died 1993
Position: Central defender

Clubs	Seasons
West Ham United	1958–59 – 1973–74
Fulham	1973–74 – 1976–77

Honours: World Cup winner 1966
FA Cup winner 1964
European Cup–Winners' Cup winner 1965
FWA Footballer of the Year 1964
PFA Merit Award 1986

International: England – 108 caps

MARTIN PETERS

Born: Plaistow, 8 November 1943
Position: Midfielder

Clubs	Seasons
West Ham United	1961–62 – 1969–70
Tottenham Hotspur	1969–70 – 1974–75
Norwich City	1974–75 – 1979–80
Sheffield United	1980–81

Honours: World Cup winner 1966
League Cup winner 1971, 1973
European Cup–Winners' Cup winner 1965
UEFA Cup winner 1972
PFA Merit Award 1986

International: England – 67 caps

NOBBY STILES

Born: Manchester, 18 May 1942
Position: Midfielder

Clubs	Seasons
Manchester United	1960–61 – 1970–71
Middlesbrough	1971–72 – 1972–73
Preston North End	1973–74 – 1974–75

Honours: World Cup winner 1966
League Championship 1965, 1967
European Cup winner 1968
PFA Merit Award 1986, 1993

International: England – 28 caps

RAY WILSON

Born: Shirebrook, 17 December 1934
Position: Left back

Clubs	Seasons
Huddersfield Town	1955–56 – 1963–64
Everton	1964–65 – 1968–69
Oldham Athletic	1969–70
Bradford City	1970–71

Honours: World Cup winner 1966
FA Cup winner 1966
PFA Merit Award 1986

International: England – 63 caps

SIR ALF RAMSEY

Born: Dagenham, 22 January 1920
Position: Full back

Clubs	Seasons
Southampton	1946–47 – 1948–49
Tottenham Hotspur	1949–50 – 1954–55

Honours: (as player) League Championship
1951
(as manager) World Cup winner 1966
League Championship 1962
PFA Merit Award 1986

International: England – 32 caps

HAROLD SHEPHERDSON

Born: Middlesbrough, 28 October 1918
Position: Centre half

Clubs	Seasons
Middlesbrough	1936–37 – 1946–47
Southend United	– –

Honours: (as coach) World Cup winner 1966
PFA Merit Award 1986

1987

CLIVE ALLEN

Born: Stepney, 20 May 1961
Position: Forward

Clubs	Seasons
QPR	1978–79 – 1979–80
Arsenal	1981–81 –
Crystal Palace	1980–81 –
Queens Park Rangers	1981–82 – 1983–84
Tottenham Hotspur	1984–85 – 1987–88
(Bordeaux – France)	
Manchester City	1989–90 – 1991–92
Chelsea	1991–92 –
West Ham United	1991–92 – 1993–94
Millwall	1994–95 –

Honours: FWA Footballer of the Year 1987
PFA Player of the Year 1987

International: England – 5 caps

TONY ADAMS

Born: Romford, 10 October 1966
Position: Central defender

Clubs	Seasons
Arsenal	1983–84 –

Honours: League Championship 1989, 1991
FA Cup winner 1993
League Cup winner 1987, 1993
European Cup–Winners' Cup winner
1994
PFA Young Player of the Year 1987

International: England – 35 caps

SIR STANLEY MATTHEWS CBE

Born: Hanley, 1 February 1915
Position: Right winger

Clubs	Seasons
Stoke City	1931–32 – 1946–47
Blackpool	1947–48 – 1961–62
Stoke City	1961–62 – 1964–65

Honours: FA Cup winner 1953
FWA Footballer of the Year 1948,
1963
European Footballer of the Year 1956
PFA Merit Award 1987

International: England – 54 caps

1988

JOHN BARNES

Born: Jamaica, 7 November 1963
Position: Forward

Clubs	Seasons
Watford	1981–82 – 1986–87
Liverpool	1987–88 –

Honours: League Championship 1988, 1990
FA Cup winner 1989
League Cup winner 1995
FWA Footballer of the Year 1988,
1990
PFA Player of the Year 1988

International: England – 77 caps

PAUL GASCOIGNE

Born: Gateshead, 27 May 1967
Position: Midfielder

Clubs	Seasons
Newcastle United	1984–85 – 1987–88
Tottenham Hotspur	1988–89 – 1991–92
(Lazio – Italy)	

Honours: FA Cup winner 1991
PFA Young Player of the Year 1988

International: England – 29 caps

BILLY BONDS MBE

Born: Woolwich, 17 September 1946
Position: Central defender/midfielder

Clubs	Seasons
Charlton Athletic	1964–65 – 1966–67
West Ham United	1967–68 – 1987–88

Honours: FA Cup winner 1975, 1980
PFA Merit Award 1988

1989

MARK HUGHES

(see 1985)

PAUL MERSON

Born: Harlesden, 20 March 1968
Position: Forward

Clubs	Seasons
Arsenal	1986–87 –
Brentford	1986–87 loan

Honours: League Championship 1989, 1991
FA Cup winner 1993
League Cup winner 1993
European Cup–Winners' Cup winner 1994
PFA Young Player of the Year 1989

International: England – 14 caps

NAT LOFTHOUSE

Born: Bolton, 27 August 1925
Position: Centre forward

Club	Seasons
Bolton Wanderers	1946–47 – 1960–61

Honours: FA Cup winner 1958
FWA Footballer of the Year 1953
PFA Merit Award 1989

International: England – 33 caps

1990

DAVID PLATT

Born: Oldham, 10 June 1966
Position: Forward

Clubs	Seasons
Manchester United	1983–84
Crewe Alexandra	1984–85 – 1987–88
Aston Villa	1987–88 – 1990–91
(Bari, Juventus, Sampdoria – Italy)	

Honours: PFA Player of the Year 1990

International: England – 52 caps

MATTHEW LE TISSIER

Born: Guernsey, 14 October 1968
Position: Forward

Club	Seasons
Southampton	1986–87 –

Honours: PFA Young Player of the Year 1990

International: England – 6 caps

PETER SHILTON OBE MBE

(see 1978)

1991

MARK HUGHES

(see 1985)

LEE SHARPE

Born: Halesowen, 27 May 1971
Position: Forward/midfielder

Clubs	Seasons
Torquay United	1987–88
Manchester United	1988–89 –

Honours: Premier League Championship 1993, 1994
FA Cup winner 1994
League Cup winner 1992
European Cup–Winners' Cup winner 1991
PFA Young Player of the Year 1991

International: England – 8 caps

TOMMY HUTCHISON

Born: Cardenden, 22 September 1947
Position: Left winger

Clubs	Seasons
(Alloa – Scotland)	
Blackpool	1967–68 – 1972–73
Coventry City	1972–73 – 1980–81
Manchester City	1980–81 – 1981–82
(Hong Kong)	
Burnley	1983–84 – 1984–85
Swansea City	1985–86 – 1990–91

Honours: PFA Merit Award 1991

International: Scotland – 17 caps

1992

GARY PALLISTER

Born: Ramsgate, 30 June 1965
Position: Central defender

Clubs	Seasons
Middlesbrough	1985–86 – 1989–90
Darlington	1985–86 loan
Manchester United	1989–90 –

Honours: Premier League Championship 1993, 1994
FA Cup winner 1990, 1994
League Cup winner 1992
European Cup–Winners' Cup winner 1991
PFA Player of the Year 1992

International: England – 17 caps

RYAN GIGGS

Born: Cardiff, 29 November 1973
Position: Forward

Club	Seasons
Manchester Utd	1990–91 –

Honours: Premier League Championship 1993, 1994
FA Cup winner 1994
League Cup winner 1992
PFA Young Player of the Year 1992, 1993

International: Wales – 13 caps

BRIAN CLOUGH OBE

Born: Middlesbrough, 21 March 1935
Position: Centre forward

Clubs	Seasons
Middlesbrough	1955–56 – 1960–61
Sunderland	1961–62 – 1964–65

Honours: (as manager) League Championship 1972, 1978
League Cup winner 1978, 1979, 1989, 1990
European Cup winner 1979, 1980
PFA Merit Award 1992

International: England – 2 caps

1993

PAUL McGRATH

Born: Ealing, 4 December 1959
Position: Central defender/midfielder

Clubs	Seasons
Manchester United	1982–83 – 1988–89
Aston Villa	1989–90 –

Honours: FA Cup winner 1985
League Cup winner 1994
PFA Player of the Year 1993

International: Republic of Ireland – 72 caps

RYAN GIGGS

(see 1992)

MANCHESTER UNITED'S 1968 EUROPEAN CUP TEAM

JOHN ASTON

Born: Manchester, 28 June 1947
Position: Left winger

Clubs	Seasons
Manchester United	1964–65 – 1971–72
Luton Town	1972–73 – 1977–78
Mansfield Town	1977–78
Blackburn Rovers	1978–79 – 1979–80

Honours: European Cup winner 1968
League Championship 1967
PFA Merit Award 1993

GEORGE BEST

Born: Belfast, 22 May 1946
Position: Forward

Clubs	Seasons
Manchester United	1963–64 – 1973–74
Stockport County	1975–76 loan
(Los Angeles – USA)	
Fulham	1976–77 – 1977–78
(Golden Bay – USA)	
Bournemouth	1982–83

Honours: European Cup winner 1968
League Championship 1965, 1967
FWA Footballer of the Year 1968
European Footballer of the Year 1968
PFA Merit Award 1993

International: Northern Ireland – 37 caps

SHAY BRENNAN

Born: Manchester, 6 May 1937
Position: Full back

Club	Seasons
Manchester United	1957–58 – 1969–70

Honours: European Cup winner 1968
League Championship 1965, 1967
PFA Merit Award 1993

International: Republic of Ireland – 19 caps

SIR BOBBY CHARLTON CBE OBE

(see 1974)

PAT CRERAND

Born: Glasgow, 19 February 1939
Position: Right half

Clubs	Seasons
Celtic	1958–59 – 1962–63
Manchester United	1962–63 – 1970–71

Honours: European Cup winner 1968
League Championship 1965, 1967
FA Cup winner 1963
PFA Merit Award 1993

International: Scotland – 16 caps

TONY DUNNE

Born: Dublin, 24 July 1941
Position: Full back

Clubs	Seasons
Manchester United	1960–61 – 1972–73
Bolton Wanderers	1973–74 – 1978–79

Honours: European Cup winner 1968
League Championship 1965, 1967
FA Cup winner 1963
PFA Merit Award 1993

International: Republic of Ireland – 33 caps

BILL FOULKES

Born: St Helens, 5 January 1932
Position: Defender

Club	Seasons
Manchester United	1952–53 – 1969–70

Honours: European Cup winner 1968
League Championship 1956, 1957,
1965, 1967
FA Cup winner 1963
PFA Merit Award 1993

International: England – 1 cap

BRIAN KIDD

Born: Manchester, 29 May 1949
Position: Forward

Clubs	Seasons
Manchester United	1967–68 – 1973–74
Arsenal	1974–75 – 1975–76
Manchester City	1976–77 – 1978–79
Everton	1978–79 – 1979–80
Bolton Wanderers	1980–81 – 1981–82

Honours: European Cup winner 1968
PFA Merit Award 1993

International: England – 2 caps

JIMMY RIMMER

Born: Southport, 10 February 1948
Position: Goalkeeper (Substitute in Final)

Clubs	Seasons
Manchester United	1967–68 – 1972–73
Swansea City	1973–74 loan
Arsenal	1973–74 – 1976–77
Aston Villa	1977–78 – 1982–83
Swansea City	1983–84 – 1985–86

Honours: League Championship 1981
European Cup winner 1982
PFA Merit Award 1993

International: England – 1 cap

DAVID SADLER

Born: Yalding, 5 February 1946
Position: Central defender

Clubs	Seasons
Manchester United	1963–64 – 1973–74
Preston North End	1973–74 – 1976–77

Honours: European Cup winner 1968
League Championship 1967
PFA Merit Award 1993

International: England – 4 caps

ALEX STEPNEY

Born: Mitcham, 18 September 1942
Position: Goalkeeper

Clubs	Seasons
Millwall	1963–64 – 1965–66
Chelsea	1966–67
Manchester United	1966–67 – 1977–78

Honours: European Cup winner 1968
League Championship 1967
FA Cup winner 1977
PFA Merit Award 1993

International: England – 1 cap

NOBBY STILES

(see 1986)

SIR MATT BUSBY CBE

(see 1980)

1994

ERIC CANTONA

Born: Paris, 24 May 1966
Position: Forward

Clubs	Seasons
(Auxerre, Martigues, Marseille, Bordeaux, Montpelier, Nimes – France)	
Leeds United	1991–92 – 1992–93
Manchester United	1992–93 –

Honours: League Championship 1992
Premier League Championship 1993, 1994
FA Cup winner 1994
PFA Player of the Year 1994

International: France 45 caps

ANDY COLE

Born: Nottingham, 15 October 1971
Position: Forward

Clubs	Seasons
Arsenal	1990–91
Fulham	1991–92 loan
Bristol City	1991–92 loan
Bristol City	1992–93
Newcastle United	1992–93 – 1994–95
Manchester United	1994–95 –

Honours: PFA Young Player of the Year 1994

International: England – 1 cap

BILLY BINGHAM MBE

Born: Belfast, 5 August 1931
Position: Right winger

Clubs	Seasons
(Glentoran – N Ireland)	
Sunderland	1950–51 – 1957–58
Luton Town	1958–59 – 1960–61
Everton	1960–61 – 1962–63
Port Vale	1963–64 – 1964–65

Honours: League Championship 1963
PFA Merit Award 1994

International: Northern Ireland – 56 caps

1995

ALAN SHEARER

Born: Newcastle, 13 August 1970
Position: Forward

Clubs	Seasons
Southampton	1987–88 – 1991–92
Blackburn Rovers	1992-93 –

Honours: PFA Player of the Year 1995
Premier League Championship 1993

International: England - 14 caps

ROBBIE FOWLER

Born: Liverpool, 9 April 1975
Position: Forward

Club	Seasons
Liverpool	1993–94 –

Honours: League Cup winner 1995
PFA Young Player of the Year 1995

GORDON STRACHAN MBE

Born: Edinburgh, 9 February 1957
Position: Midfielder

Clubs	Seasons
Dundee	1974–75 – 1976–77
Aberdeen	1977–78 – 1983–84
Manchester United	1984–85 – 1988–89
Leeds United	1988–89 – 1994–95
Coventry City	1994–95

Honours:
Scottish League Championship 1980, 1984
Scottish Cup winner 1982, 1983, 1984
European Cup–Winners' Cup winner 1983
League Championship 1992
FA Cup winner 1985
Scottish Footballer of the Year 1980
Footballer of the Year 1991
PFA Merit Award 1995

International: Scotland – 50 caps

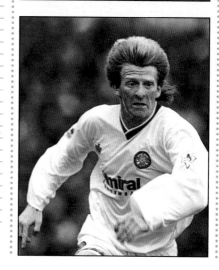

AWARD PRESENTERS

Player of the Year	Young Player of the Year	Merit Award
1974 Sir Matt Busby CBE	Don Revie OBE	Tom Finney OBE
1975 The Rt Hon Harold Wilson, The Prime Minister	Billy Wright CBE	Bill Shankly OBE
1976 HRH The Duke of Kent	Gordon Banks OBE	Joe Mercer OBE
1977 The Rt Hon The Lord Elwyn-Jones, The Lord Chancellor*	Jimmy Greaves	John Charles
1978 The Lord Ted Willis	Ron Greenwood	Ally McLeod
1979 The Rt Hon George Thomas MP	Kevin Keegan	Brian Clough
1980 The Rt Hon Norman St John Stevas MP	Ron Greenwood	Bobby Charlton CBE
1981 Sir Stanley Rous CBE	Geoff Hurst MBE	Jimmy Dickinson MBE
1982 Neil Macfarlane MP	Kevin Beattie	Cliff Lloyd OBE
1983 Bob Paisley OBE	Mike England	Roger Hunt
1984 The Rt Hon Neil Kinnock MP	Steve Coppell	Danny Blanchflower
1985 Elton John	John Hollins MBE	Trevor Brooking MBE
1986 Tony Jacklin OBE**	Pat Jennings MBE	Sir Stanley Rous CBE
1987 Sir Stanley Matthews CBE	Billy Wright CBE	Sir Walter Winterbottom CBE, OBE
1988 Bobby Robson	Bobby Charlton CBE OBE	Ted Croker
1989 The Rt Hon Denis Howell MP	Brian Talbot	Ian Greaves
1990 Jack Charlton OBE	Terry Paine MBE	Gordon Banks OBE
1991 Graham Taylor	Garth Crooks	Terry Yorath
1992 Trevor Brooking MBE	Alex Ferguson OBE	Roy McFarland
1993 Bobby Charlton CBE, OBE	Cyrille Regis	Eusebio
1994 Terry Venables	Peter Beardsley	Bryan Hamilton
1995 Kenny Dalglish MBE	Ray Wilkins MBE	Denis Law

* Trophy presented by Chris Nicholl in Sutton Coldfield.   *** Trophy presented by Howard Kendall at Goodison Park.*

ACKNOWLEDGEMENTS

The author wishes to thank PFA Chief Executive Gordon Taylor who first agreed that this book could go ahead and then provided the Foreword. PFA Commercial Executive Brian Marwood was also instrumental in getting the project off the ground and was the perfect link-man between author and Award winners. Deputy Chief Executive Brendon Batson read the manuscript and made valuable comments.

Independent scrutineer Mike Birch, of Chartered Accountants Humphreys, Bower and Gothard, gave a fascinating insight into the balloting procedure. Allan Cummings, Ian Vosper and Dick Wright each provided useful information from their own archives.

Designer Stuart Perry carried out work beyond the call of duty; and Ray Driscoll provided invaluable editorial expertise.

Thanks are also due to all those PFA Players' Player of the Year Award winners who granted interviews for this book.

Photographs supplied by Action Images, Allsport, Colorsport, Empics, The PFA and Professional Sport.